Programming Web Services with SOAP

Programming Web Services
with SOAP

James Snell, Doug Tidwell, and Pavel Kulchenko

O'REILLY®

Beijing · Cambridge · Farnham · Köln · Paris · Sebastopol · Taipei · Tokyo

Programming Web Services with SOAP
by James Snell, Doug Tidwell, and Pavel Kulchenko

Published by O'Reilly & Associates, Inc., 1005 Gravenstein Highway North, Sebastopol, CA 95472.

O'Reilly & Associates books may be purchased for educational, business, or sales promotional use. Online editions are also available for most titles (*safari.oreilly.com*). For more information contact our corporate/institutional sales department: (800) 998-9938 or *corporate@oreilly.com*.

Editor:	Nathan Torkington
Production Editor:	Colleen Gorman
Cover Designer:	Ellie Volckhausen
Interior Designer:	Melanie Wang

Printing History:

January 2002:	First Edition.

ISBN: 0-596-00095-2
[M]

Table of Contents

Preface

You'd be hard-pressed to find a buzzword hotter than *web services*. Breathless articles promise that web services will revolutionize business, open new markets, and change the way the world works. Proponents call web services "The Third-Generation Internet," putting them on a par with email and the browseable web. And no protocol for implementing web services has received more attention than SOAP, the Simple Object Access Protocol.

This book will give you perspective to make sense of all the hype. When you finish this book, you will come away understanding three things: what web services are, how they are written with SOAP, and how to use other technologies with SOAP to build web services for the enterprise.

While this book is primarily a technical resource for software developers, its overview of the relevant technologies, development models, standardization efforts, and architectural fundamentals can be easily grasped by a nontechnical audience wishing to gain a better understanding of this emerging set of new technologies.

For the technical audience, this book has several things to offer:

- A detailed walk-through of the SOAP, WSDL, UDDI, and related specifications
- Source code and commentary for sample web services
- Insights on how to address issues such as security and reliability in enterprise environments

Web services represent a powerful new way to build software systems from distributed components. But because many of the technologies are immature or only address parts of the problem, it's not a simple matter to build a robust and secure web service. A web service solution today will either dodge tricky issues like security, or will be developed using many different technologies. We have endeavored to lay a roadmap to guide you through the many possible technologies and give you sound advice for developing web services.

Will web services revolutionize everything? Quite possibly, but it's not likely to be as glamorous or lucrative, or happen as quickly as the hype implies. At the most basic level, web services are plumbing, and plumbing is never glamorous. The applications they make possible may be significant in the future, and we discuss Microsoft Passport and Peer-to-Peer (P2P) systems built with web services, but the plumbing that enables these systems will never be sexy.

Part of the fundamental utility of web services is their language independence—we come back to this again and again in the book. We show how Java, Perl, C#, and Visual Basic code can be easily integrated using the web services architecture, and we describe the underlying principles of the web service technologies that transcend the particular programming language and toolkit you choose to use.

Audience for This Book

There's a shortage of good information on web services at all levels. Managers are being bombarded with marketing hyperbole and wild promises of efficiency, riches, and new markets. Programmers have a bewildering array of acronyms thrust into their lives and are expected to somehow choose the correct system to use. On top of this confusion, there's pressure to do something with web service immediately.

If you're a programmer, we show you the big picture of web services, and then zoom in to give you low-level knowledge of the underlying XML. This knowledge informs the detailed material on developing SOAP web services. We also provide detailed information on the additional technologies needed to implement enterprise-quality web services.

Managers can benefit from this book, too. We strip away the hype and present a realistic view of what is, what isn't, and what might be. Chapter 1 puts SOAP in the wider context of the web services architecture, and Chapter 9 looks ahead to the future to see what is coming and what is needed (these aren't always the same).

Structure of This Book

We've arranged the material in this book so that you can read it from start to finish, or jump around to hit just the topics you're interested in.

Chapter 1, *Introducing Web Services,* places SOAP in the wider picture of web services, discussing Just-in-Time integration and the Web Service Technology Stack.

Chapter 2, *Introducing SOAP*, explains what SOAP does and how it does it, with constant reference to the XML messages being shipped around. It covers the SOAP envelope, headers, body, faults, encodings, and transports.

Chapter 3, *Writing SOAP Web Services*, shows how to use SOAP toolkits in Perl, Visual Basic, Java, and C# to create an elementary web service.

Chapter 4, *The Publisher Web Service*, presents our first real-world web service. Registered users may add, delete, or browse articles in a database.

Chapter 5, *Describing a SOAP Service*, introduces the Web Services Description Language (WSDL) at an XML and programmatic level, shows how WSDL makes it easier to write a web service client, and discusses complex message patterns.

Chapter 6, *Discovering SOAP Services*, shows how to use the Universal Description, Discovery, and Integration (UDDI) project and the WS-Inspection standard to publish, discover, and call web services, and features best practices for using WSDL and UDDI together.

Chapter 7, *Web Services in Action*, builds a peer-to-peer (P2P) web services application for sharing source code in Perl and Java using SOAP, WSDL, and related technologies.

Chapter 8, *Web Services Security*, describes the issues and approaches to security in web services, focusing on Microsoft Passport, XML Encryption, and Digital Signatures.

Chapter 9, *The Future of Web Services*, explains the present shortcomings in web services technologies, describes some developing standardization efforts, and identifies the future battlegrounds for web services mindshare.

Appendix A, *Web Service Standardization*, is a summary of the many varied standards for aspects of web services such as packaging, security, transactions, routing, and workflow, with pointers to online sources for more information on each standard.

Appendix B, *XML Schema Basics*, is a gentle introduction to the bits of the XML Schema specification you'll need to know to make sense of WSDL and UDDI.

Appendix C, *Code Listings*, contains full source for the programs developed in this book.

Conventions

The following typographic conventions are used in this book:

Italic
> Used for filenames, directories, email addresses, and URLs.

Constant Width
> Used for XML and code examples. Also used for constants, variables, data structures, and XML elements.

Constant Width Bold
> Used to indicate user input in examples and to highlight portions of examples that are commented upon in the text.

Constant Width Italic
> Used to indicate replaceables in examples.

Comments and Questions

We have tested and verified all of the information in this book to the best of our ability, but you may find that features have changed, that typos have crept in, or that we have made a mistake. Please let us know about what you find, as well as your suggestions for future editions, by contacting:

O'Reilly & Associates, Inc.
1005 Gravenstein Highway North
Sebastopol, CA 95472
(800) 998-9938 (in the U.S. or Canada)
(707) 829-0515 (international/local)
(707) 829-0104 (fax)

You can also send us messages electronically. To be put on the mailing list or request a catalog, send email to:

info@oreilly.com

To ask technical questions or comment on the book, send email to:

bookquestions@oreilly.com

We have a web site for the book, where we'll list examples, errata, and any plans for future editions. You can access this page at:

http://www.oreilly.com/catalog/progwebsoap/

For more information about this book and others, see the O'Reilly web site:

http://www.oreilly.com

Acknowledgments

The authors and editor would like to thank the technical reviewers, whose excellent and timely feedback greatly improved the book you read: Ethan Cerami, Tony Hong, Matt Long, Simon Fell, and Aron Roberts.

James

Thank you,

> To Paul and Doug, for their help.
> To my editor, Nathan, for his persistent badgering.
> To my wife, Jennifer, for her patience.
> To my son, Joshua, for his joy.
> And to my God, for his grace.

This book wouldn't exist without them.

Doug

I would like to thank my wonderful wife, Sheri Castle, and our amazing daughter, Lily, for their love and support. Nothing I do would be possible or meaningful without them.

Paul

I wouldn't have been able to participate in this project without my family's patience and love. My son, Daniil, was the source of inspiration for my work, and my wife, Alena, provided constant support and encouragement. Thank you!

Many thanks to Tony Hong for his sound technical advice, productive discussions, and our collaboration on projects that gave me the required knowledge and experience.

I'd like to thank James Snell for inviting me to participate in writing this book, and for the help he gave me throughout the process.

Thanks to our wonderful technical editor, Nathan Torkington, who was a delight to work with and wonderfully persistent in his efforts to get this book done and make it great.

Finally, I am fortunate to be part of two communities, Perl and SOAP. I want to thank the many people that make up those communities for the enthusiastic support, feedback, and the fresh ideas that they've provided to me—they've helped to make SOAP::Lite and the other projects I've worked on what they are now.

## CHAPTER 1

Introducing Web Services

To make best use of web services and SOAP, you must have a firm understanding of the principles and technologies upon which they stand. This chapter is an introduction to a variety of new technologies, approaches, and ideas for writing web-based applications to take advantage of the web services architecture. SOAP is one part of the bigger picture described in this chapter, and you'll learn how it relates to the other technologies described in this book: the Web Service Description Language (WSDL), the Web Service Inspection Language (WS-IL), and the Universal Description, Discovery, and Integration (UDDI) services.

What Is a Web Service?

Before we go any further, let's define the basic concept of a "web service." A *web service* is a network accessible interface to application functionality, built using standard Internet technologies. This is illustrated in Figure 1-1.

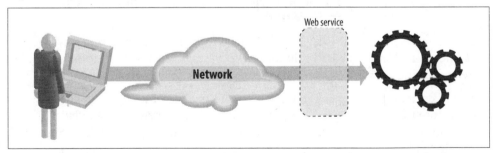

Figure 1-1. A web service allows access to application code using standard Internet technologies

In other words, if an application can be accessed over a network using a combination of protocols like HTTP, XML, SMTP, or Jabber, then it is a web service. Despite all the media hype around web services, it really is that simple.

Web services are nothing new. Rather, they represent the evolution of principles that have guided the Internet for years.

Web Service Fundamentals

As Figures 1-1 and 1-2 illustrate, a web service is an interface positioned between the application code and the user of that code. It acts as an abstraction layer, separating the platform and programming-language–specific details of how the application code is actually invoked. This standardized layer means that any language that supports the web service can access the application's functionality.

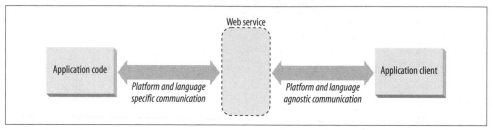

Figure 1-2. Web services provide an abstraction layer between the application client and the application code

The web services that we see deployed on the Internet today are HTML web sites. In these, the application services—the mechanisms for publishing, managing, searching, and retrieving content—are accessed through the use of standard protocols and data formats: HTTP and HTML. Client applications (web browsers) that understand these standards can interact with the application services to perform tasks like ordering books, sending greeting cards, or reading news.

Because of the abstraction provided by the standards-based interfaces, it does not matter whether the application services are written in Java and the browser written in C++, or the application services deployed on a Unix box while the browser is deployed on Windows. Web services allow for cross-platform interoperability in a way that makes the platform irrelevant.

Interoperability is one of the key benefits gained from implementing web services. Java and Microsoft Windows-based solutions have typically been difficult to integrate, but a web services layer between application and client can greatly remove friction.

There is currently an ongoing effort within the Java community to define an exact architecture for implementing web services within the framework of the Java 2 Enterprise Edition specification. Each of the major Java technology providers (Sun, IBM, BEA, etc.) are all working to enable their platforms for web services support.

Many significant application vendors such as IBM and Microsoft have completely embraced web services. IBM for example, is integrating web services support throughout their WebSphere, Tivoli, Lotus, and DB2 products. And Microsoft's new .NET development platform is built around web services.

What Web Services Look Like

Web services are a messaging framework. The only requirement placed on a web service is that it must be capable of sending and receiving messages using some combination of standard Internet protocols. The most common form of web services is to call procedures running on a server, in which case the messages encode "Call this subroutine with these arguments," and "Here are the results of the subroutine call."

Figure 1-3 shows the pieces of a web service. The application code holds all the business logic and code for actually doing things (listing books, adding a book to a shopping cart, paying for books, etc.). The Service Listener speaks the transport protocol (HTTP, SOAP, Jabber, etc.) and receives incoming requests. The Service Proxy decodes those requests into calls into the application code. The Service Proxy may then encode a response for the Service Listener to reply with, but it is possible to omit this step.

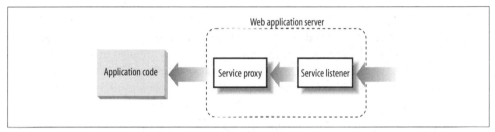

Figure 1-3. A web service consists of several key components

The Service Proxy and Service Listener components may either be standalone applications (a TCP-server or HTTP-server daemon, for instance) or may run within the context of some other type of application server. As an example, IBM's WebSphere Application Server includes built-in support for receiving a SOAP message over HTTP and using that to invoke Java applications deployed within WebSphere. In comparison, the popular open source Apache web server has a module that implements SOAP. In fact, there are implementations of SOAP for both the Palm and PocketPL Portable Digital Assistant (PDA) operating systems.

Keep in mind, however, that web services do not require a server environment to run. Web services may be deployed anywhere that the standard Internet technologies can be used. This means that web services may be hosted or used by anything from an Application Service Provider's vast server farm to a PDA.

Web services do not require that applications conform to a traditional client-server (where the server holds the data and does the processing) or n-tier development model (where data storage is separated from business logic that is separated from the user interface), although they are certainly being heavily deployed within those environments. Web services may take any form, may be used anywhere, and may serve any purpose. For instance, there are strong crossovers between peer-to-peer systems (with decentralized data or processing) and web services where peers use standard Internet protocols to provide services to one another.

Intersection of Business and Programming

Because a web service exposes an application's functionality to any client in any programming language, they raise interesting questions in both the programming and the business world.

Programmers tend to raise questions like, "How do we do two-phase commit transactions?" or "How do I do object inheritance?" or "How do I make this damn thing run faster?"—questions typically associated with going through the steps of writing code.

Business folks, on the other hand, tend to ask questions like, "How do I ensure that the person using the service is really who they say they are?" or "How can we tie together multiple web services into a workflow?" or "How can I ensure the reliability of web service transactions?" Their questions typically address business concerns.

These two perspectives go hand-in-hand with one another. Every business issue will have a software-based solution. But the two perspectives are also at odds with each other: the business processes demand completeness, trust, security, and reliability, which may be incompatible with the programmers' goals of simplicity, performance, and robustness.

The outcome is that tools for implementing web services will do so from one of these two angles, but rarely will they do so from both. For example, SOAP::Lite, the Perl-based SOAP implementation written by the coauthor of this book, Pavel Kulchenko, is essentially written for programmers. It provides a very simple set of tools for invoking Perl modules using SOAP, XML-RPC, Jabber, or any number of other protocols.

In contrast, Apache's Axis project (the next generation of Apache's SOAP implementation) is a more complex web services implementation designed to make it easier to implement processes, or to tie together multiple web services. Axis can perform the stripped down bare essentials, but that is not its primary focus.

The important thing to keep in mind is that both tools implement many of the same set of technologies (SOAP, WSDL, UDDI, and others, many of which we discuss later on), and so they are capable of interoperating with each other. The differences are in the way they interface with applications. This gives programmers a choice of how their web service is implemented, without restricting the users of that service.

Just-In-Time Integration

Once you understand the basic web services outlined earlier, the next step is to add *Just-In-Time Integration*. That is, the dynamic integration of application services based not on the technology platform the services are implemented in, but upon the business requirements of what needs to get done.

Just-In-Time Integration recasts the Internet application development model around a new framework called the web services architecture (Figure 1-4).

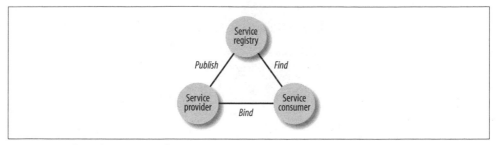

Figure 1-4. The web services architecture

In the web services architecture, the *service provider* publishes a description of the service(s) it offers via the *service registry*. The *service consumer* searches the service registry to find a service that meets their needs. The service consumer could be a person or a program.

Binding refers to a service consumer actually using the service offered by a service provider. The key to Just-in-Time integration is that this can happen at any time, particularly at runtime. That is, a client might not know which procedures it will be calling until it is running, searches the registry, and identifies a suitable candidate. This is analogous to late binding in object-oriented programming.

Imagine a purchasing web service, where consumers requisition products from a service provider. If the client program has hard-coded the server it talks to, then the service is bound at compile-time. If the client program searches for a suitable server and binds to that, then the service is bound at runtime. The latter is an example of Just-In-Time integration between services.

The Web Service Technology Stack

The web services architecture is implemented through the layering of five types of technologies, organized into layers that build upon one another (Figure 1-5).

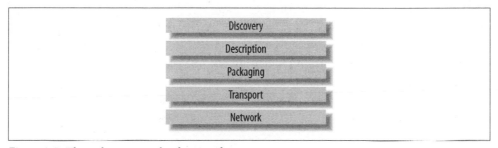

Figure 1-5. The web service technology stack

It should come as no surprise that this stack is very similar to the TCP/IP network model used to describe the architecture of Internet-based applications (Figure 1-6).

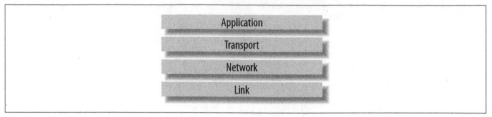

Figure 1-6. The TCP/IP network model

The additional packaging, description, and discovery layers in the web services stack are the layers essential to providing Just-In-Time Integration capability and the necessary platform-neutral programming model.

Because each part of the web services stack addresses a separate business problem, you only have to implement those pieces that make the most sense at any given time. When a new layer of the stack is needed, you do not have to rewrite significant chunks of your infrastructure just to support a new form of exchanging information or a new way of authenticating users.

The goal is total modularization of the distributed computing environment as opposed to recreating the large monolithic solutions of more traditional distributed platforms like Java, CORBA, and COM. Modularity is particularly necessary in web services because of the rapidly evolving nature of the standards. This is shown in the sample CodeShare application of Chapter 7, where we don't use the discovery layer, but we do draw in another XML standard to handle security.

Beyond the Stack

The layers of the web services stack do not provide a complete solution to many business problems. For instance, they don't address security, trust, workflow, identity, or many other business concerns. Here are some of the most important standardization initiatives currently being pursued in these areas:

XML Protocol
> The W3C XML Protocol working group is chartered with standardizing the SOAP protocol. Its work will eventually replace the SOAP protocol completely as the de facto standard for implementing web services.

XKMS
> The XML Key Management Services are a set of security and trust related services that add Private Key Infrastructure (PKI) capabilities to web services.

SAML

The Security Assertions Markup Language is an XML grammar for expressing the occurrence of security events, such as an authentication event. Used within the web services architecture, it provides a standard flexible authentication system.

XML-Dsig

XML Digital Signatures allow any XML document to be digitally signed.

XML-Enc

The XML Encryption specification allows XML data to be encrypted and for the expression of encrypted data as XML.

XSD

XML Schemas are an application of XML used to express the structure of XML documents.

P3P

The W3C's Platform for Privacy Preferences is an XML grammar for the expression of data privacy policies.

WSFL

The Web Services Flow Language is an extension to WSDL that allows for the expression of work flows within the web services architecture.

Jabber

Jabber is a new lightweight, asynchronous transport protocol used in peer-to-peer applications.

ebXML

ebXML is a suite of XML-based specifications for conducting electronic business. Built to use SOAP, ebXML offers one approach to implementing business-to-business integration services.

Discovery

The discovery layer provides the mechanism for consumers to fetch the descriptions of providers. One of the more widely recognized discovery mechanisms available is the Universal Description, Discovery, and Integration (UDDI) project. IBM and Microsoft have jointly proposed an alternative to UDDI, the Web Services Inspection Language (WS-Inspection). We will discuss both UDDI and WS-Inspection in depth (including arguments for and against their use) in Chapter 6.

Description

When a web service is implemented, it must make decisions on every level as to which network, transport, and packaging protocols it will support. A description of that service represents those decisions in such a way that the Service Consumer can contact and use the service.

The Web Service Description Language (WSDL) is the de facto standard for providing those descriptions. Other, less popular, approaches include the use of the W3C's Resource Description Framework (RDF) and the DARPA Agent Markup Language (DAML), both of which provide a much richer (but far more complex) capability of describing web services than WSDL.

We cover WSDL in Chapter 5. You can find out more information about DAML and RDF from:

> *http://daml.semanticweb.org*
> *http://www.w3.org/rdf*

Packaging

For application data to be moved around the network by the transport layer, it must be "packaged" in a format that all parties can understand (other terms for this process are "serialization" and "marshalling"). This encompasses the choice of data types understood, the encoding of values, and so on.

HTML is a kind of packaging format, but it can be inconvenient to work with because HTML is strongly tied to the presentation of the information rather than its meaning. XML is the basis for most of the present web services packaging formats because it can be used to represent the meaning of the data being transferred, and because XML parsers are now ubiquitous.

SOAP is a very common packaging format, built on XML. In Chapter 2, we'll see how SOAP encodes messages and data values, and in Chapter 3 we'll see how to write actual web services with SOAP. There are several XML-based packaging protocols available for developers to use (XML-RPC for instance), but as you might have guessed from the title of this book, SOAP is the only format we cover.

Transport

The transport layer includes the various technologies that enable direct application-to-application communication on top of the network layer. Such technologies include protocols like TCP, HTTP, SMTP, and Jabber. The transport layer's primary role is to move data between two or more locations on the network. Web services may be built on top of almost any transport protocol.

The choice of transport protocol is based largely on the communication needs of the web service being implemented. HTTP, for example, provides the most ubiquitous firewall support but does not provide support for asynchronous communication. Jabber, on the other hand, while not a standard, does provide good a asynchronous communication channel.

Network

The network layer in the web services technology stack is exactly the same as the network layer in the TCP/IP Network Model. It provides the critical basic communication, addressing, and routing capabilities.

Application

The application layer is the code that implements the functionality of the web service, which is found and accessed through the lower layers in the stack.

The Peer Services Model

The peer services model is a complimentary but alternative view of the web services architecture. Based on the peer-to-peer (P2P) architecture, every member of a group of peers shares a common collection of services and resources. A peer can be a person, an application, a device, or another group of peers operating as a single entity.

While it may not be readily apparent, the same fundamental web services components are present as in the peer services architecture. There are both service providers and service consumers, and there are service registries. The distinction between providers and consumers, however, is not as clear-cut as in the web services case. Depending on the type of service or resource that the peers are sharing, any individual peer can play the role of both a service provider and a service consumer. This makes the peer services model more dynamic and flexible.

Instant Messaging is the most widely utilized implementation of the peer services model. Every person that uses instant messaging is a peer. When you receive an invitation to chat with somebody, you are playing the role of a service provider. When you send an invitation out to chat with somebody else, you are playing the role of a service consumer. When you log on to the Instant Messaging Server, the server is playing the role of the service registry—that is, the Instant Messaging Server keeps track of where you currently are and what your instant messaging capabilities are. Figure 1-7 illustrates this.

Peer services and web services emerged and evolved separately from one another, and accordingly make use of different protocols and technologies to implement their respective models. Peer web services tie the two together by unifying the technologies, the protocols, and the models into a single comprehensive big picture. The implementation of a peer web service will be the central focus of Chapter 7.

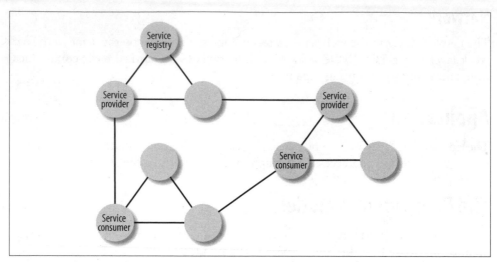

Figure 1-7. The peer web services model simply applies the concepts of the web services architecture in a peer-to-peer network

## CHAPTER 2

Introducing SOAP

SOAP's place in the web services technology stack is as a standardized packaging protocol for the messages shared by applications. The specification defines nothing more than a simple XML-based envelope for the information being transferred, and a set of rules for translating application and platform-specific data types into XML representations. SOAP's design makes it suitable for a wide variety of application messaging and integration patterns. This, for the most part, contributes to its growing popularity.

This chapter explains the parts of the SOAP standard. It covers the message format, the exception-reporting mechanism (*faults*), and the system for encoding values in XML. It discusses using SOAP over transports that aren't HTTP, and concludes with thoughts on the future of SOAP. You'll learn what SOAP does and how it does it, and get a firm understanding of the flexibility of SOAP. Later chapters build on this to show how to program with SOAP using toolkits that abstract details of the XML.

SOAP and XML

SOAP is XML. That is, SOAP is an application of the XML specification. It relies heavily on XML standards like XML Schema and XML Namespaces for its definition and function. If you are not familiar with any of these, you'll probably want to get up to speed before continuing with the information in this chapter (you can find information about each of these specifications at the World Wide Web Consortium's web site at *http://www.w3c.org*). This book assumes you are familiar with these specifications, at least on a cursory level, and will not spend time discussing them. The only exception is a quick introduction to the XML Schema data types in Appendix B.

XML Messaging

XML messaging is where applications exchange information using XML documents (see Figure 2-1). It provides a flexible way for applications to communicate, and forms the basis of SOAP.

A message can be anything: a purchase order, a request for a current stock price, a query for a search engine, a listing of available flights to Los Angeles, or any number of other pieces of information that may be relevant to a particular application.

Figure 2-1. XML messaging

Because XML is not tied to a particular application, operating system, or programming language, XML messages can be used in all environments. A Windows Perl program can create an XML document representing a message, send it to a Unix-based Java program, and affect the behavior of that Java program.

The fundamental idea is that two applications, regardless of operating system, programming language, or any other technical implementation detail, may openly share information using nothing more than a simple message encoded in a way that both applications understand. SOAP provides a standard way to structure XML messages.

RPC and EDI

XML messaging, and therefore SOAP, has two related applications: RPC and EDI. Remote Procedure Call (RPC) is the basis of distributed computing, the way for one program to make a procedure (or function, or method, call it what you will) call on another, passing arguments and receiving return values. Electronic Document Interchange (EDI) is basis of automated business transactions, defining a standard format and interpretation of financial and commercial documents and messages.

If you use SOAP for EDI (known as "document-style" SOAP), then the XML will be a purchase order, tax refund, or similar document. If you use SOAP for RPC (known, unsurprisingly, as "RPC-style" SOAP) then the XML will be a representation of parameter or return values.

The Need for a Standard Encoding

If you're exchanging data between heterogeneous systems, you need to agree on a common representation. As you can see in Example 2-1, a single piece of data like a telephone number may be represented in many different, and equally valid ways in XML.

Example 2-1. Many XML representations of a phone number

```
<phoneNumber>(123) 456-7890</phoneNumber>
<phoneNumber>
    <areaCode>123</areaCode>
    <exchange>456</exchange>
```

Example 2-1. Many XML representations of a phone number (continued)

```
    <number>7890</number>
</phoneNumber>
<phoneNumber area="123"  exchange="456"  number="7890" />
<phone area="123">
    <exchange>456</exchange>
    <number>7890</number>
</phone>
```

Which is the correct encoding? Who knows! The correct one is whatever the application is expecting. In other words, simply saying that server and client are using XML to exchange information is not enough. We need to define:

- The types of information we are exchanging
- How that information is to be expressed as XML
- How to actually go about sending that information

Without these agreed conventions, programs cannot know how to decode the information they're given, even if it's encoded in XML. SOAP provides these conventions.

SOAP Messages

A SOAP message consists of an envelope containing an optional header and a required body, as shown in Figure 2-2. The header contains blocks of information relevant to how the message is to be processed. This includes routing and delivery settings, authentication or authorization assertions, and transaction contexts. The body contains the actual message to be delivered and processed. Anything that can be expressed in XML syntax can go in the body of a message.

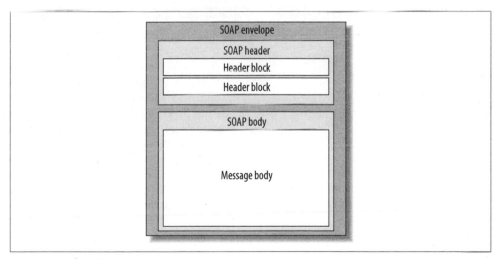

Figure 2-2. The SOAP message structure

The XML syntax for expressing a SOAP message is based on the http://www.w3.org/2001/06/soap-envelope namespace. This XML namespace identifier points to an XML Schema that defines the structure of what a SOAP message looks like.

If you were using document-style SOAP, you might transfer a purchase order with the XML in Example 2-2.

Example 2-2. A purchase order in document-style SOAP

```
<s:Envelope
 xmlns:s="http://www.w3.org/2001/06/soap-envelope">
    <s:Header>
        <m:transaction xmlns:m="soap-transaction"
                       s:mustUnderstand="true">
            <transactionID>1234</transactionID>
        </m:transaction>
    </s:Header>
    <s:Body>
        <n:purchaseOrder xmlns:n="urn:OrderService">
            <from><person>Christopher Robin</person>
                  <dept>Accounting</dept></from>
            <to><person>Pooh Bear</person>
                <dept>Honey</dept></to>
            <order><quantity>1</quantity>
                   <item>Pooh Stick</item></order>
        </n:purchaseOrder>
    </s:Body>
</s:Envelope>
```

This example illustrates all of the core components of the SOAP Envelope specification. There is the <s:Envelope>, the topmost container that comprises the SOAP message; the optional <s:Header>, which contains additional blocks of information about how the body payload is to be processed; and the mandatory <s:Body> element that contains the actual message to be processed.

Envelopes

Every Envelope element must contain exactly one Body element. The Body element may contain as many child nodes as are required. The contents of the Body element are the message. The Body element is defined in such a way that it can contain any valid, well-formed XML that has been namespace qualified and does not contain any processing instructions or Document Type Definition (DTD) references.

If an Envelope contains a Header element, it must contain no more than one, and it must appear as the first child of the Envelope, before the Body. The header, like the body, may contain any valid, well-formed, and namespace-qualified XML that the creator of the SOAP message wishes to insert.

Each element contained by the Header is called a *header block*. The purpose of a header block is to communicate contextual information relevant to the processing of a SOAP message. An example might be a header block that contains authentication credentials, or message routing information. Header blocks will be highlighted and explained in greater detail throughout the remainder of the book. In Example 2-2, the header block indicates that the document has a transaction ID of "1234".

RPC Messages

Now let's see an RPC-style message. Typically messages come in pairs, as shown in Figure 2-3: the request (the client sends function call information to the server) and the response (the server sends return value(s) back to the client). SOAP doesn't require every request to have a response, or vice versa, but it is common to see the request-response pairing.

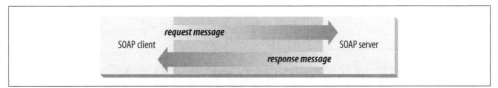

Figure 2-3. Basic RPC messaging architecture

Imagine the server offers this function, which returns a stock's price, as a SOAP service:

```
public Float getQuote(String symbol);
```

Example 2-3 illustrates a simple RPC-style SOAP message that represents a request for IBM's current stock price. Again, we show a header block that indicates a transaction ID of "1234".

Example 2-3. RPC-style SOAP message

```
<s:Envelope
 xmlns:s="http://www.w3.org/2001/06/soap-envelope">
    <s:Header>
        <m:transaction xmlns:m="soap-transaction"
                        s:mustUnderstand="true">
            <transactionID>1234</transactionID>
        </m:transaction>
    </s:Header>
    <s:Body>
        <n:getQuote xmlns:n="urn:QuoteService">
            <symbol xsi:type="xsd:string">
                IBM
            </symbol>
        </n:getQuote>
    </s:Body>
</s:Envelope>
```

Example 2-4 is a possible response that indicates the operation being responded to and the requested stock quote value.

Example 2-4. SOAP response to request in Example 2-3

```
<s:Envelope
 xmlns:s="http://www.w3.org/2001/06/soap-envelope">
    <s:Body>
        <n:getQuoteRespone
                xmlns:n="urn:QuoteService">
            <value xsi:type="xsd:float">
                98.06
            </value>
        </n:getQuoteResponse>
    </s:Body>
</s:Envelope>
```

The mustUnderstand Attribute

When a SOAP message is sent from one application to another, there is an implicit requirement that the recipient must understand how to process that message. If the recipient does not understand the message, the recipient must reject the message and explain the problem to the sender. This makes sense: if Amazon.com sent O'Reilly a purchase order for 150 electric drills, someone from O'Reilly would call someone from Amazon.com and explain that O'Reilly and Associates sells books, not electric drills.

Header blocks are different. A recipient may or may not understand how to deal with a particular header block but still be able to process the primary message properly. If the sender of the message wants to require that the recipient understand a particular block, it may add a mustUnderstand="true" attribute to the header block. If this flag is present, and the recipient does not understand the block to which it is attached, the recipient must reject the entire message.

In the getQuote envelope we saw earlier, the transaction header contains the mustUnderstand="true" flag. Because this flag is set, regardless of whether or not the recipient understands and is capable of processing the message body (the getQuote message), if it does not understand how to deal with the transaction header block, the entire message must be rejected. This guarantees that the recipient understands transactions.

Encoding Styles

As part of the overall specification, Section 5 of the SOAP standard introduces a concept known as *encoding styles*. An encoding style is a set of rules that define exactly how native application and platform data types are to be encoded into a common XML syntax. These are, obviously, for use with RPC-style SOAP.

The encoding style for a particular set of XML elements is defined through the use of the encodingStyle attribute, which can be placed anywhere in the document and applies to all subordinate children of the element on which it is located.

For example, the encodingStyle attribute on the getQuote element in the body of Example 2-5 indicates that all children of the getQuote element conform to the encoding style rules defined in Section 5.

Example 2-5. The encodingStyle attribute

```
<s:Envelope
 xmlns:s="http://www.w3.org/2001/06/soap-envelope">
 <s:Body>
  <n:getQuote xmlns:n="urn:QuoteService"
   s:encodingStyle="http://www.w3.org/2001/06/soap-encoding">
    <symbol xsi:type="xsd:string">IBM</symbol>
  </n:getQuote>
 </s:Body>
</s:Envelope>
```

Even though the SOAP specification defines an encoding style in Section 5, it has been explicitly declared that no single style is the default serialization scheme. Why is this important?

Encoding styles are how applications on different platforms share information, even though they may not have common data types or representations. The approach that the SOAP Section 5 encoding style takes is just one possible mechanism for providing this, but it is not suitable in every situation.

For example, in the case where a SOAP message is used to exchange a purchase order that already has a defined XML syntax, there is no need for the Section 5 encoding rules to be applied. The purchase order would simply be dropped into the Body section of the SOAP envelope as is.

The SOAP Section 5 encoding style will be discussed in much greater detail later in this chapter, as most SOAP applications and libraries use it.

Versioning

There have been several versions of the SOAP specification put into production. The most recent working draft, SOAP Version 1.2, represents the first fruits of the World Wide Web Consortium's (W3C) effort to standardize an XML-based packaging protocol for web services. The W3C chose SOAP as the basis for that effort.

The previous version of SOAP, Version 1.1, is still widely used. In fact, at the time we are writing this, there are only three implementations of the SOAP 1.2 specification available: SOAP::Lite for Perl, Apache SOAP Version 2.2, and Apache Axis (which is not even in beta status).

While SOAP 1.1 and 1.2 are largely the same, the differences that do exist are significant enough to warrant mention. To prevent subtle incompatibility problems, SOAP 1.2 introduces a versioning model that deals with how SOAP Version 1.1 processors and SOAP Version 1.2 processors may interact. The rules for this are fairly straightforward:

1. If a SOAP Version 1.1 compliant application receives a SOAP Version 1.2 message, a "version mismatch" error will be triggered.

2. If a SOAP Version 1.2 compliant application receives a SOAP Version 1.1 message, the application may choose to either process it according to the SOAP Version 1.1 specification or trigger a "version mismatch" error.

The version of a SOAP message can be determined by checking the namespace defined for the SOAP envelope. Version 1.1 uses the namespace `http://schemas.xmlsoap.org/soap/envelope/`, whereas Version 1.2 uses the namespace `http://www.w3.org/2001/06/soap-envelope`. Example 2-6 illustrates the difference.

Example 2-6. Distinguishing between SOAP 1.1 and SOAP 1.2

```
<!-- Version 1.1 SOAP Envelope -->
<s:Envelope
 xmlns:s="http://schemas.xmlsoap.org/soap/envelope/">
  ...
</s:Envelope>

<!-- Version 1.2 SOAP Envelope -->
<s:Envelope
 xmlns:s="http://www.w3.org/2001/06/soap-envelope">
  ...
</s:Envelope>
```

When applications report a version mismatch error back to the sender of the message, it may optionally include an `Upgrade` header block that tells the sender which version of SOAP it supports. Example 2-7 shows the `Upgrade` header in action.

Example 2-7. The Upgrade header

```
<s:Envelope xmlns:s="http://schemas.xmlsoap.org/soap/envelope/">
  <s:Header>
    <V:Upgrade xmlns:V="http://www.w3.org/2001/06/soap-upgrade">
      <envelope qname="ns1:Envelope"
                xmlns:ns1="http://www.w3.org/2001/06/soap-envelope"/>
    </V:Upgrade>
  </s:Header>
  <s:Body>
    <s:Fault>
      <faultcode>s:VersionMismatch</faultcode>
      <faultstring>Version Mismatch</faultstring>
    </s:Fault>
  </s:Body>
</s:Envelope>
```

For backwards compatibility, version mismatch errors must conform to the SOAP Version 1.1 specification, regardless of the version of SOAP being used.

SOAP Faults

A SOAP fault (shown in Example 2-8) is a special type of message specifically targeted at communicating information about errors that may have occurred during the processing of a SOAP message.

Example 2-8. SOAP fault

```
<s:Envelope xmlns:s="...">
   <s:Body>
      <s:Fault>
        <faultcode>Client.Authentication</faultcode>
        <faultstring>
           Invalid credentials
        </faultstring>
        <faultactor>http://acme.com</faultactor>
        <details>
           <!-- application specific details -->
        </details>
      </s:Fault>
   </s:Body>
</s:Envelope>
```

The information communicated in the SOAP fault is as follows:

The fault code

> An algorithmically generated value for identifying the type of error that occurred. The value must be an XML Qualified Name, meaning that the name of the code only has meaning within a defined XML namespace.

The fault string

> A human-readable explanation of the error.

The fault actor

> The unique identifier of the message processing node at which the error occurred (actors will be discussed later).

The fault details

> Used to express application-specific details about the error that occurred. This must be present if the error that occurred is directly related to some problem with the body of the message. It must not be used, however, to express information about errors that occur in relation to any other aspect of the message process.

Standard SOAP Fault Codes

SOAP defines four standard types of faults that belong to the `http://www.w3.org/2001/06/soap-envelope` namespace. These are described here:

VersionMismatch
>   The SOAP envelope is using an invalid namespace for the SOAP Envelope element.

MustUnderstand
>   A `Header` block contained a `mustUnderstand="true"` flag that was not understood by the message recipient.

Server
>   An error occurred that can't be directly linked to the processing of the message.

Client
>   There is a problem in the message. For example, the message contains invalid authentication credentials, or there is an improper application of the Section 5 encoding style rules.

These fault codes can be extended to allow for more expressive and granular types of faults, while still maintaining backwards compatibility with the core fault codes.

The example SOAP fault demonstrates how this extensibility works. The `Client.Authentication` fault code is a more granular derivative of the `Client` fault type. The "." notation indicates that the piece to the left of the period is more generic than the piece that is to the right of the period.

MustUnderstand Faults

As mentioned earlier, a header block contained within a SOAP message may indicate through the `mustUnderstand="true"` flag that the recipient of the message must understand how to process the contents of the header block. If it cannot, then the recipient must return a `MustUnderstand` fault back to the sender of the message. In doing so, the fault should communicate specific information about the header blocks that were not understood by the recipient.

The SOAP fault structure is not allowed to express any information about which headers were not understood. The `details` element would be the only place to put this information and it is reserved solely for the purpose of expressing error information related to the processing of the body, not the header.

To solve this problem, the SOAP Version 1.2 specification defines a standard `Misunderstood` header block that can be added to the SOAP fault message to indicate which header blocks in the received message were not understood. Example 2-9 shows this.

Example 2-9. The Misunderstood header

```
<s:Envelope xmlns:s="...">
   <s:Header>
      <f:Misunderstood qname="abc:transaction"
                       xmlns:="soap-transactions" />
   </s:Header>
   <s:Body>
      <s:Fault>
       <faultcode>MustUnderstand</faultcode>
       <faultstring>
           Header(s) not understood
       </faultstring>
       <faultactor>http://acme.com</faultactor>
      </s:Fault>
   </s:Body>
</s:Envelope>
```

The Misunderstood header block is optional, which makes it unreliable to use as the primary method of determining which headers caused the message to be rejected.

Custom Faults

A web service may define its own custom fault codes that do not derive from the ones defined by SOAP. The only requirement is that these custom faults be namespace qualified. Example 2-10 shows a custom fault code.

Example 2-10. A custom fault

```
<s:Envelope xmlns:s="...">
   <s:Body>
      <s:Fault xmlns:xyz="urn:myCustomFaults">
         <faultcode>xyz:CustomFault</faultcode>
         <faultstring>
             My custom fault!
         </faultstring>
      </s:Fault>
   </s:Body>
</s:Envelope>
```

Approach custom faults with caution: a SOAP processor that only understands the standard four fault codes will not be able to take intelligent action upon receipt of a custom fault. However, custom faults can still be useful in situations where the standard fault codes are too generic or are otherwise inadequate for the expression of what error occurred.

For the most part, the extensibility of the existing four fault codes makes custom fault codes largely unnecessary.

The SOAP Message Exchange Model

Processing a SOAP message involves pulling apart the envelope and doing something with the information that it carries. SOAP defines a general framework for such processing, but leaves the actual details of how that processing is implemented up to the application.

What the SOAP specification does have to say about message processing deals primarily with how applications exchange SOAP messages. Section 2 of the specification outlines a very specific message exchange model.

Message Paths and Actors

At the core of this exchange model is the idea that while a SOAP message is fundamentally a one-way transmission of an envelope from a sender to a receiver, that message may pass through various intermediate processors that each in turn do something with the message. This is analogous to a Unix pipeline, where the output of one program becomes the input to another, and so on until you get the output you want.

A SOAP intermediary is a web service specially designed to sit between a service consumer and a service provider and add value or functionality to the transaction between the two. The set of intermediaries that the message travels through is called the message path. Every intermediary along that path is known as an actor.

The construction of a message path (the definition of which nodes a message passes through) is not covered by the SOAP specification. Various extensions to SOAP, such as Microsoft's SOAP Routing Protocol (WS-Routing) have emerged to fill that gap, but there is still no standard (de facto or otherwise) method of expressing the message path. We cover WS-Routing later.

What SOAP does specify, however, is a mechanism of identifying which parts of the SOAP message are intended for processing by specific actors in its message path. This mechanism is known as "targeting" and can only be used in relation to header blocks (the body of the SOAP envelope cannot be explicitly targeted at a particular node).

A header block is targeted to a specific actor on its message path through the use of the special actor attribute. The value of the actor attribute is the unique identifier of the intermediary being targeted. This identifier may be the URL where the intermediary may be found, or something more generic. Intermediaries that do not match the actor attribute must ignore the header block.

For example, imagine that I am a wholesaler of fine cardigan sweaters. I set up a web service that allows me to receive purchase orders from my customers in the form of SOAP messages. You, one of my best customers, want to submit an order for 100 sweaters. So you send me a SOAP message that contains the purchase order.

For our mutual protection, however, I have established a relationship with a trusted third-party web service that can help me validate that the purchase order you sent really did come from you. This service works by verifying that your digital signature header block embedded in the SOAP message is valid.

When you send that message to me, it is going to be routed through this third-party signature verification service, which will, in turn, extract the digital signature, validate it, and add a new header block that tells me whether the signature is valid. The transaction is depicted in Figure 2-4.

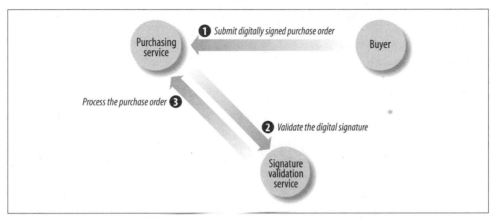

Figure 2-4. The signature validation intermediary

Now, the signature verification intermediary needs to have some way of knowing which header block contains the digital signature that it is expected to verify. This is accomplished by targeting the digital signature block to the verification service, as in Example 2-11.

Example 2-11. The actor header

```
<s:Envelope xmlns:s="...">
   <s:Header>
      <x:signature actor="uri:SignatureVerifier">
         ...
      </x:signature>
   </s:Header>
   <s:Body>
      <abc:purchaseOrder>...</abc:purchaseOrder>
   </s:Body>
</s:Envelope>
```

The actor attribute on the signature header block is how the signature verifier intermediary knows that it is responsible for processing that header block. If the message does not pass through the signature verifier, then the signature block is ignored.

The SOAP Routing Protocol

Remember, SOAP does not specify how the message is to be routed to the signature verification service, only that it should be at some point during the processing of the SOAP message. This makes the implementation of SOAP message paths a fairly difficult proposition since there is no single standard way of representing that path. The SOAP Routing Protocol (WS-Routing) is Microsoft's proposal for solving this problem.

WS-Routing defines a standard SOAP header block (see Example 2-12) for expressing routing information. Its role is to define the exact sequence of intermediaries through which a message is to pass.

Example 2-12. A WS-Routing message

```
<s:Envelope xmlns:s="...">
 <s:Header>
  <m:path xmlns:m="http://schemas.xmlsoap.org/rp/"
          s:mustUnderstand="true">
   <m:action>http://www.im.org/chat</m:action>
    <m:to>http://D.com/some/endpoint</m:to>
    <m:fwd>
     <m:via>http://B.com</m:via>
     <m:via>http://C.com</m:via>
    </m:fwd>
    <m:rev>
     <m:via/>
    </m:rev>
    <m:from>mailto:johndoe@acme.com</m:from>
    <m:id>
      uuid:84b9f5d0-33fb-4a81-b02b-5b760641c1d6
    </m:id>
  </m:path>
 </S:Header>
 <S:Body>
  ...
 </S:Body>
</S:Envelope>
```

In this example, we see the SOAP message is intended to be delivered to a recipient located at http://d.com/some/endpoint but that it must first go through both the http://b.com and http://c.com intermediaries.

To ensure that the message path defined by the WS-Routing header block is properly followed, and because WS-Routing is a third-party extension to SOAP that not every SOAP processor will understand, the mustUnderstand="true" flag can be set on the path header block.

Using SOAP for RPC-Style Web Services

RPC is the most common application of SOAP at the moment. The following sections show how method calls and return values are encoded in SOAP message bodies.

Invoking Methods

The rules for packaging an RPC request in a SOAP envelope are simple:

- The method call is represented as a single structure with each in or in-out parameter modeled as a field in that structure.
- The names and physical order of the parameters must correspond to the names and physical order of the parameters in the method being invoked.

This means that a Java method with the following signature:

```
String checkStatus(String orderCode,
                   String customerID);
```

can be invoked with these arguments:

```
result = checkStatus("abc123", "Bob's Store")
```

using the following SOAP envelope:

```
<s:Envelope xmlns:s="...">
  <s:Body>
    <checkStatus xmlns-"..."
                 s:encodingStyle="http://www.w3.org/2001/06/soap-encoding">
      <orderCode xsi:type="string">abc123</orderCode>
      <customerID xsi:type="string">
        Bob's Store
      </customerID>
    </checkStatus>
  </s:Body>
</s:Envelope>
```

The SOAP RPC conventions do not require the use of the SOAP Section 5 encoding style and xsi:type explicit data typing. They are, however, widely used and will be what we describe.

Returning Responses

Method responses are similar to method calls in that the structure of the response is modeled as a single structure with a field for each in-out or out parameter in the method signature. If the checkStatus method we called earlier returned the string new, the SOAP response might be something like Example 2-13.

Example 2-13. Response to the method call

```
<s:Envelope xmlns:s="...">
  <s:Body>
    <checkStatusResponse
      s:encodingStyle="http://www.w3.org/2001/06/soap-encoding">
      <return xsi:type="xsd:string">new</return>
    </checkStatusResponse>
  </SOAP:Body>
</SOAP:Envelope>
```

The name of the message response structure (checkStatusResponse) element is not important, but the convention is to name it after the method, with Response appended. Similarly, the name of the return element is arbitrary—the first field in the message response structure is assumed to be the return value.

Reporting Errors

The SOAP RPC conventions make use of the SOAP fault as the standard method of returning error responses to RPC clients. As with standard SOAP messages, the SOAP fault is used to convey the exact nature of the error that has occurred and can be extended to provide additional information through the use of the detail element. There's little point in customizing error messages in SOAP faults when you're doing RPC, as most SOAP RPC implementations will not know how to deal with the custom error information.

SOAP's Data Encoding

The first part of the SOAP specification outlines a standard envelope format for packaging data. The second part of the specification (specifically, Section 5) outlines one possible method of serializing the data intended for packaging. These rules outline in specific detail how basic application data types are to be mapped and encoded into XML format when embedded into a SOAP Envelope.

The SOAP specification introduces the SOAP encoding style as "a simple type system that is a generalization of the common features found in type systems in programming languages, databases, and semi-structured data." As such, these encoding rules can be applied in nearly any programming environment regardless of the minor differences that exist between those environments.

Encoding styles are completely optional, and in many situations not useful (recall the purchase order example we gave earlier in this chapter, where it made sense to ship a document and not an encoded method call/response). SOAP envelopes are designed to carry any arbitrary XML documents no matter what the body of the message looks like, or whether it conforms to any specific set of data encoding rules. The Section 5 encoding rules are offered only as a convenience to allow applications to dynamically exchange information without a priori knowledge of the types of information to be exchanged.

Understanding the Terminology

Before continuing, it is important to gain a firm understanding of the vocabulary used to describe the encoding process. Of particular importance are the terms *value* and *accessor*.

A value represents either a single data unit or combination of data units. This could be a person's name, the score of a football game, or the current temperature. An accessor represents an element that contains or allows access to a value. In the following, firstname is an accessor, and Joe is a value:

```
<firstname> Joe </firstname>
```

A compound value represents a combination of two or more accessors grouped as children of a single accessor, and is demonstrated in Example 2-14.

Example 2-14. A compound value

```
<name>
    <firstname> Joe </firstname>
    <lastname> Smith </lastname>
</name>
```

There are two types of compound values, structs (the structures we talked about earlier) and arrays. A *struct* is a compound value in which each accessor has a different name. An *array* is a compound value in which the accessors have the same name (values are identified by their positions in the array). A struct and an array are shown in Example 2-15.

Example 2-15. Structs and arrays

```
<!--A struct -->
<person>
    <firstname>Joe</firstname>
    <lastname>Smith</lastname>
</person>

<!--An array-->
<people>
    <person name='joe smith'/>
    <person name='john doe'/>
</people>
```

Through the use of the special id and href attributes, SOAP defines that accessors may either be *single-referenced* or *multireferenced*. A single-referenced accessor doesn't have an identity except as a child of its parent element. In Example 2-16, the <address> element is a single-referenced accessor.

Example 2-16. A single-referenced accessor

```
<people>
    <person name='joe smith'>
        <address>
            <street>111 First Street</street>
            <city>New York</city>
            <state>New York</state>
        </address>
    </person>
</people>
```

A multireferenced accessor uses id to give an identity to its value. Other accessors can use the href attribute to refer to their values. In Example 2-17, each person has the same address, because they reference the same multireferenced address accessor.

Example 2-17. A multireferenced accessor

```
<people>
   <person name='joe smith'>
      <address href='#address-1'
   </person>
   <person name='john doe'>
      <address href='#address-1'
   </person>
</people>
<address id='address-1'>
   <street>111 First Street</street>
   <city>New York</city>
   <state>New York</state>
</address>
```

This approach can also be used to allow an accessor to reference external information sources that are not a part of the SOAP Envelope (binary data, for example, or parts of a MIME multipart envelope). Example 2-18 references information contained within an external XML document.

Example 2-18. A reference to an external document

```
<person name='joe smith'>
   <address href='http://acme.com/data.xml#joe_smith' />
</person>
```

XML Schemas and xsi:type

The SOAP encoding rule in Section 5.1 states how to express data types within the SOAP envelope, and has caused quite a bit of confusion and challenges for SOAP implementers. Read for yourself:

> Although it is possible to use the xsi:type attribute such that a graph of values is self-describing both in its structure and that types of its values, the serialization rules permit that the types of values MAY be determinable only by reference to a schema. Such schemas MAY be in the notation described by 'XML Schema Part 1: Structures' and 'XML Schemas Part 2: Data types' or MAY be in any other notation.

English translation: SOAP defines three different ways to express the data type of an accessor.

1. Use the xsi:type attribute on each accessor, explicitly referencing the data type according to the XML Schema specification, as in this example:

```
<person>
   <name xsi:type="xsd:string">John Doe</name>
</person>
```

2. Reference an XML Schema document that defines the exact data type of a particular element within its definition, as in this example:

```
<person xmlns="personschema.xsd">
    <name>John Doe</name>
</person>
<!-- where "personschema.xsd" defines the name
        element as type=xsd:string -->
```

3. Reference some other type of schema document that defines the data type of a particular element within its definition, as in this example:

```
<person xmlns="urn:some_namespace">
    <name>John Doe</name>
</person>
<!-- where "urn:some_namespace" indicates some
        namespace in which the value of name
        elements are strings -->
```

Early SOAP implementations varied in their interpretations of this part of the SOAP specification, causing some rather nasty and annoying integration problems (ironic because SOAP's main goal is to enable interoperability). In particular, the IBM (later Apache) SOAP implementation chose the route of requiring xsi:type based typing (forgoing the other two options completely) while the Microsoft SOAP implementation chose to completely ignore the xsi:type option in favor of using schemas based on an external service description document. Since neither tool was implemented as a complete implementation of the SOAP Encoding rules, neither tool was capable of interpreting the data types encoded by the other, even though both were implemented as legal SOAP Encoding schemes. This has, fortunately, since been resolved.

In fact, there has been a large ongoing effort to improve the interoperability between SOAP implementations. For more information about this effort, see the "SOAPBuilders" group at *http://groups.yahoo.com*.

SOAP Data Types

The data types supported by the SOAP encoding style are the data types defined by the "XML Schema data types" specification. All data types used within a SOAP-encoded block of XML must either be taken directly from the XML Schema specification or derived from types therein.

SOAP encoding provides two alternate syntaxes for expressing instances of these data types within the SOAP envelope. Example 2-19 shows two equivalent expressions of an integer equaling the value "36".

Example 2-19. Alternate SOAP encoding syntaxes for typing values

```
<SOAP-ENC:int>36</SOAP-ENC:int>
<value xsi:type="xsd:int">36</value>
```

The first method is what is known as an *anonymous accessor*, and is commonly found in SOAP encoded arrays (as we will see a little later in this chapter). It's "anonymous" because the accessor's name is its type, rather than a meaningful identification for the value. The second approach is the named accessor syntax that we've already seen. Either is valid since they both can be directly linked back to the XML Schema data types.

Multiple References in XML-Encoded Data

The values a program works with are stored in memory. Variables are how programming languages let you manipulate those values in memory. Two different variables might have the same value; for instance, two integer variables could both be set to the value 42. The SOAP XML encoding for this would use single-reference XML, as in Example 2-20.

Example 2-20. Two integer variables set to 42

```
<SOAP-ENC:int>42</SOAP-ENC:int>
<SOAP-ENC:int>42</SOAP-ENC:int>
```

Sometimes, though, you need to indicate that two separate variables are stored in the same piece of memory. For instance, if this subroutine call is going to be XML encoded for SOAP, you'll need to identify the first and second parameters as being the same:

```
tweak(&i, &i);
```

You do this with Section 5's encoding rules using multiple-reference types. That is, you use the id attribute to name the value in i, then use the href attribute to identify other occurrences of that value, as in Example 2-21.

Example 2-21. Multiple-reference to indicate two parameters are the same

```
<value xsi:type="xsd:int" id="v1">42</value>
<value href="#v1" />
```

It's important to understand that even though "SOAP" originally stood for "Simple Object Access Protocol," it actually has no concept of what an object is. To SOAP, everything is data encoded into XML. Therefore there is no such thing as an "object reference" in SOAP. Rather, SOAP Section 5 Encoding specifies a set of rules for transforming an object into XML representing that object. All references to that object that must also be encoded would be done through the use of the id and href attributes.

Given Example 2-22, the SOAP encoded serialization of the Person object might look something like Example 2-23.

Example 2-22. Java code to construct an object

```
Address address = new Address( );
Person person   = new Person( );
person.setAddress(address);
```

Example 2-23. SOAP serialization of the object

```
<Person>
   <Address href="#address1" />
</Person>
<Address id="address1" />
```

Structs, Arrays, and Other Compound Types

It was mentioned previously that the difference between an array and a struct in SOAP is that in an array, each accessor in the group is differentiated only by its ordinal position in the group, whereas in the struct, each accessor is differentiated by name. This was shown in Example 2-15.

Even though many programming languages regard strings as an array of bytes, SOAP does not. A string is represented with the string data type, rather than as an array of bytes. If you do have a collection of bytes that you want to ship around, and those bytes do not represent a text string, SOAP Section 5 Encoding decrees that you should use a base64 string, as defined by the XML Schemas specification. The proper serialization of an array of arbitrary bytes, then, is shown in Example 2-24.

Example 2-24. A SOAP-encoded array of bytes

```
<some_binary_data xsi:type="SOAP-ENC:base64">
    aDF4J1K34KJjk3443kjlkj43SDF43==
</some_binary_data>
```

Regular arrays, however, are indicated as accessors of the type SOAP-ENC:Array, or a type derived from that. The type of elements that an array can contain is indicated through the use of the SOAP defined arrayType attribute, shown in Example 2-25.

Example 2-25. The arrayType attribute

```
<some_array xsi:type="SOAP-ENC:Array" SOAP-ENC:arrayType="se:string[3]">
   <se:string>Joe</se:string>
   <se:string>John</se:string>
   <se:string>Marsha</se:string>
</some_array>
```

Note the [3] appended to the end of the data type value on the arrayType attribute. The square brackets ([]) indicate the dimensions of the array, while the numbers internally represent the number of elements per dimension. In other words, [3] indicates a single dimension of 3 elements, while [3,2] indicates a two dimensional array of three elements each. SOAP Encoding supports an unlimited number of dimensions per array in addition to allowing arrays of arrays. For instance, an `arrayType` of `xsd:string[2][]` indicates an unbounded array of single dimensional string arrays, each of which contains two elements.

In Example 2-26, the data accessor is an array that contains both of the names arrays.

Example 2-26. A two-dimensional array

```
<data xsi:type="SOAP-ENC:Array" SOAP-ENC:arrayType="xsd:string[2][]">
   <names href="#names-1"/>
   <names href="#names-2"/>
</data>
<names id="names-1" xsi:type="SOAP-ENC:Array"
      SOAP-ENC:arrayType="xsd:string[2]">
  <name>joe</name>
  <name>john</name>
</names>
<names id="names-2" xsi:type="SOAP-ENC:Array"
      SOAP-ENC:arrayType="xsd:string[2]">
  <name>mike</name>
  <name>bill</name>
</names>
```

Multidimensional arrays, expressed as XML, are syntactically no different than a regular single-dimension array, with the exception of the value indicated by the `arrayType` attribute. For example, a two-dimensional array of two strings is nearly identical to a one-dimensional array of four strings (shown in Example 2-27).

Example 2-27. Comparison of two-dimensional and one-dimensional arrays

```
<names xsi:type="SOAP-ENC:Array" SOAP-ENC:arrayType="xsd:string[2,2]">
    <name xsi:type="xsd:string">a1d1</name>
    <name xsi:type="xsd:string">a2d1</name>
    <name xsi:type="xsd:string">a1d2</name>
    <name xsi:type="xsd:string">a2d2</name>
</names>

<names xsi:type="SOAP-ENC:Array" SOAP-ENC:arrayType="xsd:string[4]">
    <name xsi:type="xsd:string">a1d1</name>
    <name xsi:type="xsd:string">a2d1</name>
    <name xsi:type="xsd:string">a3d1</name>
    <name xsi:type="xsd:string">a4d1</name>
</names>
```

The value of the `arrayType` attribute distinguishes the true nature of the serialized array.

Partially Transmitted Arrays and Sparse Arrays

SOAP Encoding also includes support for *partially transmitted arrays* and *sparse arrays* through a set of additional attribute definitions.

A partially transmitted array is one in which only part of the array is serialized into the SOAP envelope. This is indicated through the use of the `SOAP-ENC:offset` attribute that provides the number or ordinals counting from zero to the first ordinal position transmitted. In other words, if you have a single-dimensional array of five elements, and you want to transmit only the last two, you would use the syntax in Example 2-28.

Example 2-28. Using SOAP-ENC:offset for partially transmitted arrays

```
<names xsi:type="SOAP-ENC:Array" SOAP-ENC:arrayType="xsd:string[5]"
      SOAP-ENC:offset="[2]">
   <name>Item 4</name>
   <name>Item 5</name>
</names>
```

Sparse arrays represent a grid of values with specified dimensions that may or may not contain any data. For example, if you have a two-dimensional array of ten items each, but only the elements at position [2,5] and [5,2] contain data, the serialization in Example 2-29 would be appropriate.

Example 2-29. SOAP serialization of sparse arrays

```
<names xsi:type="SOAP-ENC:Array" SOAP-ENC:arrayType="xsd:string[10,10]">
   <name SOAP-ENC:position="[2,5]">data</name>
   <name SOAP-ENC:position="[5,2]">data</name>
</names>
```

Null Accessors

In the sparse array example, the absence of an accessor indicates that the value of the accessor is either null or some other default value. One problem with this is the fact that the receiver of the message has no real way of knowing whether the value of the accessor really was null, or if the sender just failed to serialize the message properly.

If the receiver expects to find the accessor in the message, a better method of indicating whether an accessor contains a null value would be to use the XML Schema defined `xsi:nil="true"` attribute:

```
<name xsi:type="xsd:string" xsi:nil="true" />
```

This allows you to be far more expressive in your encoding of application data and eliminates confusion over the significance of missing elements.

SOAP Transports

As mentioned before, SOAP fits in on the web services technology stack as a standardized packaging protocol layered on top of the network and transport layers. As a packaging protocol, SOAP does not care what transport protocols are used to exchange the messages. This makes SOAP extremely flexible in how and where it is used.

As an illustration of this flexibility, SOAP::Lite—the Perl-based SOAP web services implementation written by Pavel Kulchenko—supports the ability to exchange SOAP messages through HTTP, FTP, raw TCP, SMTP, POP3, MQSeries, and Jabber. We'll show SOAP over Jabber in Chapter 3.

SOAP over HTTP

Because of its pervasiveness on the Internet, HTTP is by far the most common transport used to exchange SOAP messages. The SOAP specification even goes so far as to give special treatment to HTTP within the specification itself—outlining in specific detail how the semantics of the SOAP message exchange model map onto HTTP.

SOAP-over-HTTP is a natural match with SOAP's RPC (request-response) conventions because HTTP is a request-response-based protocol. The SOAP request message is posted to the HTTP server with the HTTP request, and the server returns the SOAP response message in the HTTP response (see Figure 2-5).

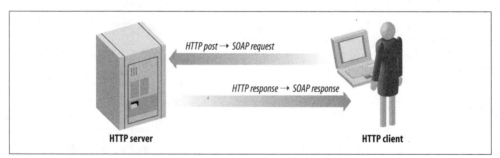

Figure 2-5. SOAP request messages are posted to the HTTP server and response messages are returned over the same HTTP connection

Example 2-30 and Example 2-31 illustrate an HTTP request and HTTP response messages that contain a SOAP message.

Example 2-30. HTTP request containing a SOAP message

```
POST /StockQuote HTTP/1.1
Content-Type: text/xml
Content-Length: nnnn
SOAPAction: "urn:StockQuote#GetQuote"

<s:Envelope xmlns:s="http://www.w3.org/2001/06/soap-envelope">
  ...
</s:Envelope>
```

Example 2-31. HTTP response containing a SOAP message

```
HTTP/1.1 200 OK
Content-Type: text/xml
Content-Length: nnnn

<s:Envelope xmlns:s="http://www.w3.org/2001/06/soap-envelope">
  ...
</s:Envelope>
```

The SOAPAction HTTP header is defined by the SOAP specification, and indicates the intent of the SOAP HTTP request. Its value is completely arbitrary, but it's intended to tell the HTTP server what the SOAP message wants to do before the HTTP server decodes the XML.

Servers can then use the SOAPAction header to filter unacceptable requests.

Contentious Issues

The conventions for sending SOAP over HTTP have always caused difficulty in the SOAP development community. There are a number of issues that seem to come up time and again. Among these are:

Should SOAP really use HTTP port 80 or should a SOAP-specific port be used?
> Because SOAP messages masquerade as traditional web traffic on port 80, firewalls generally pass them straight through. Obviously, security administrators may have a problem with this. There are no requirements that SOAP over HTTP must use port 80, but many people use it specifically to avoid being filtered by firewalls.

Is the SOAPAction header really useful?
> Because its value is arbitrary, there's no way for a server to always know the intent of a request without parsing the XML. This is an issue that has been debated ever since the SOAPAction header was first introduced in SOAP Version 1.1. The W3C working group that is standardizing SOAP is leaning towards deprecating the SOAPAction header in the next version of the protocol.

When a client fault occurs while processing a SOAP message, should the server send a HTTP 500 "Server Error" back to the client or a HTTP 200 "OK" response with a SOAP fault included?
> This is an interesting question of semantics. A client fault in SOAP is obviously an application level error, and not the result of a server error. The HTTP 500 Server Error response however, is the default response required for all SOAP faults, regardless of the fault code. The general consensus on this question has been that consistency is most important. Despite the fact that client fault types are not Server Errors, the 500 Server Error code is still the right response when HTTP is used for the transport.

Should a SOAP specific URL scheme be used rather than the traditional http:// scheme used for web pages?

This question, like the one dealing with the use of port 80, directly addresses the question of whether or not SOAP web services should masquerade as more traditional HTTP-based services. Some have maintained that a new soap:// URL scheme is required. Microsoft's SOAP Routing Protocol even goes so far as to define such a scheme.

While HTTP is the most popular transport for SOAP message, it is not without problems. HTTP was not designed as a transport for XML messages, and there are times when the two protocols don't mesh perfectly. That said, it remains the most popular transport for SOAP, although Microsoft's .NET makes heavy use of SOAP-over-Instant Messaging and this may challenge HTTP's supremacy.

## CHAPTER 3

Writing SOAP Web Services

In Chapter 2, we looked under the hood of SOAP at the XML underneath. In this chapter, we demonstrate how to create, deploy, and use SOAP web services using toolkits for Java, Perl, and Microsoft's new .NET platform. We cover the installation, configuration, and use of SOAP::Lite for Perl, Apache SOAP for Java, and Microsoft .NET for C#.

The task of *creating* and *deploying* web services is really not all that difficult, nor is it all that different than what developers currently do in more traditional web applications. The tendency on all platforms is to automate more and more of the gory details and tedious work in creating web services. Most programmers don't need to know the exact details of encodings and envelopes; instead, they'll simply use a SOAP toolkit such as those described here.

Web Services Anatomy 101

In Chapter 1, we touched briefly on the fact that a web service consists of three components: a listener to receive the message, a proxy to take that message and translate it into an action to be carried out (such as invoking a method on a Java object), and the application code to implement that action.

The listener and proxy components should be completely transparent to the application code, if properly implemented. The ideal situation in most cases is that the code doesn't even know it is being invoked through a web service interface, but that is not always possible, or desirable.

A good example of a seamless, simple web services implementation is the SOAP::Lite for Perl written by Pavel Kulchenko. This package allows any installed Perl module to be automatically deployed as a web service without any work on the part of the module developer. The proxy can automatically load and invoke any subroutine in any module.

SOAP Implementations and Toolkits

There is a surprisingly long list of SOAP implementations available to developers. In this book, we have chosen to focus on three of the most popular tools: Apache SOAP for Java, SOAP::Lite for Perl, and Microsoft .NET. No matter which toolkit you use, the fundamental process of creating, deploying, and using SOAP web services is the same.

A comprehensive and up-to-date listing of all known SOAP implementations and toolkits can be found by visiting either *http://www.soaplite.com* or *http://www. soapware.org*. There are SOAP toolkits for all the popular programming languages and environments (Java, C#, C++, C, Perl, PHP, and Python, just to name a few).

Handling SOAP Messages

The integration of SOAP toolkits varies with the transport layer. Some implement their own HTTP servers. Some expect to be installed as part of a particular web server, so that rather than serving up a web page, the HTTP daemon hands the SOAP message to the toolkit's proxy component, which does the work of invoking the code behind the web service (see Figure 3-1).

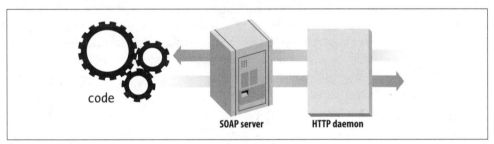

Figure 3-1. The HTTP daemon passes the request to the SOAP proxy, which then invokes the code behind the web service

Still other SOAP toolkits support a pluggable transport mechanism that allows you to select different transport protocols by doing hardly anything more than setting a property value. SOAP::Lite is a good example of this with its support for FTP, HTTP, IO, Jabber, SMTP, POP3, TCP, and MQSeries transports.

Whether the transport is built-in or pluggable, all SOAP toolkits provide the proxy component, which parses and interprets the SOAP message to invoke application code. The proxy must understand how to deal with things like encoding styles, translation of native types of data in to XML (and vice versa), whether headers in the SOAP message that have the `mustUnderstand="true"` flag set are actually understood—basically, everything that is covered in Chapter 2.

When the proxy component is handed a SOAP message by a listener, it must do three things:

1. Deserialize the message, if necessary, from XML into some native format suitable for passing off to the code.

2. Invoke the code.

3. Serialize the response to the message (if one exists) back into XML and hand it back to the transport listener for delivery back to the requester.

Despite differences in how various SOAP implementations accomplish these tasks, all SOAP web service tools follow this same simple pattern.

Deploying Web Services

Deploying a web service involves telling the proxy component which code to invoke when a particular type of message is received. In other words, the proxy component has to know that a getQuote message is going to be handled by the samples.QuoteServer Java class or the QuoteServer.pm Perl module. Once this has happened, clients can access the server, send the message, and trigger a call to application code.

Web service tools have different deployment mechanisms. SOAP::Lite requires that the Perl module be in @INC, Perl's module search path. Apache's SOAP implementation requires a deployment descriptor file, which describes the Java class and rules for mapping Java objects used in the service to their XML equivalents. This file must be added to a deployed services registry used by Apache SOAP (see Figure 3-2).

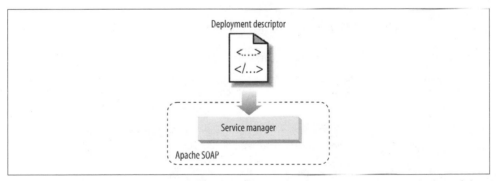

Figure 3-2. Unlike SOAP::Lite, where the server program contains a description of which modules are to be deployed as services, Apache SOAP uses a separate deployment descriptor file

Creating Web Services in Perl with SOAP::Lite

Perl, like most languages, hides the programmer from the complexities of SOAP with a toolkit. The SOAP::Lite toolkit is one of the most complete implementations of

SOAP available, supporting both Versions 1.1 and 1.2 of SOAP. It has strong support for alternate transports (FTP, HTTP, IO, Jabber, SMTP, POP3, TCP, and MQSeries), which we'll use later to demonstrate SOAP over Jabber.

Installing SOAP::Lite

SOAP::Lite, like many Perl modules, is available on the Comprehensive Perl Archive Network (CPAN). CPAN is a network of web and FTP sites with identical content—the source to thousands of Perl modules. You can access CPAN through a Perl command-line client or via the Web at *http://www.cpan.org*. See *http://www.cpan.org/misc/cpan-faq.html#How_install_Perl_modules* for information on installing Perl modules.

Example 3-1 shows a sample installation of SOAP::Lite using the interactive CPAN command-line shell.

Example 3-1. Installing SOAP::Lite with the CPAN shell

```
C:\book>perl -MCPAN -e shell
cpan shell -- CPAN exploration and modules installation (v1.59_54)
cpan> install SOAP::Lite
```

(You may be walked through configuring the CPAN shell if this is the first time you have run it.) The CPAN shell will connect to a CPAN site and download the source for SOAP::Lite. Once downloaded, the shell will attempt to build the module. SOAP::Lite has a series of interactive steps to configure the module, shown in Example 3-2. You can either use a default configuration or manually select from a menu of options to build a custom configuration.

Example 3-2. SOAP::Lite's interactive configuration

```
We are about to install SOAP::Lite and for your convenience will provide you with list of
modules and prerequisites, so you'll be able to choose only modules you need for your
configuration.

XMLRPC::Lite, UDDI::Lite, and XML::Parser::Lite are included by default. Installed
transports can be used for both SOAP::Lite and XMLRPC::Lite.

Client (SOAP::Transport::HTTP::Client)                              [yes]
Client HTTPS/SSL support
   (SOAP::Transport::HTTP::Client, require OpenSSL)                 [no]
Client SMTP/sendmail support (SOAP::Transport::MAILTO::Client)      [yes]
Client FTP support (SOAP::Transport::FTP::Client)                   [yes]
Standalone HTTP server (SOAP::Transport::HTTP::Daemon)              [yes]
Apache/mod_perl server (SOAP::Transport::HTTP::Apache, require Apache)[no]
FastCGI server (SOAP::Transport::HTTP::FCGI, require FastCGI)       [no]
POP3 server (SOAP::Transport::POP3::Server)                         [yes]
IO server (SOAP::Transport::IO::Server)                             [yes]
MQ transport support (SOAP::Transport::MQ)                          [no]
JABBER transport support (SOAP::Transport::JABBER)                  [no]
```

Example 3-2. SOAP::Lite's interactive configuration (continued)

```
MIME messages [required for POP3, optional for HTTP]
    (SOAP::MIMEParser)                                              [no]
SSL support for TCP transport (SOAP::Transport::TCP)               [no]
Compression support for HTTP transport (SOAP::Transport::HTTP)     [no]

Do you want to proceed with this configuration? [yes]
```

In most cases, the default configuration is adequate. We, however, are going to make a slight change to the configuration in order to demonstrate the use of Jabber as a transport protocol for SOAP. To indicate this, answer "no" to the question "Do you want to proceed with this configuration?" Press the Enter key to accept the default options for each of the configuration items until you get to the one that asks whether you plan to use the Jabber transport support module. Answer "yes" and press Enter. The CPAN shell will then make sure that all of the prerequisites and support modules for using Jabber are installed. You may select the default options for the remainder of the installation process.

The Hello Server

No book introducing a new programming system can get by without including a Hello World sample illustrating how easy the system is to use.

Start by creating the Hello World Perl module shown in Example 3-3.

Example 3-3. Hello.pm

```
# Hello.pm - simple Hello module
package Hello;
sub sayHello {
  shift;              # remove class name
  return "Hello " . shift;
}
1;
```

This module will be the code that sits behind our web service interface. There are several approaches you can take with SOAP::Lite to deploy this module as a web service.

If you already have a CGI-capable web server (and most people do) you can simply create the CGI script shown in Example 3-4.

Example 3-4. hello.cgi

```
#!/usr/bin/perl -w
# hello.cgi - Hello SOAP handler
use SOAP::Transport::HTTP;
SOAP::Transport::HTTP::CGI
 -> dispatch_to('Hello::(?:sayHello)')
 -> handle
;
```

This CGI script is the glue that ties the listener (the HTTP server daemon) to the proxy (the SOAP::Lite module). With this glue, SOAP::Lite will dispatch any received request to the Hello World module's sayHello operation.

Perl will need to find the Hello module, though. If you don't have permission to install Hello into one of Perl's default module directories (print @INC to see what they are), use the lib pragma to tell Perl to look in the directory containing the Hello module. If the module is in /home/pavel/lib then simply add this use line to hello.cgi:

```
use lib '/home/pavel/lib';
```

Your SOAP web service is deployed and ready for action.

The Hello Client

To test your Hello web service, simply use the client script in Example 3-5.

Example 3-5. hw_client.pl

```
#!/usr/bin/perl -w
# hw_client.pl - Hello client
use SOAP::Lite;
my $name = shift;
print "\n\nCalling the SOAP Server to say hello\n\n";
print "The SOAP Server says: ";
print SOAP::Lite
  -> uri('urn:Example1')
  -> proxy('http://localhost/cgi-bin/helloworld.cgi')
  -> sayHello($name)
  -> result . "\n\n";
```

Running this script should give you the following results:

```
% perl hw_client.pl James

Calling the SOAP Server to say hello
The SOAP Server says: Hello James
%
```

We see here a complete SOAP web service. Granted, it doesn't do much, but that wasn't the point. The point was that the process we followed (create the code, deploy the service, invoke the service) is the same regardless of the service we're implementing, the tools we're using, or the complexity of the service.

A Visual Basic Client

To prove that it really is SOAP that we're passing around here, the Visual Basic Script in Example 3-6 uses the Microsoft XML Parser's ability to send XML directly over HTTP to exchange SOAP messages back and forth with the Hello World service.

Example 3-6. hw_client.vbs

```
Dim x, h
Set x = CreateObject("MSXML2.DOMDocument")
x.loadXML "<s:Envelope xmlns:s='http://schemas.xmlsoap.org/soap/envelope/' xmlns:
xsi='http://www.w3.org/1999/XMLSchema-instance' xmlns:xsd='http://www.w3.org/1999/
XMLSchema'><s:Body><m:sayHello xmlns:m='urn:Example1'><name xsi:type='xsd:string'>James</
name></m:sayHello></s:Body></s:Envelope>"
msgbox x.xml, , "Input SOAP Message"
Set h = CreateObject("Microsoft.XMLHTTP")
h.open "POST", "http://localhost:8080"
h.send (x)
while h.readyState <> 4
wend
msgbox h.responseText,,"Output SOAP Message"
```

Running the Visual Basic script should demonstrate two things to you: invoking
SOAP web services is easy to do, and it doesn't matter which language you use. Perl
and Visual Basic strings are being interchanged over HTTP.

In the next example, there are two messages exchanged between the requester and
the service provider. The request, encoding the service we're calling (sayHello) and
the parameter (James), is shown in Example 3-7, and the response containing Hello
James is shown in Example 3-8.

Example 3-7. Hello request

```
<s:Envelope
  xmlns:s="http://schemas.xmlsoap.org/soap/envelope/"
  xmlns:xsi="http://www.w3.org/1999/XMLSchema-instance"
  xmlns:xsd="http://www.w3.org/1999/XMLSchema">
  <s:Body>
    <m:sayHello xmlns:m='urn:Example1'>
      <name xsi:type='xsd:string'>James</name>
    </m:sayHello>
  </s:Body>
</s:Envelope>
```

Example 3-8. Hello response

```
<s:Envelope
  xmlns:s="http://www.w3.org/2001/06/soap-envelope"
  xmlns:xsi="http://www.w3.org/1999/XMLSchema-instance"
  xmlns:xsd="http://www.w3.org/1999/XMLSchema">
  <s:Body>
    <n:sayHelloResponse xmlns:n="urn:Example1">
      <return xsi:type="xsd:string">
        Hello James
      </return>
    </n:sayHelloResponse>
  </s:Body>
</s:Envelope>
```

Changing Transports

SOAP::Lite supports many transport protocols. Let's modify the Hello World sample so that it can be invoked using Jabber. This demonstrates the modular nature of the web services stack, where the packaging can be independent of the transport. You might deploy a web service over Jabber to take advantage of the presence and identity features that Jabber provides.

Create an instance of the SOAP-aware Jabber server built into SOAP::Lite using the script in Example 3-9.

Example 3-9. sjs, the SOAP Jabber server

```perl
#!/usr/bin/perl -w
# sjs - soap jabber server

use SOAP::Transport::JABBER;

my $server = SOAP::Transport::JABBER::Server
  -> new('jabber://soaplite_server:soapliteserver@jabber.org:5222')
  -> dispatch_to('Hello')
;

print "SOAP Jabber Server Started\n";
do { $server->handle } while sleep 1;
```

Then, modify the client script we used earlier to point to the Jabber address of the service, as shown in Example 3-10.

Example 3-10. sjc, the SOAP Jabber client

```perl
#!/usr/bin/perl -w
# sjc - soap jabber client

use SOAP::Lite;

my $name = shift;
print "\n\nCalling the SOAP Server to say hello\n\n";
print "The SOAP Server says: ";
print SOAP::Lite
  -> uri('urn:Example1')
  -> proxy('jabber://soaplite_client:soapliteclient@jabber.org:5222/' .
           'soaplite_server@jabber.org/')
  -> sayHello($name)
  -> result . "\n\n";
```

The soaplite_server and soaplite_client accounts are registered with *Jabber.org*, so this example should work as typed. To avoid confusion when everyone reading this book tries the example at the same time, you should register your own Jabber IDs at *http://www.jabber.org*.

Now, in case you're curious as to how Jabber is capable of carrying SOAP messages, Example 3-11 is the text of the sayHello message sent by the previous script. As you can see, the SOAP message itself is embedded into the Jabber message element. This demonstrates the flexibility of both protocols.

Example 3-11. Jabber message with SOAP payload

```
<iq to="soapproxy@johndoe.ibm.com/soaprouter" id="6" type="get">
  <query xmlns="soap-message">
    <s:Envelope
      xmlns:s="http://schemas.xmlsoap.org/soap/envelope/"
      xmlns:xsi="http://www.w3.org/2001/XMLSchema-instance"
      xmlns:xsd="http://www.w3.org/2001/XMLSchema">
      <s:Body>
        <m:sayHello xmlns:m="urn:Example1">
          <name xsi:type="xsd:string">James</name>
        </m:sayHello>
      </s:Body>
    </s:Envelope>
  </query>
</iq>
```

Creating Web Services in Java with Apache SOAP

Creating web services in Java is more work than in Perl with SOAP::Lite, but the process is essentially the same. To illustrate how it's done, let's create the same Hello World web service and deploy it using the Apache SOAP tools.

Apache SOAP is the Apache Software Foundation's implementation of the SOAP protocol. It is designed to run as a servlet within any Java HTTP Server. As such, it implements only the proxy part of the message handling process. Like SOAP::Lite, Apache SOAP's list of features is impressive, sharing many of the same benefits as its Perl-based counterpart.

Installing Apache SOAP

Apache SOAP can be used as both a client and provider of SOAP web services. A server-side installation of Apache SOAP involves placing some *.jar* files in your classpath. You will need a separate web server that supports Servlets and Java Server Pages, such as Apache's Tomcat (*http://jakarta.apache.org/tomcat/*).

The Apache SOAP homepage, *http://xml.apache.org/soap/index.html*, has links to both source-only and precompiled distributions of the toolkit. Installing the precompiled binary distribution is as simple as downloading a Zip archive and extracting it into a directory.

On the client, three *.jar* files from the distribution (*soap.jar*, *mail.jar*, and *activation.jar*) must be present in your classpath. Also present must be any Java API for XML Parsing (JAXP) aware XML parser, such as Xerces Version 1.4 (*http://xml.apache.org/ xerces-j/*).

Assuming that you installed Apache SOAP *.jar* files in the *C:\book\soap* directory, set your SOAP_LIB environment variable to *C:\book\soap\lib*. Adding the *.jar* files to your classpath then entails:

```
set CLASSPATH = %CLASSPATH%;%SOAP_LIB%\soap.jar
set CLASSPATH = %CLASSPATH%;%SOAP_LIB%\mail.jar
set CLASSPATH = %CLASSPATH%;%SOAP_LIB%\activation.jar
```

Or, in the Unix Bourne shell (*/bin/sh*):

```
CLASSPATH = $CLASSPATH;$SOAP_LIB/soap.jar
CLASSPATH = $CLASSPATH;$SOAP_LIB/mail.jar
CLASSPATH = $CLASSPATH;$SOAP_LIB/activation.jar
```

The exact steps for a server installation will depend on which web application server you are using, but the process is essentially the same. The first step is to ensure the same three *.jar* files are located in your application server's classpath.

If your application server supports the use of web application archives (WAR files), simply use the *soap.war* file that ships with Apache SOAP. Apache Tomcat supports this. The Apache SOAP documentation includes detailed installation instructions for Tomcat and a number of other environments.

If you intend to use the Bean Scripting Framework (BSF) to make script-based web services, you need to ensure that *bsf.jar* and *js.jar* (a BSF JavaScript implementation) are also in the web application server's classpath.

The vast majority of problems encountered by new Apache SOAP users are related to incorrect classpaths. If you encounter problems writing web services with Apache SOAP, be sure to start your debugging by checking your classpath!

The Hello Server

We're going to do the same things we did in Perl: create the code, deploy the service, and use the service. Example 3-12 shows the Java code for the Hello class.

Example 3-12. Hello.java

```
package samples;
public class Hello {
    public String sayHello(String name) {
        return "Hello " + name;
    }
}
```

Compile the Java class and put it somewhere in your web server's classpath.

Deployment Descriptor

Next we must create a *deployment descriptor* to tell the Apache SOAP implementation everything it needs to know to dispatch sayHello messages to the samples.Hello class. This is shown in Example 3-13.

Example 3-13. Deployment descriptor for samples.Hello

```
<dd:service xmlns:dd="http://xml.apache.org/xml-soap/deployment" id="urn:Example1">
  <dd:provider type="java"
               scope="Application"
               methods="sayHello">
    <dd:java class="samples.Hello"
             static="false" />
  </dd:provider>
  <dd:faultListener>
    org.apache.soap.server.DOMFaultListener
  </dd:faultListener>
  <dd:mappings />
</dd:service>
```

The information contained within a deployment descriptor is fairly basic. There is the class name of the Java code being invoked (<dd:java class="samples.Hello" static="false" />), and an indication of the session scope of the service class (application or session scope, as defined by the Java Servlet specification), an indication of which faultListener to use (used to declare how faults are handled by the SOAP engine), and a listing of Java-to-XML type mappings. We will demonstrate later how the type mappings are defined.

Apache SOAP supports the use of *pluggable providers* that allow web services to be implemented not only as Java classes, but as Enterprise Java Beans, COM Classes, and Bean Scripting Framework scripts. Full information about how to use pluggable providers is available in the documentation and not covered here.

While simple in structure, deployment descriptor files must be created for every web service that you want to deploy. Thankfully, there are tools available that automate that process, but they still require the developer to walk through some type of wizard to select the Java class, the methods, and the type mappings. (A *type mapping* is an explicit link between a type of XML data and a Java class, and the Java classes that are used to serialize or deserialize between those types.)

Once the file is created, you have to deploy it with the Apache SOAP service manager. There are two ways to do this: you can use the Service Manager Client or, if you're using the XML-based Service Manager that ships with Apache SOAP, modify the deployment registry directly.

The first method requires executing the following command:

```
% java org.apache.soap.server.ServiceManagerClient http://hostname:port/soap/servlet/
rpcrouter deploy foo.xml
```

Where *hostname:port* is the hostname and port that your web service is listening on.

One interesting fact you should notice here is that the Apache Service Manager is itself a web service, and that deployment of a new service takes place by sending a SOAP message to the server that includes the deployment descriptor. While this is handy, it's not necessarily all that secure (considering the fact that it would allow anybody to deploy and undeploy services on your web server). To disable this, set the SOAPInterfaceEnabled option in the *soap.xml* configuration file to false. This will prevent the ServiceManagerClient from working.

The second approach will only work if you're using the XML Configuration Manager. This component allows you to store deployment information in an XML file. This file is located in the *web-apps* folder where your Apache SOAP servlet is located.

The XML is nothing more than a root element that contains all of the deployment descriptors for all of the services deployed. To deploy the Hello World service, simply take the deployment descriptor we wrote earlier and append it to this list. The next time that the SOAP servlet is started, the service manager will be reinitialized and the new service will be ready for use. A sample configuration file is given in Example 3-14.

Example 3-14. Apache SOAP configuration file

```
<root>
  <dd:service xmlns:dd="http://xml.apache.org/xml-soap/deployment"
              id="urn:Example1">
    <dd:provider type="java"
                 scope="Application"
                 methods="sayHello">
      <dd:java class="samples.Hello"
               static="false" />
    </dd:provider>
    <dd:faultListener>
     org.apache.soap.server.DOMFaultListener
    </dd:faultListener>
    <dd:mappings />
  </dd:service>
</root>
```

The Hello Client

To invoke the Hello World service, use the Java class in Example 3-15.

Example 3-15. Hello client in Java

```
import java.io.*;
import java.net.*;
import java.util.*;
import org.apache.soap.*;
import org.apache.soap.rpc.*;
```

Example 3-15. Hello client in Java (continued)

```
public class Example1_client {

  public static void main (String[] args)
      throws Exception {

    System.out.println("\n\nCalling the SOAP Server to say hello\n\n");
    URL url = new URL (args[0]);
    String name = args[1];

    Call call = new Call ();
    call.setTargetObjectURI("urn:Example1");
    call.setMethodName("sayHello");
    call.setEncodingStyleURI(Constants.NS_URI_SOAP_ENC;);
    Vector params = new Vector ();
    params.addElement (new Parameter("name", String.class, name, null));
    call.setParams (params);

    System.out.print("The SOAP Server says: ");

    Response resp = call.invoke(url, "");

    if (resp.generatedFault ()) {
      Fault fault = resp.getFault ();
      System.out.println ("\nOuch, the call failed: ");
      System.out.println ("  Fault Code   = " + fault.getFaultCode ());
      System.out.println ("  Fault String = " + fault.getFaultString ());
    } else {
      Parameter result = resp.getReturnValue ();
      System.out.print(result.getValue ());
      System.out.println();
    }
  }
}
```

The amount of code to accomplish this relatively simple operation may seem surprising (nine lines to actually initialize and invoke the web services call). Java will never be as terse as Perl and other scripting languages, but it has other strengths. Also, various Java-based SOAP toolkits such as The Mind Electric's GLUE and IBM's Web Services ToolKit support dynamic proxy interfaces that cut down the amount of code necessary to invoke web services. Those interfaces, however, generally require additional mechanisms, such as WSDL, to simplify the programming interface. We will take a look at these dynamic proxies later in Chapter 5. For now, if you compile and run this class, you'll end up with the same result that we saw in the Perl example:

```
% java samples.Hello http://localhost/soap/servlet/rpcrouter James

Calling the SOAP Server to say hello
The SOAP Server says: Hello James

%
```

Your Java web service is finished. If you have both the Perl and Java versions installed, run the Perl client script again but point it at the Java version of the Hello World service (the modified script is shown in Example 3-16). You'll see that everything still works.

Example 3-16. hw_jclient.pl, the Perl client for the Java Hello World server

```perl
#!/usr/bin/perl -w
# hw_jclient.pl - java Hello client
use SOAP::Lite;
my $name = shift;
print "\n\nCalling the SOAP Server to say hello\n\n";
print "The SOAP Server says: ";
print SOAP::Lite
  -> uri('urn:Example1')
  -> proxy('http://localhost/soap/servlet/rpcrouter James')
  -> sayHello($name)
  -> result . "\n\n";
```

Which will produce the expected result:

```
% perl hw_client.pl James

Calling the SOAP Server to say hello
The SOAP Server says: Hello James

%
```

The TCPTunnelGui Tool

One very useful tool that comes bundled with Apache SOAP is TCPTunnelGui, a debugging tool that lets a developer view the SOAP messages that are being sent to and returned from a SOAP web service. The tool is a proxy—it listens on the local machine and forwards traffic to and from the real SOAP server. The contents of the messages passing through the local port will be displayed in the graphical interface.

Launch the tool by typing:

```
% java org.apache.soap.util.net.TcpTunnelGui listenport tunnelhost tunnelport
```

Listenport is the local TCP/IP port number you want the tool to open and listen to requests. *Tunnelhost* is the address of the server (either DNS or IP address) where the traffic is to be redirected, and *tunnelport* is the port number at tunnelhost.

For example, assume your Hello World service is deployed at *http://www.example.com/soap/servlet/rpcrouter*. To view the messages sent to and from that service by redirecting traffic through local TCP/IP port 8080, launch the TCPTunnelGui tool with the following parameters:

```
% java org.apache.soap.util.net.TcpTunnelGui 8080 http://www.example.com 80
```

And now direct the Hello World SOAP requests to `http://localhost:8080/soap/servlet/rpcrouter`.

Figure 3-3 shows TCPTunnelGui displaying the SOAP messages for each request to the Hello World service.

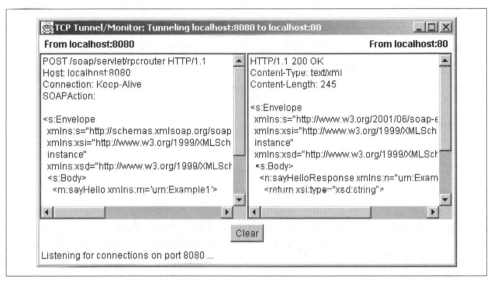

Figure 3-3. The TCPTunnelGui Tool showing the SOAP messages sent to and from the Hello World service

TCPTunnelGui is an extremely valuable tool for anybody wanting to learn how SOAP Web services work (or debugging why a service doesn't work!).

Creating Web Services In .NET

For web service developers working strictly on the Windows platform, Microsoft's .NET development platform offers built-in support for easily creating and deploying SOAP web services. Let's walk through how you create the Hello World service using C#, the new Java-like programming language designed specifically for use with .NET.

Installing .NET

The first thing you need to do is download and install the Microsoft .NET SDK Beta 2 from *http://msdn.microsoft.com*. This free distribution contains everything you need to create and run any .NET application, including .NET Web Services.

There are, however, several prerequisites that you need:

1. You must be running Windows 2000, Windows NT 4.0, Windows 98, or Windows Millennium Edition.

2. You must have Microsoft Internet Explorer Version 5.01 or higher.

3. You must have the Microsoft Data Access Components (Version 2.6 or higher) installed.

4. And you must have Microsoft Internet Information Server (IIS) installed and running. .NET Web services can only be deployed within the IIS environment.

The .NET Framework SDK installation is a fairly automatic process, with an easy-to-use installation wizard. Once installed, we can create the Hello World service.

Introducing .NET

Before we get into exactly how web services are created in .NET, let's take a quick walk through the .NET architecture to help put things into perspective.

First and foremost, .NET is a runtime environment similar to the Java Virtual Machine. Code packages, called *assemblies*, can be written in several .NET specific versions of popular programming languages like Visual Basic, C++, C#, Perl, Python, and so on. Assemblies run within a managed, hierarchically organized runtime called the "Common Language Runtime" that deals with all of the low-level memory and system management details (see Figure 3-4).

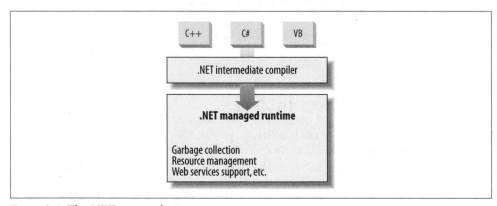

Figure 3-4. The .NET managed runtime

Currently, .NET runs basically as an extension to the existing COM environment upon which the current versions of Windows are built. As such, .NET can be utilized anywhere COM can be used, including within Microsoft's Internet Information Server (IIS) environment.

.NET web services are specific types of .NET assemblies that are specially flagged for export as web services. These assemblies are either contained within or referenced from a new type of server-side script called an *.asmx* file. The .NET extensions to IIS recognize files ending in *.asmx* as web services and automatically export the functions of the referenced assemblies.

The process is simple:

1. Write the code.
2. Save the code in an *.asmx* file.
3. Move the *.asmx* file to your IIS web server.
4. Invoke your web service.

Saying Hello

.NET introduces a programming language called C#. We'll develop our example web service in C#, but remember that .NET makes it just as easy to develop in Visual Basic, C++, and other languages.

Example 3-17 defines the .NET Hello World service. You can use an ordinary text editor to create this file.

Example 3-17. HelloWorld.asmx, a C# Hello World Service

```
<%@ WebService Language="C#" Class="Example1" %>

using System.Web.Services;

[WebService(Namespace="urn:Example1")]
public class Example1 {

    [ WebMethod ]
    public string sayHello(string name) {
        return "Hello " + name;
    }

}
```

Notice how similar the code looks to the Java version we created earlier. At heart, a function that appends two strings isn't rocket science. The bracketed sections (<% %> and [ ]) tell the .NET runtime that this code is intended to be exported as a SOAP web service.

The <% WebService Language="C#" Class="Example1" %> line tells .NET that we are exporting one web service, written in C#, implemented by the Example1 class.

The using line imports a module, in this case the standard web services classes.

The [WebService(Namespace="urn:Example1")] line is optional, but allows us to declare various attributes of the web service being deployed. In this instance, we are setting an explicit namespace for the web service rather than allowing .NET to assign a default (which, by the way, will always be http://tempuri.org/). Other attributes you can set for the web service include the name and textual description of the service.

The [WebMethod] line sets an attribute that flags the methods in the class to be exposed as part of the web service. As with the WebService attribute previously, we could use this line to define various custom properties about the web service operation. Options include whether to buffer the response of the operation; if buffered, how long to keep it buffered; whether to maintain a session state for the operation; whether transactions are supported on the method; what the exported name of the operation is; and a textual description of the operation. In the case of the Hello World example, we have no need to set any of these options, so we simply leave it alone.

What will .NET do with all of this information? It's actually quite simple. Whenever a *.asmx* file is requested by a client through IIS, the .NET runtime will first compile the code for the service if it hasn't done so already. The compiled code is temporarily cached in memory and recompiled every time a change is made to the *.asmx* file or the IIS server is restarted.

Next, the .NET runtime will determine what type of request is being made. There are several choices:

1. The request may be for information about the web service.

2. The request may be for information about one of the methods exported by the web service.

3. Or, the request may be to invoke an operation on the web service. .NET allows the operations to be invoked one of three different ways: through an HTTP-GET operation, through an HTTP-POST operation, or through the use of SOAP messages. .NET is one of the only web services platforms that allow web services to be invoked using multiple protocols.

Deploying the Service

Save the *HelloWorld.asmx* file to a location in your IIS web root. Take note of the *.asmx* file's URL. For example, if your Microsoft IIS server is installed at *c:\inetpub* (the default installation location), the web root is *c:\inetpub\wwwroot*. If you saved the *.asmx* file directly to this location, the URL of the *.asmx* file will be *http:// localhost/helloworld.asmx*, where *localhost* is the DNS name or IP address of your IIS server. Once you've completed this step, your .NET web service is deployed.

Ensure that your .NET environment and web service are fully operational by launching your favorite web browser and navigating to *http://localhost/HelloWorld.asmx*. If all goes well, you should be presented with an automatically generated HTML page that documents the Hello World service you just created (see Figure 3-5).

These pages are generated dynamically whenever an HTTP-GET request is received for the deployed *.asmx* file. You do not have to do anything to create these pages.

Clicking on the "sayHello" link will yield a detailed description of how to invoke the sayHello operation using SOAP, HTTP-GET, and HTTP-POST, as well as a simple HTML form for testing the operation (see Figure 3-6).

Figure 3-5. Automatically generated documentation for the .NET web service

Figure 3-6. Auto-generated documentation for the sayHello operation

To test the service, either type your name in the test form at the top of the automatically generated documentation page (see Figure 3-7), or navigate your browser to *http://localhost/helloworld.asmx/sayHello?name=yourname*.

Either method should generate the response shown in Figure 3-8.

If you get the "Hello James" message, you're ready to move on.

Figure 3-7. Ensure that the service works using the Test form

Figure 3-8. A typical HTTP-GET web service response

Invoking the Service Using SOAP

Creating a SOAP client for the Hello World service using .NET is, surprisingly, harder than creating the service itself. There are tools to make it easier (we will explore them briefly in Chapter 5), but for now we'll go through the steps manually so you know what is going on.

Again using your favorite text editor, create *HelloWorld.cs* (the *.cs* extension indicates C# source code) from Example 3-18.

Example 3-18. HelloWorld.cs, a C# HelloWorld client

```
// HelloWorld.cs

using System.Diagnostics;
using System.Xml.Serialization;
```

Example 3-18. HelloWorld.cs, a C# HelloWorld client (continued)

```
using System;
using System.Web.Services.Protocols;
using System.Web.Services;

[System.Web.Services.WebServiceBindingAttribute(
    Name="Example1Soap",
    Namespace="urn:Example1")]
public class Example1 :
            System.Web.Services.Protocols.SoapHttpClientProtocol {

    public Example1() {
        this.Url = "http://localhost/helloworld.asmx ";
    }

    [System.Web.Services.Protocols.SoapDocumentMethodAttribute(
        "urn:Example1/sayHello",
        RequestNamespace="urn:Example1",
        ResponseNamespace="urn:Example1",
        Use=System.Web.Services.Description.SoapBindingUse.Literal,
        ParameterStyle=System.Web.Services.Protocols.SoapParameterStyle.Wrapped)]
    public string sayHello(string name) {
        object[] results = this.Invoke("sayHello",
                                       new object[] {name});
        return ((string)(results[0]));
    }

    public static void Main(string[] args) {
        Console.WriteLine("Calling the SOAP Server to say hello");
        Example1 example1 = new Example1();
        Console.WriteLine("The SOAP Server says: " +
                          example1.sayHello(args[0]));
    }
}
]
```

The [System.Web.Services.WebserviceBindingAttribute] line tells the .NET managed runtime that this particular .NET assembly is going to be used to invoke a web service. When the assembly is compiled, .NET will automatically supply the infrastructure to make the SOAP request work.

Subclassing System.Web.Services.Protocols.SOAPHttpClientProtocol tells the .NET runtime which protocol you want to use (SOAP over HTTP in this case). Within the constructor for this class, set the URL for the web service (the assignment to *this.Url*).

The rest of the class declares a proxy for the sayHello operation, specifies various attributes of the web services invocation, calls the invoke method, and returns the result.

Lastly, we create the main entry point for the C# application. The entry point does nothing more than create an instance of our client class and invoke the proxy sayHello operation, outputting the results to the console.

Compile the client to a *HelloWorld.exe* application:

```
C:\book>csc HelloWorld.cs
```

To invoke the web service, simply type:

```
C:\book>HelloWorld yourname
```

You will be greeted with the same result we saw previously with the Java and Perl versions of the Hello World service:

```
Calling the SOAP Server to say hello
The SOAP Server says: Hello James
```

Interoperability Issues

At the time of this writing, .NET's SOAP implementation still has a few issues that need to be worked out, primarily in the area of interoperability.

Slight variations between the way .NET implements SOAP and SOAP::Lite's implementation of SOAP, for example, cause some difficulty in allowing the two to work together out of the box. To illustrate the problem, follow the steps shown here. One would think that everything would work fine, but it doesn't. I'll point out why after we walk through it.

First, launch the Java TcpTunnelGui tool that ships with Apache SOAP, specifying port 8080 as the local listening port, and redirecting to whatever server you have your *HelloWorld.asmx* file deployed to:

```
C:\book>start java org.apache.soap.util.net.TcpTunnelGui 8080
        localhost 80
```

Then, modify the Perl Hello World client to point to the *HelloWorld.asmx* file, but replace the server part of the URL with `localhost:8080`.

When you run the Perl script:

```
C:\book>perl hello_client1.pl James
```

The result is not what you would expect. The script ends without ever displaying the "Hello James" result. If you take a look at the TcpTunnelGui tool, you'll see that the SOAP message is sent, but the .NET runtime rejects the request and issues a SOAP fault in response. This is shown in Example 3-19.

Example 3-19. SOAP fault from .NET

```
<?xml version="1.0" encoding="utf-8"?>
<soap:Envelope xmlns:soap="http://schemas.xmlsoap.org/soap/envelope/">
  <soap:Body>
    <soap:Fault>
      <faultcode>soap:Client</faultcode>
      <faultstring>
          System.Web.Services.Protocols.SoapException: Server did
          not recognize the value of HTTP Header SOAPAction:
```

Example 3-19. SOAP fault from .NET (continued)

```
        urn:Example#sayHello.
        at System.Web.Services.Protocols.SoapServerProtocol.Initialize()
        at  System.Web.Services.Protocols.ServerProtocolFactory.Create(
        Type type, HttpContext context, HttpRequest request,
        HttpResponse response)
      </faultstring>
      <detail />
    </soap:Fault>
  </soap:Body>
</soap:Envelope>
```

.NET requires that the HTTP SOAPAction header be used to exactly identify the operation on which service is being invoked. .NET requires the format of the SOAPAction header to be the service namespace, followed by a forward slash, followed by the name of the operation, or urn:Example/sayHello. Notice, though, that SOAP::Lite's default is to use a pound sign (#) to separate the service namespace from the name of the operation. This wasn't an issue when we were invoking Java services with SOAP::Lite because Apache SOAP simply ignores the SOAPAction header altogether.

To fix this problem, we must explicitly tell SOAP::Lite how to format the SOAP-Action header. To do so, make the change to the client script highlighted in Example 3-20.

Example 3-20. Fragment showing change to Perl client script

```
print SOAP::Lite
  -> uri('urn:Example1')
  -> on_action(sub{sprintf '%s/%s', @_ })
  -> proxy('http://localhost:8080/helloworld/example1.asmx')
  -> sayHello($name)
  -> result . "\n\n";
```

The on_action method in SOAP::Lite allows the developer to override the default behavior and specify a new format for the SOAPAction header.

However, even with this change there's still a problem. The script will appear to run, but rather than returning the expected Hello James string, all that will be returned is Hello. The name is missing from the response! This happens because .NET requires all parameters for a method call to be named and typed explicitly, whereas Perl does not do this by default.

Again, take a look at the TcpTunnelGui tool and look at the SOAP message sent to the HelloWorld.asmx service from SOAP::Lite. This is shown in Example 3-21.

Example 3-21. The Perl-generated SOAP request sent to the .NET service

```
<SOAP-ENV:Envelope
  xmlns:SOAP-ENC="http://schemas.xmlsoap.org/soap/encoding/"
  SOAP-ENV:encodingStyle="http://schemas.xmlsoap.org/soap/encoding/"
  xmlns:SOAP-ENV="http://schemas.xmlsoap.org/soap/envelope/"
```

```
    xmlns:xsi="http://www.w3.org/1999/XMLSchema-instance"
    xmlns:xsd="http://www.w3.org/1999/XMLSchema">

  <SOAP-ENV:Body>
    <namesp1:sayHello xmlns:namesp1="urn:Hello">
      <c-gensym3 xsi:type="xsd:string">
         James
      </c-gensym3>
    </namesp1:sayHello>
  </SOAP-ENV:Body>
</SOAP-ENV:Envelope>
```

Notice the oddly named `c-gensym3` element that contains the input parameter. Because Perl is a scripting language that does not support strong typing or strict function signatures, method parameters do not have names, nor do they have types. When SOAP::Lite creates the SOAP message it automatically generates an element name and sets all parameters to the `string` data type. .NET doesn't like this behavior. If the C# method is written to take a `String` parameter called `name` it expects to find an element in the SOAP envelope called `name` with a type of `xsi:type="xsd:string"`. In XML, that would be as shown in Example 3-22.

Example 3-22. A SOAP request encoded by .NET

```
<SOAP-ENV:Envelope
  xmlns:SOAP-ENC="http://schemas.xmlsoap.org/soap/encoding/"
  SOAP-ENV:encodingStyle="http://schemas.xmlsoap.org/soap/encoding/"
  xmlns:SOAP-ENV="http://schemas.xmlsoap.org/soap/envelope/"
  xmlns:xsi="http://www.w3.org/1999/XMLSchema-instance"
  xmlns:xsd="http://www.w3.org/1999/XMLSchema">

  <SOAP-ENV:Body>
    <namesp1:sayHello xmlns:namesp1="urn:Hello">
      <name xsi:type="xsd:string">
         James
      </name>
    </namesp1:sayHello>
  </SOAP-ENV:Body>
</SOAP-ENV:Envelope>
```

The .NET beta also did not properly recognize that the `name` element is declared as part of the same namespace as its parent `sayHello` element. This is a standard rule of XML namespaces. To get SOAP::Lite working with .NET, we must tell SOAP::Lite the name, type, and namespace of each of the parameters we are passing into the operation, as shown in Example 3-23.

Example 3-23. Perl client modified to work with .NET

```
use SOAP::Lite;

my $name = shift;
```

Example 3-23. Perl client modified to work with .NET (continued)

```
print "\n\nCalling the SOAP Server to say hello\n\n";
print "The SOAP Server says: ";

print SOAP::Lite
   -> uri('urn:Example1')
   ->on_action(sub{sprintf '%s/%s', @_ })
   ->proxy('http://localhost:8080/helloworld/example1.asmx')
   ->sayHello(SOAP::Data->name(name => $name->type('string')
                        ->uri('urn:Example1'))
   ->result . "\n\n";
```

Now, run the script and you will see that everything works as expected.

Developers who are writing and using web services that may be accessed by a wide variety of SOAP implementations need to be aware that inconsistencies like this will exist between the various toolkits and you need to be prepared to deal with them. As web services become more complex and more mission critical, it is important to have a clear understanding of how to manage these issues. Over time, the more popular SOAP implementations will be honed to a point where they will work together seamlessly, but with many of these implementations still being released as beta and sometimes alpha code status, you must be aware that issues will exist. Luckily, as we will see in Chapter 5, there are workarounds available for some of these problems.

CHAPTER 4
The Publisher Web Service

The Publisher web service is a demonstration of a more complex web service modeled after the one used by the SOAP Web Services Resource Center (*http://www. soap-wrc.com*). This service demonstrates techniques for implementing more complicated forms of web services. It builds on the Hello World example from Chapter 3.

Overview

The Publisher web service manages a database of important news items, articles, and resources that relate to SOAP and web services in general.

A Perl-based service allows registered users to post, delete, or browse items, and to manage their registration information. We've also implemented an interactive Java shell client that uses the Apache SOAP client.

The supported operations are:

register
    Create a new user account.
modify
    Modify a user account.
login
    Start a user session.
post
    Post a new item to the database.
remove
    Remove an item from the database.
browse
    Browse the database by item type. The data can be returned in either a publisher-specific XML format or as a Rich Site Summary (RSS) channel.

Publisher Service Security

Security in the Publisher service is handled through a login operation that returns an authorization token to the user. This token consists of a user ID, email address, login time, and a MD5 digest that the user must include in all operations that require that the user be authenticated, namely the post and remove operations (see Figure 4-1).

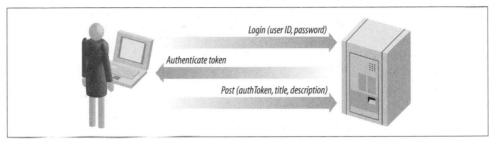

Figure 4-1. When registered users log in, they will be given an authentication token that they must use whenever they post or remove an item in the database

In the login operation, the user's ID and password are sent (in plain text) to the publisher service where they are validated. The service then creates an authentication token and returns it to the user. While not very secure, this illustrates one way that authentication can occur in SOAP-based web services. That is, rather than using transport-level security mechanisms, such as HTTP authentication, security can be built into the web services interface directly. In Chapter 5, we will discuss several much more secure and robust security mechanisms for web services.

The Publisher Operations

The operations exposed by the Publisher service are fairly straightforward. If we cast these operations in a Java interface, they would look like Example 4-1.

Example 4-1. The Publisher interface in Java

```
public Interface Publisher {

  public boolean register (String email,
                           String password,
                           String firstName,
                           String lastName,
                           String title,
                           String company,
                           String url);

  public boolean modify   (String email,
                           String newemail,
                           String password,
                           String firstName,
                           String lastName,
```

Example 4-1. The Publisher interface in Java (continued)

```
                              String title,
                              String company,
                              String url);

  public AuthInfo login     {String id,
                              String password);

  public int post           (AuthInfo authinfo,
                              String type,
                              String title,
                              String description);

  public boolean remove     (AuthInfo authinfo,
                              int itemID);

  public org.w3c.dom.Document browse (
                              String type,
                              String format,
                              int maxRows);
}
```

The Publisher Server

The Publisher Perl module uses the Perl DBI package and DBD::CSV package, both of which are available from CPAN and installed the same way SOAP::Lite is installed. The code discussed in the next section should be contained in a single Perl module called `Publisher.pm`, shown in full in Appendix C.

The code is quite straightforward. We create a database to store the news, articles, and resource items, and the list of users who will use the service. After the database is created, we define the operations for manipulating that database. Those operations are not exported. The deployed code is in the last half of the script, managing user logins and exposing the various operations that the web service will support.

The Preamble

Example 4-2 defines the code's namespace, loads the database module, and defines a convenience function for accessing the database handle. Data is stored in a comma-separated text file, but you can change that to a relational database by changing the `"DBI:CSV:..."` string to the data source specifier for a MySQL or a similar database.

Example 4-2. Publisher preamble

```
package Publisher;

use strict;

package Publisher::DB;
```

Example 4-2. Publisher preamble (continued)

```
use DBI;
use vars qw($CONNECT);

$CONNECT = "DBI:CSV:f_dir=/home/book;csv_sep_char=\0";
my $dbh;

sub dbh {
  shift;
  unless ($dbh) {
    $dbh = DBI->connect(shift || $CONNECT);
    $dbh->{'RaiseError'} = 1;
  }
  return $dbh;
}
```

Data Tables

Example 4-3 creates the data tables for storing information about the members and items managed by the Publisher service.

Example 4-3. Create data tables

```
sub create {
  my $dbh = shift->dbh;

  $dbh->do($_) foreach split /;/, '

CREATE TABLE members (
  memberID   integer,
  email      char(100),
  password   char(25),
  firstName  char(50),
  lastName   char(50),
  title      char(50),
  company    char(50),
  url        char(255),
  subscribed integer
);

CREATE TABLE items (
  itemID      integer,
  memberID    integer,
  type        integer,
  title       char(255),
  description char(512),
  postStamp   integer
)

';

}
```

Once the tables are created, we need to write the code for manipulating the data in those tables. These methods, shown in Example 4-4, are private and will not be exposed as part of our web service. Only the first few methods are shown in full. Consult Appendix C for the full source.

Example 4-4. Methods to manipulate data in tables

```
sub insert_member {
  my $dbh = shift->dbh;
  my $newMemberID = 1 + $dbh->selectrow_array(
    "SELECT memberID FROM members ORDER BY memberID
    DESC");

  my %parameters = (@_, memberID => $newMemberID, subscribed => 0);
  my $names = join ', ', keys %parameters;
  my $placeholders = join ', ', ('?') x keys %parameters;

  $dbh->do("INSERT INTO members ($names) VALUES
          ($placeholders)", {}, values %parameters);
  return $newMemberID;
}

sub select_member {
  my $dbh = shift->dbh;
  my %parameters = @_;

  my $where = join ' AND ', map {"$_ = ?"} keys %parameters;
  $where = "WHERE $where" if $where;

  # returns row in array context and first element (memberID) in scalar
  return $dbh->selectrow_array("SELECT * FROM members
          $where", {}, values %parameters);
}

sub update_member {}

sub insert_item {}

sub select_item {}

sub select_all_items {}

sub delete_item {}
```

Utility Functions

Now we start defining the actual Publisher web service. Example 4-5 shows several private utility functions, primarily for dealing with the creation and validation of the authorization tokens used as part of the Publisher service's security model (discussed later).

Example 4-5. Utility functions

```
package Publisher;

use POSIX qw(strftime);

@Publisher::ISA = qw(SOAP::Server::Parameters);

use Digest::MD5 qw(md5);

my $calculateAuthInfo = sub {
  return md5(join '', 'unique (yet persistent) string', @_);
};

my $checkAuthInfo = sub {
  my $authInfo = shift;
  my $signature = $calculateAuthInfo->(@{$authInfo}{qw(memberID email time)});
  die "Authentication information is not valid\n" if $signature ne $authInfo->{signature};
  die "Authentication information is expired\n" if time() > $authInfo->{time};
  return $authInfo->{memberID};
};

my $makeAuthInfo = sub {
  my($memberID, $email) = @_;
  my $time = time()+20*60;
  my $signature = $calculateAuthInfo->($memberID, $email, $time);
  return +{memberID => $memberID, time => $time, email => $email, signature => $signature};
};
```

Register a New User

Example 4-6 shows the code for the exported operation that registers new users.

Example 4-6. Exported method to register a new user

```
sub register {
  my $self = shift;
  my $envelope = pop;
  my %parameters = %{$envelope->method() || {}};

  die "Wrong parameters: register(email, password, firstName, " .
      "lastName [, title][, company][, url])\n"
    unless 4 == map {defined} @parameters{qw(email password firstName
lastName)};

  my $email = $parameters{email};
  die "Member with email ($email) already registered\n"
    if Publisher::DB->select_member(email -> $email);
  return Publisher::DB->insert_member(%parameters);
}
```

Modify User Information

Example 4-7 is the operation that allows users to modify their information.

Example 4-7. Exported subroutine to modify a user's information

```
sub modify {
  my $self = shift;
  my $envelope = pop;
  my %parameters = %{$envelope->method() || {}};

  my $memberID = $checkAuthInfo->($envelope->valueof('//authInfo'));
  Publisher::DB->update_member($memberID, %parameters);
  return;
}
```

User Login

Example 4-8 is the operation that validates a user's ID and password and issues an authentication token.

Example 4-8. Exported method to validate a user and issue a token

```
sub login {
  my $self = shift;
  my %parameters = %{pop->method() || {}};

  my $email = $parameters{email};
  my $memberID = Publisher::DB->select_member(email => $email, password => $parameters{password});
  die "Credentials are wrong\n" unless $memberID;
  return bless $makeAuthInfo->($memberID, $email) => 'authInfo';
}
```

Posting an Item

Example 4-9 shows the method that posts a new item to the database.

Example 4-9. Exported method to post a new item

```
my %type2code = (news => 1, article => 2, resource => 3);
my %code2type = reverse %type2code;

sub postItem {
  my $self = shift;
  my $envelope = pop;
  my $memberID = $checkAuthInfo->($envelope->valueof('//authInfo'));
  my %parameters = %{$envelope->method() || {}};

  die "Wrong parameter(s): postItem(type, title, description)\n"
    unless 3 == map {defined} @parameters{qw(type title description)};

  $parameters{type} = $type2code{lc $parameters{type}}
                                 or die "Wrong type of item ($parameters{type})\n";
  return Publisher::DB->insert_item(memberID => $memberID, %parameters);
}
```

Removing Items

Example 4-10 shows the exported method for removing items from the database. Only the user who added an item can remove it.

Example 4-10. Exported method to remove an item from the database

```
sub removeItem {
  my $self = shift;
  my $memberID = $checkAuthInfo->(pop->valueof('//authInfo'));
  die "Wrong parameter(s): removeItem(itemID)\n" unless @_ == 1;

  my $itemID = shift;
  die "Specified item ($itemID) can't be found or removed\n"
    unless Publisher::DB->select_item(memberID => $memberID, itemID => $itemID);
  Publisher::DB->delete_item($itemID);
  return;
}
```

Browsing

Users can browse the item database using either a Publisher service-specific XML format or the popular Rich Site Summary (RSS) format used extensively across the Internet.

Example 4-11, while looking fairly complex, creates the appropriate XML structures depending on the format requested by the caller.

Example 4-11. Code to support browsing in proprietary and RSS formats

```
my $browse = sub {
  my $envelope = pop;
  my %parameters = %{$envelope->method() || {}};

  my ($type, $format, $maxRows, $query) = @parameters{qw(type format maxRows query)};
  $type = {all => 'all', %type2code}->{lc($type) || 'all'}
          or die "Wrong type of item ($type)\n";
  # default values
  $maxRows ||= 25;
  $format ||= 'XML';
  my $items = Publisher::DB->select_all_items($type ne 'all' ? (type => $type) : ());
  my %members;
  my @items = map {
    my ($type, $title, $description, $date, $memberID) = @$_;
    my ($email, $firstName, $lastName) = @{
      $members{$memberID} ||= [Publisher::DB->select_member(memberID =>
      $memberID)]
    }[1,3,4];
    +{
      $format =~ /^XML/ ? (
        type       => $code2type{$type},
        title      => $title,
```

```perl
          description => $description,
          date        => strftime("%Y-%m-%d", gmtime($date)),
          creator     => "$firstName $lastName ($email)"
      ) : (
          category    => $code2type{$type},
          title       => "$title by $firstName $lastName ($email) on "
                         . strftime("%Y-%m-%d", gmtime($date)),
          description => $description,
      )
    }
  } @{$items}[0..(!$query && $maxRows <= $#$items ? $maxRows-1 : $#$items)];

  if ($query) {
    my $regexp = join '', map {
      /\s+and\s+/io ? '&&' : /\s+or\s+/io ? '||' : /[()]/ ? $_ : $_ ? '/'
      . quotemeta($_) . '/o' : ''
    } split /(\(|\)|\s+and\s+|\s+or\s+)/io, $query;
    eval "*checkfor = sub { for (\@_) { return 1 if $regexp; } return }"
        or die;
    @items = grep {checkfor(values %$_)} @items;
    splice(@items, $maxRows <= $#items ? $maxRows : $#items+1);
  }

  return $format =~ /^(XML|RSS)str$/
    ? SOAP::Serializer
        -> autotype(0)
        -> readable(1)
        -> serialize(SOAP::Data->name(($1 eq 'XML' ? 'itemList' : 'channel')
                     => \SOAP::Data->name(item => @items)))
    : [@items];
};

sub browse {
  my $self = shift;
  return SOAP::Data->name(browse => $browse->(@_));
}
```

Search

The search operation is similar to the browse operation with the exception that users are allowed to specify a keyword filter to limit the number of items returned. It is shown in Example 4-12.

Example 4-12. Exported method to search the database

```perl
sub search {
  my $self = shift;
  return SOAP::Data->name(search => $browse->(@_));
}
```

Deploying the Publisher Service

To deploy the Publisher service, you need to do two things. First, create the database that is going to store the information. Do so by running the script in Example 4-13.

Example 4-13. Program to create the database

```
#!/usr/bin/perl -w
use Publisher;
Publisher::DB->create;
```

This will create two files in the current directory, called *members* and *items*.

Next, create the CGI script that will listen for SOAP messages and dispatch them to SOAP::Lite and the Publisher module. This is given in Example 4-14.

Example 4-14. Publisher.cgi, SOAP proxy for the Publisher module

```
#!/bin/perl -w

use SOAP::Transport::HTTP;
use Publisher;

$Publisher::DB::CONNECT =
  "DBI:CSV:f_dir=d:/book;csv_sep_char=\0";
$authinfo = 'http://www.soaplite.com/authInfo';
my $server = SOAP::Transport::HTTP::CGI
  -> dispatch_to('Publisher');
$server->serializer->maptype({authInfo => $authinfo});
$server->handle;
```

The dispatch_to method call instructs the SOAP::Lite package which methods to accept, and in which module those methods can be found.

Copy the CGI script to your web server's *cgi-bin* directory and install the *Publisher.pm*, *members*, and *items* files in your Perl module directory. The Publisher web service is now ready for business.

The Java Shell Client

The Java shell client is a simple interface for interacting with the Publisher web service. A typical session is shown in Example 4-15. Notice that once the shell is started, the user must log on prior to posting new items.

Example 4-15. A sample session with the Java shell client

```
C:\book>java Client http://localhost/cgi-bin/Publisher.cgi

Welcome to Publisher!
> help
```

Example 4-15. A sample session with the Java shell client (continued)

```
Actions: register | login | post | remove | browse
> login

What is your user id: james@soap-wrc.com

What is your password: abc123xyz

Attempting to login...
james@soap-wrc.com is logged in

> post

What type of item [1 = News, 2 = Article, 3 = Resource]: 1

What is the title:
Programming Web Services with SOAP, WSDL and UDDI

What is the description:
A cool new book about Web services!

Attempting to post item...
Posted item 46

> quit

C:\book>
```

To create the shell, you need to create two Java classes: one for the shell itself
(Client.java), and the other to keep track of the authorization token issued by the
Publisher service when you log in (AuthInfo.java).

The Authentication Class

The preamble to the authInfo class is shown in Example 4-16.

Example 4-16. The authInfo class

```java
// authInfo.java

import org.w3c.dom.Document;
import org.w3c.dom.Element;

public class authInfo {
  private int memberID;
  private long time;
  private String email;
  private byte [] signature;

  public authInfo() { }

  public authInfo(int memberID, long time, String email, byte[] signature) {
```

Example 4-16. The authInfo class (continued)

```
    this.memberID = memberID;
    this.time = time;
    this.email = email;
    this.signature = signature;
  }
```

The class has the usual get and set accessors. Example 4-17 shows the first four methods, and stubs the rest. For the full source, see Appendix C.

Example 4-17. authInfo accessors

```
  public void setMemberID(int memberID) {
    this.memberID = memberID;
  }

  public int getMemberID( ) {
    return memberID;
  }

  public void setTime(long time) {
    this.time = time;
  }

  public long getTime( ) {
    return time;
  }

  public void setEmail(String email) {}
  public String getEmail( ) {}
  public void setSignature(byte [] signature) {}
  public byte [] getSignature( ) {}
  public String toString( ) {}

  public void serialize(Document doc) {
    Element authEl = doc.createElementNS(
                    "http://www.soaplite.com/authInfo",
                    "authInfo");
    authEl.setAttribute("xmlns:auth", "http://www.soaplite.com/authInfo");
    authEl.setPrefix("auth");

    Element emailEl = doc.createElement("email");
    emailEl.appendChild(doc.createTextNode(auth.getEmail( )));

    Element signatureEl = doc.createElement("signature");
    signatureEl.setAttribute("xmlns:enc", Constants.NS_URI_SOAP_ENC);
    signatureEl.setAttribute("xsi:type", "enc:base64");
    signatureEl.appendChild(doc.createTextNode(
                            Base64.encode(auth.getSignature( ))));

    Element memberIdEl = doc.createElement("memberID");
    memberIdEl.appendChild(doc.createTextNode(
                            String.valueOf(auth.getMemberID( ))));
```

Example 4-17. authInfo accessors (continued)

```
    Element timeEl = doc.createElement("time");
    timeEl.appendChild(doc.createTextNode(
                       String.valueOf(auth.getTime())));

    authEl.appendChild(emailEl);
    authEl.appendChild(signatureEl);
    authEl.appendChild(memberIdEl);
    authEl.appendChild(timeEl);
    doc.appendChild(authEl);
  }
}
```

The serialize method creates an XML representation of the authInfo class instance that looks like Example 4-18.

Example 4-18. Sample serialization from the authInfo class

```
<auth:authInfo xmlns:auth="http://www.soaplite.com/authInfo">
   <email>johndoe@acme.com</email>
   <signature> <!-- Base64 encoded string --> </signature>
   <memberID>123</memberID>
   <time>2001-08-10 12:04:00 PDT (GMT + 8:00)</time>
</auth:authInfo>
```

The Client Class

The Client class is straightforward. There are utility routines for working with the SOAP client object, some code to handle authentication and login, methods to make a SOAP call for each of the operations the user might wish to perform, and then a main routine to handle the interface with the user.

Preamble

The preamble to the Client class is shown Example 4-19.

Example 4-19. The Client class

```
// Client.java
import java.io.*;
import java.net.*;
import java.util.*;
import javax.xml.parsers.DocumentBuilderFactory;
import javax.xml.parsers.DocumentBuilder;
import org.w3c.dom.*;

import org.apache.soap.util.xml.*;
import org.apache.soap.*;
import org.apache.soap.encoding.*;
import org.apache.soap.encoding.soapenc.*;
import org.apache.soap.rpc.*;
```

Example 4-19. The Client class (continued)

```java
public class Client {

  private URL url;
  private String uri;
  private authInfo authInfo;

  public Client (String url, String uri) throws Exception {
    try {
      this.uri = uri;
      this.url = new URL(url);
    } catch (Exception e) {
      throw new Exception(e.getMessage());
    }
  }
}
```

The initCall method in Example 4-20 initializes the Apache SOAP client.

Example 4-20. The initCall method

```java
private Call initCall () {
  Call call = new Call();
  call.setEncodingStyleURI(Constants.NS_URI_SOAP_ENC);
  call.setTargetObjectURI(uri);
  return call;
}
```

The invokeCall method shown in Example 4-21 makes the calls to the Publisher service. This is similar to the Hello World service example that we provided earlier.

Example 4-21. The invokeCall method

```java
private Object invokeCall (Call call)
    throws Exception {
  try {
    Response response = call.invoke(url, "");
    if (!response.generatedFault()) {
      return response.getReturnValue() == null
        ? null :
        response.getReturnValue().getValue();
    } else {
      Fault f = response.getFault();
      throw new Exception("Fault = " +
                          f.getFaultCode() + ", " +
                          f.getFaultString());
    }
  } catch (SOAPException e) {
    throw new Exception("SOAPException = " +
                        e.getFaultCode() + ", " +
                        e.getMessage());
  }
}
```

Authentication

The makeAuthHeader operation in Example 4-22 creates a SOAP header block that contains an authentication token. This operation must be called every time that somebody wishes to post or remove items in the Publisher service.

It works by simply creating a DOM document, instructing the authInfo class to serialize itself to that document (see the serialize operation on the authInfo class in Example 4-18), and adding the authentication information to the headers.

Example 4-22. The makeAuthHeader method

```
public Header makeAuthHeader (authInfo auth)
   throws Exception {
  if (auth == null) { throw new Exception("Oops,
    you are not logged in. Please login first"); }
  DocumentBuilderFactory dbf = DocumentBuilderFactory.newInstance( );
  dbf.setNamespaceAware(true);
  dbf.setValidating(false);
  DocumentBuilder db = dbf.newDocumentBuilder( );
  Document doc = db.newDocument( );
  auth.serialize(doc);
  Vector headerEntries = new Vector( );
  headerEntries.add(doc.getDocumentElement( ));
  Header header = new Header( );
  header.setHeaderEntries(headerEntries);
  return header;
}
```

User login

Example 4-23 shows the login operation. Notice that before we invoke the request, we must tell Apache SOAP which deserializer to use for the authentication token that will be returned if the operation is a success. The BeanSerializer is a utility class that comes with Apache SOAP for translating XML into instances of Java classes that conform to the Java Bean standard. We must explicitly inform Apache SOAP that we want all authInfo XML elements found in a SOAP message within the http://www.soaplite.com/Publisher namespace to be deserialized using the BeanSerializer class. If we don't, an error occurs whenever an authInfo element is found in the SOAP envelope.

We earlier brought up the topic of type mappings in Apache SOAP but never really explained what they are or how they work. A type mapping is a link between some type of native data type (such as a Java class) and the way that data type appears as XML. Serializers and deserializers are special pieces of code capable of translating between the two. The SOAPMappingRegistry is a collection of all type mappings and their corresponding serializers and deserializers.

In Apache SOAP, we have to declare a type mapping whenever we want to use any data type other than primitive built-in data types (e.g., strings, integers, floats, etc.).

Example 4-23. The login method

```
public void login (String email, String password) throws Exception {
  Call call = initCall( );

  SOAPMappingRegistry smr =
        new SOAPMappingRegistry( );
  BeanSerializer beanSer = new BeanSerializer( );
  smr.mapTypes(Constants.NS_URI_SOAP_ENC,
              new QName("http://www.soaplite.com/Publisher",
                        "authInfo"),
              authInfo.class, beanSer, beanSer);

  Vector params = new Vector ( );
  params.add(new Parameter("email", String.class,
            email, null));
  params.add(new Parameter("password",
            String.class, password, null));
  call.setParams(params);
  call.setMethodName("login");
  call.setSOAPMappingRegistry(smr);
  authInfo = (authInfo) invokeCall(call);
  System.out.println(authInfo.getEmail( ) + " logged in.");
}
```

Wrappers to call the remote operations

Although the shell client has methods for each of the operations of the Publisher web
service, it doesn't necessarily have to. We've done it in this example to ensure you
get a clear picture of the way the SOAP envelope gets built and used. This would be
easier, though, if we had a mechanism for creating a more dynamic proxy similar to
the one provided by SOAP::Lite. In Chapter 5 we will demonstrate a Java proxy built
on top of Apache SOAP that does just that.

The operations in Example 4-24 all follow a very simple pattern: initialize the SOAP
call, set the parameters, and invoke the SOAP call.

Example 4-24. Wrappers for the remote operations

```
public void register (String email,
                      String password,
                      String firstName,
                      String lastName,
                      String title,
                      String company,
                      String url) throws Exception {
  Call call = initCall( );

  Vector params = new Vector ( );
  params.add(new Parameter("email", String.class, email, null));
  params.add(new Parameter("password", String.class, password, null));
  params.add(new Parameter("firstName", String.class, firstName, null));
  params.add(new Parameter("lastName", String.class, lastName, null));
```

Example 4-24. Wrappers for the remote operations (continued)

```
  if (url != null)
            params.add(new Parameter("url", String.class, url, null));
  if (title != null)
            params.add(new Parameter("title", String.class, title, null));
  if (company != null)
            params.add(new Parameter("company", String.class, company, null));
  call.setParams(params);
  call.setMethodName("register");
  invokeCall(call);
  System.out.println("Registered.");
}

public void postItem (String type,
                      String title,
                      String description)
                      throws Exception {
  Call call = initCall();
  Vector params = new Vector ();
  params.add(new Parameter("type", String.class, type, null));
  params.add(new Parameter("title", String.class, title, null));
  params.add(new Parameter("description", String.class, description, null));
  call.setParams(params);
  call.setMethodName("postItem");
  call.setHeader(makeAuthHeader(authInfo));
  Integer itemID = (Integer)invokeCall(call);
  System.out.println("Posted item " + itemID + ".");
}

public void removeItem (Integer itemID);
public void browse (String type,
                    String format,
                    Integer maxRows);
```

The main routine

Now that the basic operations for interacting with the web service have been defined, we need to create the code for the Publisher shell (Example 4-25). This code does nothing more than provide users with a menu of things that can be done with the Publisher service. In a loop we get input from the user, decide what they want to do, and do it.

Because none of this code deals directly with the invocation and use of the Publisher web service, significant pieces were removed for the sake of brevity. The entire code sample can be found in Appendix C.

Example 4-25. The main method

```
public static void main(String[] args) {
  String myname = Client.class.getName();

  if (args.length < 1) {
```

Example 4-25. The main method (continued)

```java
        System.err.println("Usage:\n  java " + myname + " SOAP-router-URL");
        System.exit (1);
    }

    try {
      Client client = new Client(args[0], "http://www.soaplite.com/Publisher");

      InputStream in = System.in;
      InputStreamReader isr = new
            InputStreamReader(in);
      BufferedReader br = new BufferedReader(isr);
      String action = null;
      while (!("quit".equals(action))) {
        System.out.print("> ");
        action = br.readLine( );

        if ("register".equals(action)) {
            // code hidden for brevity
            client.register(email, password, firstName, lastName,
                            title, company, url);
        }

        if ("login".equals(action)) {
            // code hidden for brevity
            client.login(id,pwd);
        }

        if ("post".equals(action)) {
            // code hidden for brevity
            client.postItem(type, title, desc);
        }

        if ("remove".equals(action)) {
        // code hidden for brevity
            client.removeItem(Integer.valueOf(id));
            } catch (Exception ex) {
               System.out.println("\nCould not remove item!");
            }
            System.out.println( );
        }

        if ("browse".equals(action)) {
        // code hidden for brevity
            client.browse(type, format, ival);
            } catch (Exception ex) {
               System.out.println(ex);
               System.out.println("\nCould not browse!");
            }
        }

        if ("help".equals(action)) {
            System.out.println("\nActions: register | login | post | remove | browse");
```

Example 4-25. The main method (continued)

```
        }
      }
    } catch (Exception e) {
      System.err.println("Caught Exception: " + e.getMessage( ));
    }
  }
}
```

Deploying the Client

Once the code is written, compile it and launch it with the following command:

```
C:\book>java Client http://localhost/cgi-bin/Publisher.cgi
```

Replace localhost with the name of the web server where the Publisher CGI script is deployed. Figure 4-2 shows the shell in action.

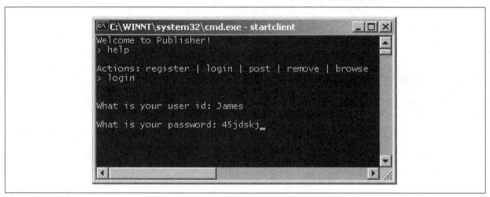

Figure 4-2. The Publisher shell at runtime

## CHAPTER 5

Describing a SOAP Service

Having seen the basic steps in implementing web services, you're now ready to explore technologies that make it easier to use web services that have already been deployed. Specifically, this chapter focuses on the Web Service Description Language (WSDL), which makes possible automated code-generation tools to simplify building clients for existing web services. WSDL also forms an integral component of the discovery process we'll see in Chapter 6.

Describing Web Services

The introduction of web services in Chapter 1 mentioned that one of the key things that sets web services apart from other types of applications is that they can be made self-describing. Here, we describe what that means.

Every application exposes some type of functionality; you invoke that functionality through various types of operations. Those operations require you to provide specific pieces of information. Once the operation is complete, the application may return information back to you. This entire exchange must be conducted using some agreed upon protocol for packaging the information and sending it back and forth. However, most applications typically require you, the developer, to describe how all of this is supposed to happen. The specific details of how a service is implemented become entrenched in the application. If any changes need to be made, the application must be changed and recompiled. These applications are not very flexible.

With web services, though, it is possible to allow applications to discover all of this information dynamically while the application is being run. This ability makes changes easier to accommodate and much less disruptive.

The SOAP specification does not address description. The de facto standard specification used to make web services self-describing is the Web Services Description Language (WSDL). Using WSDL, a web service can describe everything about what it does, how it does it, and how consumers of that web service can go about using it.

There are several advantages to using WSDL:

1. WSDL makes it easier to write and maintain services by providing a more structured approach to defining web service interfaces.

2. WSDL makes it easier to consume web services by reducing the amount of code (and potential errors) that a client application must implement.

3. WSDL makes it easier to implement changes that will be less likely to "break" SOAP client applications. Dynamic discovery of WSDL descriptions allows such changes to be pushed down automatically to clients using WSDL so that potentially expensive modifications to the client code don't have to be made every time a change occurs.

WSDL is not perfect, however. Currently, there is no support for versioning of WSDL descriptions, so web services providers and consumers need to be aware that when significant changes to a WSDL description occur, there may very well be problems propagated down to the client. For the most part, however, WSDL descriptions should be treated in a similar manner to traditional object interfaces—where the definition of the service, once put into production, is immutable and cannot be changed.

Another key point is that, for the most part, web service developers will not be required to manually create WSDL descriptions of their services. Many toolkits include tools for generating WSDL automatically from existing application components.

Microsoft's .NET platform, for example, will automatically generate a WSDL description of deployed *.asmx* services simply by appending *?WSDL* to the URL of the *.asmx* file. If you have .NET and the *HelloWorld.asmx* service from Chapter 3, open your web browser and append the *?WSDL* to the end of the service's URL. You will see a dynamically generated WSDL description of the Hello World service, shown in Figure 5-1.

Keep in mind that not every web services toolkit includes WSDL support; third party add-ons may be required. IBM supplies an extension to Apache SOAP called the Web Services ToolKit that provides comprehensive WSDL support on top of Apache SOAP. WSIF, another IBM tool that we will take a look at in just a minute, is another example of a WSDL-enabling add-on for Apache SOAP. Apache Axis, when complete, will include built-in support for the use and creation of WSDL documents.

Although you can, and many do, use SOAP without WSDL, WSDL descriptions of your services make life easier for consumers of those services.

A Quick Example

To demonstrate quickly the difference that using a WSDL description of a web service can make in terms of the amount of code necessary to access a web service from

Figure 5-1. Automatically generated WSDL description for the .NET Hello World service

Java, let's create a WSDL description for the Hello World web service and use the IBM Web Service Invocation Framework (WSIF) tools to invoke it. WSIF is a Java package that provides a WSDL-aware layer on top of Apache SOAP, allowing us to call SOAP services easily given only a WSDL description. It can be downloaded from *http://alphaworks.ibm.com/tech/wsif*. Within this service description, we will point to the Perl-based Hello World service created in Chapter 3.

The WSDL file begins with a preamble, then defines some messages that will be exchanged. This preamble is shown in Example 5-1.

Example 5-1. WSDL preamble

```
<?xml version="1.0" encoding="UTF-8"?>
<wsdl:definitions name="HelloWorldDescription"
    targetNamespace="urn:HelloWorld"
    xmlns:tns="urn:HelloWorld"
    xmlns:soap="http://schemas.xmlsoap.org/wsdl/soap/"
    xmlns:wsdl="http://schemas.xmlsoap.org/wsdl/">
```

Example 5-1. WSDL preamble (continued)

```
<wsdl:message name="sayHello_IN">
  <part name="name" type="xsd:string" />
</wsdl:message>
<wsdl:message name="sayHello_Out">
  <part name="greeting" type="xsd:string" />
</wsdl:message>
```

Next, the WSDL defines how a method translates into messages. This is shown in Example 5-2.

Example 5-2. WSDL showing how a method corresponds to messages

```
<wsdl:portType name="HelloWorldInterface">
  <wsdl:operation name="sayHello">
    <wsdl:input message="tns:sayHello_IN" />
    <wsdl:output message="tns:sayHello_OUT" />
  </wsdl:operation>
</wsdl:portType>
```

Then the WSDL defines how the method is implemented (see Example 5-3).

Example 5-3. WSDL showing the implementation of the method

```
<wsdl:binding name="HelloWorldBinding"
              type="tns:HelloWorldInterface">
  <soap:binding style="rpc"
   transport="http://schemas.xmlsoap.org/soap/http"
   />
  <wsdl:operation name="sayHello">
    <soap:operation soapAction="urn:Hello" />
    <wsdl:input>
      <soap:body use="encoded"
                 namespace="urn:Hello"
                 encodingStyle=http://schemas.xmlsoap.org/soap/encoding/
      />
    </wsdl:input>
    <wsdl:output>
      <soap:body use="encoded"
                 namespace="urn:Hello"
                 encodingStyle=http://schemas.xmlsoap.org/soap/encoding/
      />
    </wsdl:output>
  </wsdl:operation>
</wsdl:binding>
```

And finally the WSDL says where the service is hosted (Example 5-4).

Example 5-4. WSDL showing the location of the service

```
<wsdl:service name="HelloWorldService">
  <wsdl:port name="HelloWorldPort"
             binding="tns:HelloWorldBinding">
```

Example 5-4. WSDL showing the location of the service (continued)

```
    <!-- location of the Perl Hello World Service -->
    <soap:address
      location="http://localhost:8080" />
  </wsdl:port>
 </wsdl:service>
</wsdl:definitions>
```

The values of the name attributes in WSDL (e.g., `HelloWorldInterface` and `HelloWorldBinding`) are completely arbitrary. There are no defined naming conventions you should follow.

The complete WSDL document, shown in full in Appendix C, would be placed either in a well-known or, as we will explain Chapter 6, a discoverable location on your web server so that it may be retrieved using a simple HTTP-GET request. Once that is done, we can invoke the WSIF `DynamicInvoker` class to invoke the web service. This can be done using a single command-line operation:

```
C:\book>java clients.DynamicInvoker http://localhost/sayhello.wsdl sayHello James
```

Which will produce the output:

```
Hello James
```

This is a big difference compared to the code we used in Chapter 3 to invoke the exact same service. The WSDL description allowed the WSIF tools to automatically figure out what needed to be done with the Apache SOAP tools in order to send the message and process the results, and you didn't have to write a single line of code. While this is a fairly simple example (you won't be able to use a single command line for every web service that uses WSDL and WSIF, as we will demonstrate later), it does stress the point: we use WSDL because it makes it easier to write web services.

Anatomy of a Service Description

A web service description describes the abstract interface through which a service consumer communicates with a service provider, as well as the specific details of how a given web service has implemented that interface. It does so by defining four types of things: data, messages, interfaces, and services.

A *service* (`HelloWorldService` in our example) is a collection of *ports* (addresses implementing the service; see `HelloWorldPort` in the example). A port has both an abstract definition (the *port type*) and a concrete definition (the *binding*). Port types function as the specification of the software interface (`HelloWorldInterface` in this example), and are composed of collections of *operations* (the individual method signatures) that define the ordered exchanges of *messages* (`sayHello_IN` and `sayHello_OUT` in the example). Bindings say which protocols are used by the port, including the packaging protocol (SOAP in this case). A message is a logical collection of named *parts* (data values) of a particular type. The type of part is defined using some standard data typing mechanism such as the XML Schema specification.

The structure of a web service description is illustrated in Figure 5-2.

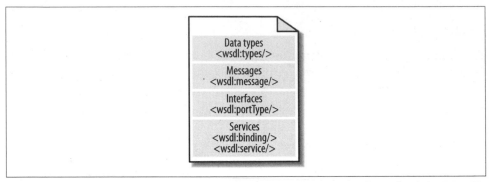

Figure 5-2. A service description describes four basic things about a web service: the data types, the messages, the interfaces, and the services

Defining Data Types and Structures with XML Schemas

Interoperability between applications on various operating system platforms and programming languages is most often hindered because one system's "integer" may not be exactly the same as another system's "integer." Because different operating systems and programming languages have different definitions of what particular base (or primitive) data types are not only called, but also how they are expressed when sent out over the wire, those operating systems and programming languages cannot communicate with each other.

To allow seamless cross-platform interoperability, there must be a mechanism by which the service consumer and the service provider agree to a common set of types and the textual representation of the data stored in them. The web services description provides the framework through which the common data types may be defined.

In WSDL, the primary method of defining these shared data types is the W3C's XML Schema specification. WSDL is, however, capable of using any mechanism to define data types, and may actually leverage the type definition mechanisms of existing programming languages or data interchange standards. No matter what type definition mechanism is used, both the service consumer and the service provider must agree to it or the service description is useless. That is why the authors of the WSDL specification chose to use XML Schemas—they are completely platform neutral.

If you're unfamiliar with the XML Schema data representation system, now would be a good time to read the quick introduction in Appendix B.

Interestingly, while XML Schemas are used to define the data types, the message that is actually sent does not have to be serialized as XML. For example, if we decide to use a standard HTML form to invoke a web service, the input message will not be in XML syntax. The XML Schema specification itself recognizes that a schema may be used to describe data that is not serialized as an XML document instance, as evidenced by Section 2 of the XML Schema specification primer (*http://www.w3.org/TR/ xmlschema-0/*):

> The purpose of a schema is to define a class of XML documents, and so the term "instance document" is often used to describe an XML document that conforms to a particular schema. In fact, neither instances nor schemas need to exist as documents per se—they may exist as streams of bytes sent between applications, as fields in a database record, or as collections of XML Infoset "Information Items." —XML Schema Part 0: Primer, Section 2

So, if the data can be expressed as XML, regardless of whether it actually *is* expressed as XML, then XML Schemas can be used to describe the rules that define the data.

Using XML Schemas in WSDL

Once the data types are defined, they must be referenced within a WSDL description. Do so either by embedding the schema directly within the `<wsdl:types />` element, or by importing the schema using the `<wsdl:import />` element. While both approaches are valid, many WSDL-enabled tools do not yet properly support `<wsdl: import />`. The `<wsdl:types />` method is by far the most common. Examples of both approaches are shown here.

With `import`, you must declare the namespace that the XML Schema defines, then import the XML Schema document. This is shown in Example 5-5.

Example 5-5. Using import to reference a type definition

```
<?xml version="1.0" encoding="UTF-8"?>
<wsdl:definitions name="HelloWorldDescription"
   targetNamespace="urn:HelloWorld"
   xmlns:tns="urn:HelloWorld"
   xmlns:types="urn:MyDataTypes"
   xmlns:soap="http://schemas.xmlsoap.org/wsdl/soap/"
   xmlns:wsdl="http://schemas.xmlsoap.org/wsdl/">

   <wsdl:import namespace="urn:MyDataTypes"
               location="telephonenumber.xsd" />

</wsdl:definitions>
```

Example 5-6 is the same definition but with the XML Schema embedded directly into the WSDL description.

Example 5-6. Embedding XML Schema directly to define types

```
<?xml version="1.0" encoding="UTF-8"?>
<wsdl:definitions name="HelloWorldDescription"
    targetNamespace="urn:HelloWorld"
    xmlns:tns="urn:HelloWorld"
    xmlns:types="urn:MyDataTypes"
    xmlns:soap="http://schemas.xmlsoap.org/wsdl/soap/"
    xmlns:wsdl="http://schemas.xmlsoap.org/wsdl/">

    <wsdl:types>
      <xsd:schema xmlns:xsd="http://www.w3.org/2000/10/XMLSchema"
                  targetNamespace="urn:MyDataTypes"
                  elementFormDefault="qualified">
        <xsd:complexType name="telephoneNumberEx">
          <xsd:complexContent>
            <xsd:restriction base="telephoneNumber">
              <xsd:sequence>
                <xsd:element name="countryCode">
                  <xsd:simpleType>
                    <xsd:restriction base="xsd:string">
                      <xsd:pattern value="\d{2}"/>
                    </xsd:restriction>
                  </xsd:simpleType>
                </xsd:element>
                <xsd:element name="area">
                  <xsd:simpleType>
                    <xsd:restriction base="xsd:string">
                      <xsd:pattern value="\d{3}"/>
                    </xsd:restriction>
                  </xsd:simpleType>
                </xsd:element>
                <xsd:element name="exchange">
                  <xsd:simpleType>
                    <xsd:restriction base="xsd:string">
                      <xsd:pattern value="\d{3}"/>
                    </xsd:restriction>
                  </xsd:simpleType>
                </xsd:element>
                <xsd:element name="number">
                  <xsd:simpleType>
                    <xsd:restriction base="xsd:string">
                      <xsd:pattern value="\d{4}"/>
                    </xsd:restriction>
                  </xsd:simpleType>
                </xsd:element>
              </xsd:sequence>
            </xsd:restriction>
          </xsd:complexContent>
        </xsd:complexType>
      </xsd:schema>
    </wsdl:types>

</wsdl:definitions>
```

Describing the Web Service Interface

Web service interfaces are generally no different from interfaces defined in object-oriented languages. There are input messages (the set of parameters passed into the operation), output messages (the set of values returned from the operation), and fault messages (the set of error conditions that may arise while the operation is being invoked). In WSDL, a web service interface is known as a *port type*.

With this in mind, let's look again at the WSDL that we used earlier to describe the Hello World service. The relevant parts are shown in Example 5-7.

Example 5-7. Describing the Hello World service

```
<definitions ...>
  <wsdl:message name="sayHello_IN">
    <part name="name" type="xsd:string" />
  </wsdl:message>

  <wsdl:message name="sayHello_Out">
    <part name="greeting" type="xsd:string" />
  </wsdl:message>

  <wsdl:portType name="HelloWorldInterface">
    <wsdl:operation name="sayHello">
      <wsdl:input message="tns:sayHello_IN" />
      <wsdl:output message="tns:sayHello_OUT" />
    </wsdl:operation>
  </wsdl:portType>
  ...
</definitions>
```

The portType element defines the interface to the Hello World service. This interface consists of a single operation that has both an input and an expected output. The input is a message of type sayHello_IN, consisting of a single part called name of type string.

WSDL portTypes do not support inheritance. It would be nice to be able to do something along the lines of Example 5-8, but it's not supported yet.

Example 5-8. Attempting inheritance with WSDL

```
<wsdl:definitions>
  <wsdl:portType name="HelloWorldInterface">
    <wsdl:operation name="sayHello" />
  </wsdl:portType>
  <wsdl:portType name="HelloWorldInterfaceEx"
              extends="HelloWorldInterface">
    <wsdl:operation name="sayGoodbye" />
  </wsdl:portType>
</wsdl:definitions>
```

The goal would be to have SayHelloInterfaceEx inherit the sayHello operation defined in HelloWorldInterface. You can't do that in WSDL right now, but support for some form of inheritance is being considered for future versions of the specification.

Describing the Web Service Implementation

WSDL can also describe the implementation of a given port type. This description is generally divided into two parts: the binding, which describes how an interface is bound to specific transport and messaging protocols (such as SOAP and HTTP), and the service, which describes the specific network location (or locations) where an interface has been implemented.

Binding Web Service Interfaces

Just as in Java, COM, or any object-oriented language, interfaces must be implemented in order to be useful. In WSDL, the word for implementation is *binding*: the interfaces are bound to specific network and messaging protocols. In WSDL, this is represented by the binding element, shown in Example 5-9.

Example 5-9. Binding an interface to specific protocols

```
<wsdl:binding name="HelloWorldBinding"
              type="tns:HelloWorldInterface">

 <soap:binding style="rpc"
   transport="http://schemas.xmlsoap.org/soap/http"/>

 <wsdl:operation name="sayHello">
   <soap:operation soapAction="urn:Hello" />

   <wsdl:input>
     <soap:body use="encoded"
                namespace="..."
                encodingStyle="..." />
   </wsdl:input>
   <wsdl:output>
     <soap:body use="encoded"
                namespace="..."
                encodingStyle="..." />
   </wsdl:output>
 </wsdl:operation>
</wsdl:binding>
```

This creates a new binding definition, representing a SOAP-over-HTTP implementation of the HelloWorldInterface port type. A SOAP-aware web services platform would use this information and the information contained in the port type and data type definitions to construct the appropriate SOAP envelopes for each operation.

The only difference between the binding element and the portType element is the addition of the <soap:binding />, <soap:operation />, and <soap:body /> elements. These are the pieces that tell us how the messages are to be packaged. An instance of the input message for the sayHello operation bound to SOAP, using the earlier definition, would look something like Example 5-10.

Example 5-10. Instance of the message

```
<s:Envelope xmlns:s="...">
  <s:Body>
    <m:sayHello xmlns:m="urn:Hello">
      <name>John</name>
    </m:sayHello>
  </s:Body>
</s:Envelope>
```

The various soap: prefixed elements indicate exactly how the SOAP protocol is to be applied to the Hello World interface:

<soap:binding />

Defines the transport protocol and the style of the SOAP message. There are two styles: *RPC* and *document*. RPC indicates a SOAP message conforming to the SOAP RPC convention. Document indicates a SOAP messaging carrying some arbitrary package of XML data.

<soap:operation />

Defines the value of the SOAPAction header when the HTTP transport protocol is used.

<soap:body />

Specifies how the parts of the abstract WSDL message definition will appear in the body of the SOAP message by defining whether the parts are encoded (following the rules of some encoding style) or literal (arbitrary XML not necessarily following any defined set of encoding rules).

<soap:fault />

While not shown in the previous example, this element specifies the contents of the SOAP fault detail element. It works exactly like the <soap:body /> element, defining how the detail part of the message will appear in the SOAP envelope.

<soap:header />

Specifies how parts of the message will appear in the header of the SOAP message.

<soap:headerfault />

Specifies how fault information pertaining to specific headers will appear in the header of the SOAP fault message returned to the sender.

<soap:address />

Specifies the network location where the SOAP web service has been deployed.

Alternatively, the binding could have specified a different packaging protocol for the messages—HTTP-GET, for instance. In this case, the binding element will include elements that describe how the message will appear within an HTTP URL. This is shown in Example 5-11.

Example 5-11. WSDL binding to HTTP-GET

```
<wsdl:binding name="HelloWorldBinding"
              type="tns:HelloWorldInterface">
 <http:binding verb="GET"/>
 <wsdl:operation name="sayHello">
    <http:operation location="sayHello" />
    <wsdl:input>
      <http:urlEncoded />
    </wsdl:input>
    <wsdl:output>
      <mime:content type="text/plain" />
    </wsdl:output>
 </wsdl:operation>
</wsdl:binding>
```

Each of the `http:` and `mime:` prefixed elements specify exactly how the port type is to be implemented. For example, the `<http:urlEncoded />` element indicates that all of the parts of the input message will appear as query string extensions to the service URL. An instance of this binding would appear as:

```
http://www.acme.com/sayHello?name=John
```

With the response message represented as nothing more than a stream of data with a MIME content type of text/plain.

```
HTTP/1.1 200 OK
Server: Microsoft-IIS/5.0
Content-Type: text/plain;
Content-Length: 11

Hello James
```

Describing the Location of a Web Service

The final piece of information that a WSDL service implementation description must provide is the network location where the web service is implemented. This is done by linking a specific protocol binding to a specific network address in the WSDL service and port elements, as shown in Example 5-12.

Example 5-12. Linking a binding to a network address

```
<wsdl:service name="HelloWorldService">
  <wsdl:port name="HelloWorldPort"
             binding="tns:HelloWorldBinding">
    <soap:address location="http://localhost:8080" />
```

Example 5-12. Linking a binding to a network address (continued)

```
  </wsdl:port>
</wsdl:service>
```

In this example, we see that the Hello World service can be invoked through the use of SOAP messages, as defined by the `HelloWorldBinding` implemented at *http://localhost:8080*.

One interesting aspect of WSDL is that a service may define multiple ports, each of which may implement a different binding at a different network location. It is possible, for example, to create a single WSDL service description for our three Hello World services written in Perl, Java, and .NET, as shown in Example 5-13.

Example 5-13. Multiple instances of the same server

```
<wsdl:service name="HelloWorldService">
  <wsdl:port name="HelloWorldPort_Perl"
             binding="tns:HelloWorldBinding">
    <soap:address location="http://localhost:8080" />
  </wsdl:port>
  <wsdl:port name="HelloWorldPort_Java"
             binding="tns:HelloWorldBinding">
    <soap:address location="http://localhost/soap/servlet/rpcrouter" />
  </wsdl:port>
  <wsdl:port name="HelloWorldPort_NET"
             binding="tns:HelloWorldBinding">
    <soap:address location="http://localhost/helloworld.asmx" />
  </wsdl:port>
</wsdl:service>
```

At this point the WSDL has described everything that a service consumer needs to know in order to invoke the Hello World web service we created in Chapter 3.

Understanding Messaging Patterns

A messaging pattern describes the sequence of messages exchanged between the service consumer and the service provider. The web services architecture supports two fundamental types of message patterns: single-message exchange and multiple-message exchange.

The definition of each pattern is based on whether the service provider or the service consumer is the first to initiate the exchange of messages, and whether there is an expected response to that initial message. Figure 5-3 illustrates two common message patterns.

Understanding these messaging patterns is an essential part of understanding how to build effective and useful web services.

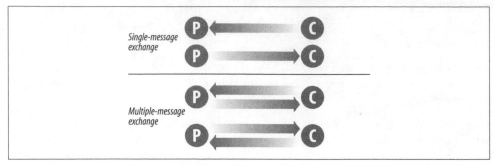

Figure 5-3. Two patterns of message exchange between the service provider (P) and the service consumer (C)

Single-Message Exchange

A single-message exchange involves just that—a single message exchanged between the service consumer and the service provider. They are analogous to functions that do not have return values. The message may originate with either the service provider or the service consumer.

To express a single-message exchange pattern in WSDL, define the abstract operation within the portType where the exchange will take place, as shown in Example 5-14.

Example 5-14. Single-message pattern in WSDL

```
<portType name="...">
  <operation name="Consumer_to_Provider">
    <input message="..." />
  </operation>
  <operation name="Provider_to_Consumer">
    <output message="..." />
  </operation>
</portType>
```

In WSDL, the <input /> element is used to express the exchange of a message from the service consumer to the service provider. The <output /> element is used to express the exchange of a message in the opposite direction, from the provider to the consumer.

Multiple-Message Exchange

And, obviously, multiple-message exchanges involve two or more messages between the service consumer and the service provider. These types of transactions range in complexity from simple function-style exchanges (calling a method on an object and returning a single result value), to a complex choreography of messages passed back and forth. The current version of WSDL, however, is only capable of expressing the simple function-style exchanges, as in Example 5-15.

Example 5-15. Function-style exchanges in WSDL

```
<portType name="...">
  <operation name="Consumer_to_Provider_to_Consumer">
    <input message="..." />
    <output message="..." />
  </operation>
  <operation name="Provider_to_Consumer_to_Provider">
    <output message="..." />
    <input message="..." />
  </operation>
</portType>
```

Again, all <input /> messages originate with the service consumer and all <output /> messages originate with the service provider.

Complex Multiple-Message Exchanges

By itself, WSDL is only capable of describing very rudimentary message exchange patterns. WSDL lacks the added ability to specify not only what messages to exchange in any given operation, but also the sequencing of operations themselves. Quite often, for example, it may be useful to specify that a service consumer must login before attempting to deleteAllRecords. WSDL has no way to describe such sequencing rules. A future version of WSDL may allow such sequencing to be defined, either natively or through various extensibility mechanisms. Specifications such as IBM's Web Services Flow Language (WSFL) and Microsoft's XLANG (pronounced "slang") have also been designed to deal with such sequencing issues from the point of view of a workflow process. These specifications will not be covered in this book.

Intermediaries

In Chapter 2 we discussed actors and message paths. A message path is the path a SOAP message takes on its way from the service consumer to the service requester. This path may be through several intermediary web services called actors, each of which may do something when it receives the message.

Intermediaries do not change the exchange pattern for a given operation. For example, a request-response operation between the service consumer and the service requester is still a request-response style operation. The only difference is that the request and the response messages may make a few additional stops on their way to their final destination. WSDL does not yet provide any facilities for communicating the path that a message is to take.

CHAPTER 6

Discovering SOAP Services

Once a WSDL description of a web service has been created, a service consumer must be able to locate it in order to be able to use it. This is known as *discovery*, the topic of this chapter. In particular, we look at the Universal Description, Discovery, and Integration (UDDI) project and the new Web Services Inspection Language.

WSDL provides a service consumer with all the information they need to interact with a service provider. But how can a consumer learn of services to use? The UDDI project is an industry effort to define a searchable registry of services and their descriptions so that consumers can automatically discover the services they need.

UDDI has two parts: a registry of all a web service's metadata (including a pointer to the WSDL description of a service), and a set of WSDL port type definitions for manipulating and searching that registry.

The latest UDDI specification is Version 2.0. In this book, however, we focus completely on Version 1.0. Version 2.0 has not yet been widely implemented and there is very little support available for it.

UDDI is not the only option for service discovery. IBM and Microsoft have recently announced the Web Services Inspection Language (WS-Inspection), an XML-based language that provides an index of all the web services at a given web location.

The first part of this chapter will focus primarily on UDDI. The last half will briefly introduce WS-Inspection and demonstrate its role inService Discovery.

The UDDI Registry

The UDDI registry allows a business to publicly list a description of itself and the services it provides. Potential consumers of those services can locate them based on taxonomical information, such as what the service does or what industry the service targets.

The registry itself is defined as a hierarchy of business, service, and binding descriptions expressed in XML.

Business Entity

The business entity structure represents the provider of web services. Within the UDDI registry, this structure contains information about the company itself, including contact information, industry categories, business identifiers, and a list of services provided. Example 6-1 shows a fictitious business's UDDI registry entry.

Example 6-1. A UDDI business entry

```
<businessEntity businessKey="uuid:C0E6D5A8-C446-4f01-99DA-70E212685A40"
                operator="http://www.ibm.com"
                authorizedName="John Doe">
  <name>Acme Company</name>
  <description>
    We create cool Web services
  </description>
  <contacts>
    <contact useType="general info">
      <description>General Information</description>
      <personName>John Doe</personName>
      <phone>(123) 123-1234</phone>
      <email>jdoe@acme.com</email>
    </contact>
  </contacts>
  <businessServices>
    ...
  </businessServices>
  <identifierBag>
    <keyedReference
        TModelKey="UUID:8609C81E-EE1F-4D5A-B202-3EB13AD01823"
        name="D-U-N-S"
        value="123456789" />
  </identifierBag>
  <categoryBag>
    <keyedReference
        TModelKey="UUID:C0B9FE13-179F-413D-8A5B-5004DB8E5BB2"
        name="NAICS"
        value="111336" />
  </categoryBag>
</businessEntity>
```

Business Services

The business service structure represents an individual web service provided by the business entity. Its description includes information on how to bind to the web service, what type of web service it is, and what taxonomical categories it belongs to. Example 6-2 show a possible business service structure for the Hello World web service.

Example 6-2. Hello World business structure in UDDI

```
<businessService serviceKey="uuid:D6F1B765-BDB3-4837-828D-8284301E5A2A"
                 businessKey="uuid:C0E6D5A8-C446-4f01-99DA-70E212685A40">
```

Example 6-2. Hello World business structure in UDDI (continued)

```
    <name>Hello World Web Service</name>
    <description>A friendly Web service</description>
    <bindingTemplates>
      ...
    </bindingTemplates>
    <categoryBag />
</businessService>
```

Notice the use of the Universally Unique Identifiers (UUIDs) in the businessKey and serviceKey attributes. Every business entity and business service is uniquely identified in all UDDI registries through the UUID assigned by the registry when the information is first entered.

Binding Templates

Binding templates are the technical descriptions of the web services represented by the business service structure. A single business service may have multiple binding templates. The binding template represents the actual implementation of the web service (it is roughly equivalent to the service element we saw in WSDL). Example 6-3 shows a binding template for Hello World.

Example 6-3. A binding template for Hello World

```
<bindingTemplate serviceKey="uuid:D6F1B765-BDB3-4837-828D-8284301E5A2A"
                 bindingKey="uuid:C0E6D5A8-C446-4f01-99DA-70E212685A40">
  <description>Hello World SOAP Binding</description>
  <accessPoint URLType="http">
    http://localhost:8080
  </accessPoint>
  <TModelInstanceDetails>
    <TModelInstanceInfo
          TModelKey="uuid:EB1B645F-CF2F-491f-811A-4868705F5904">
      <instanceDetails>
        <overviewDoc>
          <description>
            references the description of the
            WSDL service definition
          </description>
          <overviewURL>
            http://localhost/helloworld.wsdl
          </overviewURL>
        </overviewDoc>
      </instanceDetails>
    </TModelInstanceInfo>
  </TModelInstanceDetails>
</bindingTemplate>
```

Because a business service may have multiple binding templates, the service may specify different implementations of the same service, each bound to a different set of protocols or a different network address.

TModels

A TModel is a way of describing the various business, service, and template structures stored within the UDDI registry. Any abstract concept can be registered within UDDI as a TModel. For instance, if you define a new WSDL port type, you can define a TModel that represents that port type within UDDI. Then, you can specify that a given business service implements that port type by associating the TModel with one of that business service's binding templates.

A TModel representing the HelloWorldInterface port type looks like Example 6-4.

Example 6-4. A TModel for Hello World

```
<TModel TModelKey="uuid:xyz987..."
        operator="http://www.ibm.com"
        authorizedName="John Doe">
  <name>HelloWorldInterface Port Type</name>
  <description>
    An interface for a friendly Web service
  </description>
  <overviewDoc>
    <overviewURL>
      http://localhost/helloworld.wsdl
    </overviewURL>
  </overviewDoc>
</TModel>
```

Federated UDDI Registries

At its core, UDDI is comprised of a global network of linked (*federated*) registries that all implement the same SOAP-based web service interface for publishing and locating web services. Figure 6-1 illustrates this.

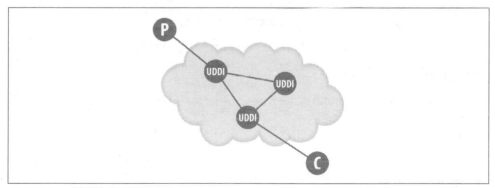

Figure 6-1. UDDI registries can be linked to provide a rudimentary distributed search capability

Private UDDI Registries

As an alternative to using the public federated network of UDDI registries available on the Internet, companies or industry groups may choose to implement their own private UDDI registries. These exclusive services would be designed for the sole purpose of allowing members of the company or of the industry group to share and advertise services amongst themselves.

The key to this, however, is that whether the UDDI registry is part of the global federated network or a privately owned and operated registry, the one thing that ties it all together is a common web services API for publishing and locating businesses and services advertised within the UDDI registry.

The UDDI Interfaces

A registry is no use without some way to access it. The UDDI standard specifies two SOAP interfaces for service consumers and service providers to interact with the registry. Service consumers use InquireSOAP to find a service, and service providers use PublishSOAP to list a service. These services are described with WSDL. The following explanation of the SOAP APIs refers to the WSDL, but abbreviates some of the repetitive parts. The full WSDL specification of the UDDI API is given in Appendix B.

The core of the UDDI interfaces is the UDDI XML Schema definitions. These define the fundamental UDDI data types, for instance, the businessDetail, which communicates detailed information about registered business entities. The UDDI XML Schema must be imported into the WSDL description from its network location at *http://www.uddi.org/schema/2001/uddi_v1.xsd*, as shown in Example 6-5.

Example 6-5. Importing the WSDL description

```
<import namespace="urn:uddi-org:api"
 location="http://www.uddi.org/schema/2001/uddi_v1.xsd"
 />
```

The Publisher Interface

The Publisher interface defines sixteen operations for a service provider managing its entries in the UDDI registry:

get_authToken
> Retrieves an authorization token. It works exactly like the authorization token we used in the Publisher example in Chapter 3. All of the Publisher interface operations require that a valid authorization token be submitted with the request.

discard_authToken
> Tells the UDDI registry to no longer accept a given authorization token. This step is equivalent to logging out of the system.

save_business
> Creates or updates a business entity's information contained in the UDDI registry.

save_service
> Creates or updates information about the web services that a business entity provides.

save_binding
> Creates or updates the technical information about a web service's implementation.

save_TModel
> Creates or updates the registration of abstract concepts managed by the UDDI registry.

delete_business
> Removes the given business entities from the UDDI registry completely.

delete_service
> Removes the given web services from the UDDI registry completely.

delete_binding
> Removes the given web service technical details from the UDDI registry.

delete_TModel
> Removes the specified TModels from the UDDI registry.

get_registeredInfo
> Returns a summary of everything the UDDI registry is currently keeping track of for the user, including all businesses, all services, and all TModels.

In the WSDL, these methods correspond to messages based on the underlying UDDI data types, as in Example 6-6.

Example 6-6. UDDI method definition

```
<message name="bindingDetail">
 <part name="body"
       element="uddi:bindingDetail" />
</message>

<message name="businessDetail">
 <part name="body"
       element="uddi:businessDetail" />
</message>
```

The other standard messages are similarly defined.

Finally, we define the port type itself, creating the interface through which modifications can be made to the UDDI registry. Again, only a few definitions have been shown in full detail in Example 6-7, as they all follow the same pattern.

Example 6-7. Representative Publisher operation definitions

```
<portType name="PublishSoap">
  <operation name="delete_binding">
    <input   message="tns:delete_binding" />
    <output message="tns:dispositionReport" />
    <fault   name="error"
             message="tns:dispositionReport" />
  </operation>

  <operation name="delete_business">
    <input   message="tns:delete_business" />
    <output message="tns:dispositionReport" />
    <fault   name="error"
             message="tns:dispositionReport" />
  </operation>

  <operation name="delete_service">
    <input   message="tns:delete_service" />
    <output message="tns:dispositionReport" />
    <fault   name="error"
             message="tns:dispositionReport" />
  </operation>

  <operation name="delete_TModel"> ...
  <operation name="discard_authToken"> ...
  <operation name="get_authToken"> ...
  <operation name="get_registeredInfo"> ...
  <operation name="save_binding"> ...
  <operation name="save_business"> ...
  <operation name="save_service"> ...
  <operation name="save_TModel"> ...
  <operation name="validate_categorization"> ...
  </portType>
</definitions>
```

The Inquiry Interface

The inquiry interface defines ten operations for searching the UDDI registry and retrieving details about specific registrations:

find_binding
: Returns a list of web services that match a particular set of criteria based on the technical binding information.

find_business
: Returns a list of business entities that match a particular set of criteria.

find_ltservice
: Returns a list of web services that match a particular set of criteria.

find_TModel
: Returns a list of TModels that match a particular set of criteria.

get_bindingDetail

> Returns the complete registration information for a particular web service binding template.

get_businessDetail

> Returns the registration information for a business entity, including all services that entity provides.

get_businessDetailExt

> Returns the complete registration information for a business entity.

get_serviceDetail

> Returns the complete registration information for a web service.

get_TModelDetail

> Returns the complete registration information for a TModel.

InquireSOAP defines the web service interface for searching the UDDI registry. Example 6-8 shows the method definitions for find_binding, find_business, and find_service.

Example 6-8. InquireSOAP

```
<portType name="InquireSoap">
  <operation name="find_binding">
    <input   message="tns:find_binding" />
    <output message="tns:bindingDetail" />
    <fault   name="error"
             message="tns:dispositionReport" />
  </operation>

  <operation name="find_business">
    <input   message="tns:find_business" />
    <output message="tns:businessList" />
    <fault   name="error"
             message="tns:dispositionReport" />
  </operation>

  <operation name="find_service">
    <input   message="tns:find_service" />
    <output message="tns:serviceList" />
    <fault   name="error"
             message="tns:dispositionReport" />
  </operation>
```

The message definitions are as straightforward as in the Publisher interface. Example 6-9 shows the first three. Consult Appendix C for the full list.

Example 6-9. Inquiry message definitions

```
<message name="authToken">
  <part name="body"
        element="uddi:authToken" />
```

Example 6-9. Inquiry message definitions (continued)

```
    </message>

    <message name="bindingDetail">
      <part name="body"
            element="uddi:bindingDetail" />
    </message>

    <message name="businessDetail">
      <part name="body"
            element="uddi:businessDetail" />
    </message>
```

Using UDDI to Publish Services

There are several toolkits, both open and closed source, that provide an implementation of the UDDI Publish and Inquiry interfaces. We'll walk you through using an open source package from IBM called UDDI4J (UDDI for Java). You can download this package from *http://oss.software.ibm.com/developerworks/projects/uddi4j*.

The steps for using UDDI4J to publish web services are:

1. Register the service provider as a UDDI business entity.
2. Specify the categories and identifiers that apply to your business entity entry.
3. Register the web service as a UDDI business service.
4. Specify the categories that apply to your business service entry.
5. Register the implementation details of your web service, including the network location where the service is deployed.

The UDDI data model lets us do all these steps in a single operation.

Registration Program

A Java program to publish the Hello World service is given in Appendix C. We'll step you through the highlights, which demonstrate how to use the UDDI4J toolkit.

You use UDDI4J through a proxy object, which handles the underlying SOAP encoding and decoding. You should initialize the proxy to the UDDI registry as shown in Example 6-10.

Example 6-10. Initializing the UDDI Proxy

```
UDDIProxy proxy = new UDDIProxy();
proxy.setPublishURL("https://www-3.ibm.com/services/uddi/testregistry/protect/
    publishapi");
```

UDDI4J defines classes for the UDDI data types. They have straightforward accessors, so you prepare the business entity record as in Example 6-11.

Example 6-11. Specifying the business entity

```
BusinessEntity business = new BusinessEntity( );
business.setName("O'Reilly and Associates");
```

Similarly you can specify the categories and identifiers for this business entity. In Example 6-12, we use a North American Industry Classification System (NAICS) category code of 11194.

Example 6-12. Specifying categories and identifiers for the business entity

```
CategoryBag cbag = new CategoryBag( );
KeyedReference cat = new KeyedReference( );
cat.setTModelKey("UUID:C0B9FE13-179F-413D-8A5B-5004DB8E5BB2");
cat.setKeyName("NAICS");
cat.setKeyValue("11194");
cbag.getKeyedReferenceVector( ).add(cat);
business.setCategoryBag(cbag);
```

In Example 6-13, we prepare the identifiers for the business entity. We specify a Dun and Bradstreet number that may be used to identify the business entity (it's fictitious, but you get the idea). Because you can have more than one identifier for a business, UDDI4J defines an IdentifierBag class that holds the individual identifiers.

Example 6-13. Business entity identifiers

```
IdentifierBag ibag = new IdentifierBag( );
KeyedReference id = new KeyedReference( );
id.setTModelKey("UUID:8609C81E-EE1F-4D5A-B202-3EB13AD01823");
id.setKeyName("D-U-N-S");
id.setKeyValue("1234567890");
ibag.getKeyedReferenceVector( ).add(id);
business.setIdentifierBag(ibag);
```

Prepare the business service record as in Example 6-14.

Example 6-14. Initializing the business service record

```
BusinessServices services = new BusinessServices( );
BusinessService service = new BusinessService( );
service.setName("Hello World Service");
services.getBusinessServiceVector( ).add(service);
business.setBusinessServices(services);
```

Example 6-15 shows the initialization of the binding templates. The binding template specifies the protocols implemented by a service and the network location. It is the UDDI equivalent to the WSDL binding and service port definition.

Example 6-15. Initializing the binding templates

```
BindingTemplates bindings = new BindingTemplates( );
BindingTemplate binding = new BindingTemplate( );
AccessPoint accessPoint = new AccessPoint( );
```

Example 6-15. Initializing the binding templates (continued)

```
accessPoint.setText("http://localhost:8080");
accessPoint.setURLType("HTTP");
binding.setAccessPoint(accessPoint);
bindings.getBindingTemplateVector( ).add(binding);
service.setBindingTemplates(bindings);
```

Example 6-16 logs onto the UDDI registry and registers the business entity.

Example 6-16. Registering the business entity

```
AuthToken token = proxy.get_authToken("james", "semaj");
Vector businesses = new Vector( );
businesses.add(business);
proxy.save_business(token.getAuthInfo().getText( ), businesses);
```

How to Register

You'll need two things before you can use the registration program:

1. You must have a valid user account with the UDDI registry you choose. You acquire one by registering through the HTML-form interface provided by the specific UDDI registry provider.

2. You must have Apache SOAP Version 2.1 or higher in your Java classpath (UDDI4J uses Apache SOAP). To meet this requirement, make sure that *soap. jar*, *mail.jar*, and *activation.jar* are all in your classpath.

There are three common situations that cause an error registering a service:

1. A company may already exist with the specified name.

2. There may be some problem with the information defined.

3. You might not have proper permissions to perform the requested action.

The SOAP Envelope for the Registration

The SOAP envelope sent to the UDDI registry includes all of the registration information for the business entity, as seen in Example 6-17.

Example 6-17. SOAP envelope for the registration

```
<SOAP-ENV:Envelope
    xmlns:SOAP-ENV="http://schemas.xmlsoap.org/soap/envelope/"
    xmlns:xsi="http://www.w3.org/1999/XMLSchema-instance"
    xmlns:xsd="http://www.w3.org/1999/XMLSchema">
  <SOAP-ENV:Body>

    <save_business generic="1.0" xmlns="urn:uddi-org:api">
      <authInfo>test</authInfo>
      <businessEntity>
        <name>O'reilly and Associates</name>
```

Example 6-17. SOAP envelope for the registration (continued)

```
      <businessServices>
       <businessService>
        <name>Hello World Service</name>
        <bindingTemplates>
         <bindingTemplate>
          <accessPoint
               urlType="HTTP">http://localhost:8080</accessPoint>
         </bindingTemplate>
        </bindingTemplates>
       </businessService>
      </businessServices>
      <identifierBag>
       <keyedReference keyName="D-U-N-S"
               keyValue="1234567890"
               TModelKey="UUID:8609C81E-EE1F-4D5A-B202-3EB13AD01823"/>
      </identifierBag>
      <categoryBag>
       <keyedReference keyName="NAICS"
               keyValue="11194"
               TModelKey="UUID:C0B9FE13-179F-413D-8A5B-5004DB8E5BB2"/>
      </categoryBag>
     </businessEntity>
    </save_business>
</SOAP-ENV:Body>

</SOAP-ENV:Envelope>
```

Other Issues

Operations like save_business are destructive. In other words, when you tell the UDDI registry to save a business entity, the registry will use the information you provide to replace all other information on that business entity that exists in the registry. There are two ways around this:

1. Retrieve the complete business entity record from the UDDI registry prior to making any changes to the information (e.g., publishing a new service). Make all changes directly to the record received from the registry. Saving stores your modified record.

2. Save only the specific parts you are changing. For example, if you already have a business entity registration at a UDDI registry, and all you want to do is register a new service, then you should use the save_service operation rather than save_business. This cuts down on the amount of data being moved around and compartmentalizes the changes being made.

Example 6-18 uses save_service to localize changes.

Example 6-18. Changing only some fields in the registry

```
// Initialize the proxy to the UDDI registry
UDDIProxy proxy = new UDDIProxy( );
```

Example 6-18. Changing only some fields in the registry (continued)

```
proxy.setPublishURL("https://www-3.ibm.com/services/uddi/testregistry/protect/publishapi");

// Prepare the business service record
BusinessServices services = new BusinessServices();
BusinessService service = new BusinessService();
service.setBusinessKey("uuid:C0E6D5A8-C446-4f01-99DA-70E212685A40");
service.setName("Hello World Service");
services.getBusinessServiceVector().add(service);

// Prepare the binding templates
BindingTemplates bindings = new BindingTemplates();
BindingTemplate binding = new BindingTemplate();
AccessPoint accessPoint = new AccessPoint();
accessPoint.setText("http://localhost:8080");
accessPoint.setURLType("HTTP");
binding.setAccessPoint(accessPoint);
bindings.getBindingTemplateVector().add(binding);
service.setBindingTemplates(bindings);

// Logon to UDDI registry and register
AuthToken token = proxy.get_authToken("username", "password");
Vector services = new Vector();
services.add(service);
proxy.save_service(token.getAuthInfo().getText(), services);
```

The only real difference is the absence of the business entity and the addition of the service.setBusinessKey line. This tells the UDDI registry which business entity to update. This ID is generated automatically by the UDDI registry and returned to the client when the business entity registration is created.

Using UDDI to Locate Services

UDDI4J can also be used to locate services that have been published within a UDDI registry. The process involves the use of several find operations such as find_business, find_service, and find_binding.

Appendix C has a program to search for a business entity and navigate the results of that operation to find out information about the services provided by that entity. We'll discuss the highlights.

FindQualifiers modifies the search operations by indicating whether case-sensitive searching is required, whether the results should be sorted ascending or descending, and whether exact name matching is required. The last argument in all of the find operations is the maximum number of results to return. Passing in the number zero indicates that all matching results should be returned. Example 6-19 sets up FindQualifiers to look for the O'Reilly business.

Example 6-19. FindQualifiers to look for O'Reilly

```
FindQualifiers fqs = new FindQualifiers( );
FindQualifier fq = new FindQualifier( );
fq.setText(FindQualifier.sortByNameAsc);
BusinessList list = proxy.find_business("O'Reilly", fqs, 0);
```

Matching business entities are returned along with a listing of the services offered. The listing includes the name and unique identifier of the service. Use the UUID to drill down and get more information about the service, as in Example 6-20.

Example 6-20. Fetching more information about the service

```
BusinessInfos infos = list.getBusinessInfos( );
for (Iterator i = infos.getBusinessInfoVector().iterator( ); i.hasNext( );) {
    BusinessInfo info = (BusinessInfo)i.next( );
    System.out.println("Business name: " + info.getName( ));
  for (Iterator j = info.getServiceInfos().getServiceInfoVector().iterator( );
      j.hasNext( );) {

        ServiceInfo sinfo = (ServiceInfo)j.next( );
        System.out.println("\tService name: " + sinfo.getName( ));
    }
}
```

To retrieve more specific information about a given service, use the get_serviceDetail operation and pass in the unique identifier of the service you are requesting:

```
ServiceDetail detail = proxy.get_serviceDetail(serviceKey);
```

Using the information contained in the service detail, a client can connect to and invoke the web service.

Generating UDDI from WSDL

Because there are some variances and overlapping in how WSDL and UDDI support the description of web services, the industry coalition that is driving UDDI has released a document describing the best practices to follow when using UDDI and WSDL together to enable dynamic discovery of web service descriptions. It basically defines how to use a WSDL description to generate the UDDI registration for a service.

First, divide the WSDL description into two parts (two separate WSDL files). The first file becomes the interface description. It includes the data types, messages, port types, and bindings. The second file is known as the implementation description. It includes only the service definition. The implementation description imports the interface description using the <wsdl:import /> mechanism.

Interface Description

Example 6-21 is the interface description for our Hello World example.

Example 6-21. HelloWorldInterfaceDescription.wsdl

```
<?xml version="1.0" encoding="UTF-8"?>
<wsdl:definitions name="HelloWorldInterfaceDescription"
   targetNamespace="urn:HelloWorldInterface"
  xmlns:tns="urn:HelloWorldInterface"
  xmlns:soap="http://schemas.xmlsoap.org/wsdl/soap/"
  xmlns:wsdl="http://schemas.xmlsoap.org/wsdl/">
  <wsdl:message name="sayHello_IN">
    <part name="name" type="xsd:string" />
  </wsdl:message>
  <wsdl:message name="sayHello_Out">
    <part name="greeting" type="xsd:string" />
  </wsdl:message>

  <wsdl:portType name="HelloWorldInterface">
    <wsdl:operation name="sayHello">
      <wsdl:input message="tns:sayHello_IN" />
      <wsdl:output message="tns:sayHello_OUT" />
    </wsdl:operation>
  </wsdl:portType>

  <wsdl:binding name="HelloWorldBinding"
                type="tns:HelloWorldInterface">
    <soap:binding style="rpc"
     transport="http://schemas.xmlsoap.org/soap/http"
    />
    <wsdl:operation name="sayHello">
      <soap:operation soapAction="urn:Hello" />
      <wsdl:input>
        <soap:body use="encoded"

        namespace="urn:Hello"
        encodingStyle="http://schemas.xmlsoap.org/soap/encoding/" />
      </wsdl:input>
      <wsdl:output>
        <soap:body use="encoded"
                   namespace="urn:Hello"
                   encodingStyle="http://schemas.xmlsoap.org/soap/encoding/" />
      </wsdl:output>
    </wsdl:operation>
  </wsdl:binding>
</wsdl:definitions>
```

Implementation Description

Example 6-22 is the WSDL implementation description for our Hello World example.

Example 6-22. HelloWorldImplementationDescription.wsdl

```
<?xml version="1.0" encoding="UTF-8"?>
<wsdl:definitions name="HelloWorldImplementationDescription"
   targetNamespace="urn:HelloWorldImplementation"
   xmlns:tns="urn:HelloWorldImplementation"
   xmlns:hwi="urn:HelloWorldInterface"
   xmlns:soap="http://schemas.xmlsoap.org/wsdl/soap/"
   xmlns:wsdl="http://schemas.xmlsoap.org/wsdl/">

  <wsdl:import namespace="urn:HelloWorldInterface"
               location="HelloWorldInterfaceDescription.wsdl" />

  <wsdl:service name="HelloWorldService">
    <wsdl:port name="HelloWorldPort"
               binding="hwi:HelloWorldBinding">
      <!-- location of the Perl Hello World Service -->
      <soap:address
        location="http://localhost:8080" />
    </wsdl:port>
  </wsdl:service>

</wsdl:definitions>
```

Registering

Register the interface description as a UDDI TModel. You've seen NAICS categories
and D-U-N-S identifiers as TModels. Another type of TModel is a WSDL description of
a service interface.

To register the interface as a TModel, create a TModel structure and use the save_
TModel operation as in Example 6-23.

Example 6-23. Registering the interface description as a TModel

```
TModel TModel = new TModel();
TModel.setName("Hello World Interface");
```

The OverviewDoc is a pointer to the interface WSDL description, held on a publicly
available web server. Example 6-24 shows how to set this.

Example 6-24. Setting the OverviewDoc

```
OverviewDoc odoc = new OverviewDoc();
// localhost == the name of the server where
// the WSDL can be accessed
odoc.setOverviewURL("http://localhost/HelloWorldInterface.wsdl");
TModel.setOverviewDoc(odoc);
```

Indicate that this TModel represents a WSDL interface description by creating a category reference with a TModelKey of uuid:C1ACF26D-9672-4404-9D70-39B756E62AB4, a
key name of uddi-org:types, and a key value of wsdlSpec, as shown in Example 6-25.

Example 6-25. Marking the TModel as WSDL

```
CategoryBag cbag = new CategoryBag( );
KeyedReference kr = new KeyedReference( );
kr.setTModelKey("uuid:C1ACF26D-9672-4404-9D70-39B756E62AB4");
kr.setKeyName("uddi-org:types");
kr.setKeyValue("wsdlSpec");
```

Example 6-25 shows how to call the save_TModel operation to register the TModel.

Example 6-26. Calling the save_TModel operation

```
UDDIProxy proxy = new UDDIProxy( );
proxy.setPublishURL(
"https://www-3.ibm.com/services/uddi/
                        testregistry/protect/publishapi");
AuthToken token = proxy.get_authToken("james", "semaj");
Vector TModels = new Vector( );
TModels.add(TModel);
TModelDetail detail = proxy.save_TModel(token.getAuthInfo().getText( ), TModels);
```

The save_TModel operation returns a copy of the TModel record just registered, including the automatically generated unique identifier. We keep that unique key for the next step, as shown in Example 6-27.

Example 6-27. Retaining unique key

```
TModel = (TModel)detail.getTModelVector( ).elementAt(0);
String TModelKey = TModel.getTModelKey( );
```

Now say what the service is and where it lives, as in Example 6-28.

Example 6-28. Defining a service, binding template, and access point for the service

```
BusinessService service = new BusinessService( );
service.setBusinessKey(businessKey);
service.setName("HelloWorldService");

BindingTemplates templates = new BindingTemplates( );
BindingTemplate template = new BindingTemplate( );
templates.getBindingTemplateVector( ).add(template);
service.setBindingTemplates(templates);

AccessPoint accessPoint = new AccessPoint( );
accessPoint.setURLType("HTTP");
accessPoint.setText("http://localhost:8080");
template.setAccessPoint(accessPoint);
```

Example 6-29 specifies that this service is an instance of the HelloWorld-InterfaceDescription TModel just registered. The variable TModelKey is the unique identifier fetched in Example 6-27.

Example 6-29. Associate service with TModel

```
TModelInstanceDetails details = new TModelInstanceDetails( );
TModelInstanceInfo instance = new TModelInstanceInfo( );
instance.setTModelKey(TModelKey);
```

Provide a link to the WSDL implementation description as in Example 6-30. This, like the interface description, needs to be located at some publicly available web address.

Example 6-30. Linking to WSDL implementation description

```
InstanceDetails instanceDetails = new InstanceDetails( );
OverviewDoc odoc = new OverviewDoc( );
odoc.setOverviewURL("http://localhost/HelloWorldImplementationDescription.wsdl");
instanceDetails.setOverviewDoc(odoc);
instance.setInstanceDetails(instanceDetails);
details.getTModelInstanceInfoVector( ).add(instance);
template.setTModelInstanceDetails(details);
```

Once the registration is prepared, initialize the proxy and call the save_service operation to register the business service. Example 6-31 shows this, in abbreviated form. See Appendix C for the full source.

Example 6-31. Saving the service information

```
UDDIProxy proxy = new UDDIProxy( );
// ...abbreviated
proxy.save_service(authInfo, services);
```

By following these guidelines, WSDL and UDDI can be made to work very well together.

Using UDDI and WSDL Together

Once the WSDL-defined web service is published into a UDDI registry, it is possible to build highly dynamic service proxies. The IBM Web Services ToolKit, for example, provides built-in support for locating services in UDDI and invoking those services through a dynamically configured WSDL-based proxy.

To show you more of what is going on behind the scenes, however, we're going to use UDDI4J and WSIF together to implement the same type of functionality.

The steps are simple:

1. Locate the Hello World service in the UDDI registry.
2. Access the WSDL description for the Hello World service.
3. Invoke the Hello World service.

All this is done on the client side. Nothing has to be done on the server for this to work.

First, write the code to locate the Hello World service in UDDI. Example 6-32 searches with FindQualifiers and takes the first result offered by the UDDI server.

Example 6-32. Locating a Hello World service

```
UDDIProxy proxy = new UDDIProxy();
FindQualifiers fq = new FindQualifiers();

ServiceList list = proxy.find_service(businessKey, "HelloWorldService", fq, 0);
ServiceInfos infos = list.getServiceInfos();

ServiceInfo info = (ServiceInfo)infos.getServiceInfoVector().elementAt(0);
String serviceKey = info.getServiceKey();
```

With the unique identifier of the matching service, Example 6-33 goes to the UDDI registry to retrieve the business service. The binding template for that service then identifies the implementation to use.

Example 6-33. Locating an implementation

```
ServiceDetail detail = proxy.get_serviceDetail(serviceKey);
BusinessService service = (BusinessService)detail.
    getBusinessServiceVector().elementAt(0);

BindingTemplate template = (BindingTemplate)service.
    getBindingTemplates().getBindingTemplateVector().elementAt(0);
TModelInstanceDetails details = template.getTModelInstanceDetails();
TModelInstanceInfo instance = details.getTModelInstanceInfoVector().elementAt(0);
InstanceDetails instanceDetails  = instance.getInstanceDetails();

OverviewDoc odoc = instanceDetails.getOverviewDoc();
String wsdlpath = odoc.getOverviewURLString();
```

WSDL in hand, Example 6-34 uses WSIF to invoke the web service.

Example 6-34. Invoking the web service with WSIF

```
Definition def = WSIFUtils.readWSDL(null, wsdlPath);
Service service = WSIFUtils.selectService(def, null, "HelloWorldService");
PortType portType = WSIFUtils.selectPortType(def, null, "HelloWorldInterface");

WSIFDynamicPortFactory dpf = new WSIFDynamicPortFactory(def, service, portType);
WSIFPort port = dpf.getPort();
```

Typically, message creation is done behind the scenes, out of the sight of the programmer. Example 6-35 shows this.

Example 6-35. Creating messages with WSIF

```
WSIFMessage input = port.createInputMessage();
WSIFMessage output = port.createOutputMessage();
WSIFMessage fault = port.createFaultMessage();
```

Example 6-36 calls the Hello World service.

Example 6-36. Invoking Hello World

```
WSIFPart namePart = new WSIFJavaPart(String.class, args[0]);
input.setPart("name", namePart);

System.out.println("Calling the SOAP Server to say hello!\n");
System.out.print("The SOAP Server says: ");
port.executeRequestResponseOperation("sayHello", input, output, fault);

WSIFPart greetingPart = output.getPart("greeting");
String greeting = (String)greetingPart.getJavaValue();
System.out.print(greeting + "\n");
```

Running this produces the same output we saw in the other Hello World services examples (shown in Example 6-37).

Example 6-37. Output from the WSDL, UDDI, and WSIF Hello World client

```
C:\book>java wsdluddiExample James
Calling the SOAP Server to say hello!

The SOAP Server says: Hello James
```

The program dynamically discovered, inspected, and bound to the Hello World web services. We didn't program the client knowing which implementation we'd use. While the client was in Java, there's no reason we couldn't have written it in any language. C#, Visual Basic, and Perl all have UDDI and WSDL extensions.

The Web Service Inspection Language (WS-Inspection)

While UDDI is the best-known mechanism for service discovery, it is neither the only mechanism nor always the best tool for the job. In many cases, the complexity and scope of UDDI is overkill if all that is needed is a simple pointer to a WSDL document or a services URL endpoint. Recognizing this, IBM and Microsoft got together and worked out a proposal for a new Web Service Inspection Language that can be used to create a simple index of service descriptions at a given network location.

An example WS-Inspection document is illustrated in Example 6-38. It contains a reference to a single service (Hello World) with two descriptions—one WSDL-based description and one UDDI-based description.

Example 6-38. A simple WS-Inspection document

```xml
<?xml version="1.0"?>
<inspection
   xmlns="http://schemas.xmlsoap.org/ws/2001/10/inspection/"
   xmlns:uddi="http://schemas.xmlsoap.org/ws/2001/10/inspection/uddi/">

<service>
 <abstract>The Hello World Service</abstract>

 <description
   referencedNamespace="http://schemas.xmlsoap.org/wsdl/"
   location="http://example.com/helloworld.wsdl"/>

 <description referencedNamespace="urn:uddi-org:api">
   <uddi:serviceDescription
      location="http://www.example.com/uddi/inquiryapi">
   <uddi:serviceKey>
      4FA28580-5C39-11D5-9FCF-BB3200333F79
    </uddi:serviceKey>
   </uddi:serviceDescription>
  </description>
 </service>

<link
   referencedNamespace="http://schemas.xmlsoap.org/ws/2001/10/inspection/"
   location="http://example.com/moreservices.wsil"/>

</inspection>
```

Once created, WS-Inspection documents should be placed in a well-known or easily-discoverable location on your web server. In fact, the WS-Inspection specification defines that, at a minimum, an inspection document called *Inspection.wsil* should be available at the root the server: for instance, *http://www.ibm.com/inspection.wsil*. This allows potential clients of those services to locate inspection documents easily and thereby discover the services being advertised.

The relationship between UDDI and WS-Inspection is simple. UDDI is a phone book. If you need a plumber to fix the pipes under your kitchen sink but do not know of a good one to call, you open the phone book and find one. If you need a web service that implements a particular WSDL defined port type for processing purchase orders for ball bearings, you can submit a request to a UDDI registry to find an appropriate service. WS-Inspection, however, is useful if you already know the service provider you want to use (e.g., you already know which plumber who want to call so you dont have to look in the phonebook). You'd simply refer to the WS-Inspection document published by the service provider to find the location of the services they are offering.

WS-Inspection Syntax

The syntax of a WS-Inspection document is simple. The root inspection element contains a collection of abstract, link, and service elements. The abstract element provides for simple documentation throughout the WS-Inspection document. The link element allows the inspection document to link to other external inspection documents or even other discovery mechanisms (such as a UDDI registry) where additional information can be found. The service element represents a web service being offered by the publisher of the inspection document.

The service element itself is a collection of abstract and description elements. You can describe a service in several ways. WS-Inspection allows all a service's descriptions to be listed. You can provide extended information about each service description using XML extensibility. Example 6-38, for instance, contains both a WSDL and UDDI-based description.

WS-Inspection will be submitted for standardization at some point. For now, both IBM and Microsoft have implemented support for it in their web services offerings and other web service toolkit vendors are considering doing the same. Because of its usefulness and simple syntax, WS-Inspection is likely to develop favorable support.

## CHAPTER 7

Web Services in Action

In the previous chapters, we've been building a picture of the technologies and methodologies around SOAP web services. In this chapter, we apply the discussion to the real-world implementation of a SOAP web service. You'll see how SOAP and WSDL are deployed, and also how to draw in other XML technologies to solve problems that SOAP and WSDL do not address.

The service we'll develop is the CodeShare Service Network, a simple set of peer-to-peer web services for sharing application source code. While we develop that code, we'll stop to take a look at security, and how to implement it when SOAP and WSDL don't cover it.

The CodeShare implementation we show here provides a way for people to share source code. We use digital signatures to verify the identity of clients, and keep a central registry of the files people are offering. Rather than a single web service, the CodeShare application comprises a number of different small interfaces, a common web services design. Each interface can be implemented in any language that supports SOAP, and we used a mixture of Perl and Java to demonstrate this. CodeShare is an example of a peer web service. In the peer-to-peer (P2P) model, the Internet isn't viewed as a network of *clients* accessing the resources of a *server*. Rather, it's a cooperative network of *peers* sharing resources equally and evenly. The lines are blurred between the service provider and the service consumer, with no application required to have just a single role.

Peer web services uses already-deployed web services technologies to provide P2P services.

The CodeShare Service Network

The CodeShare Service Network is a very simple example of peer web services. It provides an environment where developers may easily share source code with the rest of the world.

Overview

There are three important CodeShare components: the owner of the code being shared, the requester of the code, and the CodeShare server that serves as clearing-house for the code and as an authentication authority that code owners can use to control access to the code that they are sharing. The relationships between the components are shown in Figure 7-1.

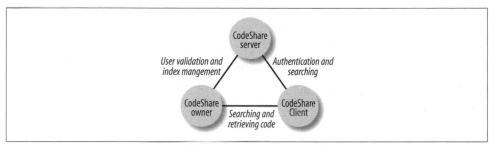

Figure 7-1. The CodeShare architecture

Here is the typical use scenario:

1. The developers of some code decide to share that code publicly. They do so by updating their local project *index.xml* file, indicating the files they wish to share.

2. The developers log onto the CodeShare server to update their entry in the master index maintained at the server.

3. The developers then start their CodeShare owner service (a local SOAP HTTP daemon).

4. Whenever users wish to find code being shared, they have two options: they can connect to the developer's CodeShare owner service directly and execute four basic operations: search, list, info, and get; or they can connect to the Code-Share server and search the master index. Doing so will result in a list of all CodeShare owner services sharing code that matches the search request. All get operations point directly to the owner service to retrieve the source code being shared.

5. At times, developers may wish to restrict who is allowed to access the code they are sharing. To do so, they simply add the names of all authorized users to their *index.xml* (all users are registered with the CodeShare server). Whenever a user tries to retrieve the restricted code, the owner service will check first to see if the user has logged into the CodeShare server and if so, whether they are allowed access.

Prerequisites

There are a few things that you need to have set up on your system before you can run this example:

SOAP::Lite Version 5.1 and all prerequisites
> Instructions on how to install this are given in Chapter 3.

DBI and DBD:CSV
> These are Perl SQL database modules used by the CodeShare owner server. Install them by typing `install DBI` and `install DBD::CSV` in the CPAN shell.

A Servlet-enabled web server
> We recommend Apache's Jakarta Tomcat Version 3.22. Tomcat can be downloaded from *http://jakarta.apache.org*.

Apache Xerces 1.4 or any other JAXP-enabled XML parser
> JAXP is the Java API for XML Processing (*http://xml.apache.org/xercesj*).

Apache SOAP
> At the time of writing, the latest version was 2.2, which has a bug you will need to fix. Download the source distribution of Apache SOAP. The changes and the build process are described in the next section of this chapter.

The latest version of the IBM XML Security Suite
> This is available from IBM's alphaWorks web site (*http://alphaworks.ibm.com/tech/xmlsecuritysuite*). Once downloaded, unzip the distribution and put the *XSS4J.jar* file into your application server's classpath.

Fixing the bug in Apache SOAP 2.2

The problem in Version 2.2 of Apache SOAP causes invalid XML to be produced in some situations. CodeShare happens to cause one of those situations. The bug fix detailed here has been submitted and it should not be necessary to make this fix in versions of Apache SOAP after 2.2.

Assuming that you have already downloaded the source distribution of the Apache SOAP source code, locate a file called *DOM2Writer.java*, in the *%SOAP_HOME%\ java\src\org\apache\soap\util\xml* folder. ($SOAP_HOME will be in the directory where the unzipped contents of the distribution were downloaded.)

At line 172, replace the lines in Example 7-1 with those in Example 7-2.

Example 7-1. Code in DOM2Writer.java to replace

```
out.print(' ' + attr.getNodeName() +"=\"" + normalize(attr.getValue()) + '\"');
```

Example 7-2. New code for DOM2Writer.java

```
if (attr.getNodeName().startsWith("xmlns:") &&
    !(NS_URI_XMLNS.equals(attr.getNamespaceURI()))) {
```

Example 7-2. New code for DOM2Writer.java (continued)

```
String attrName = attr.getNodeName( );
String prefix= attrName.substring(attrName.indexOf(":")+1);
try
    {
        String namespaceURI =
            (String)namespaceStack.lookup(prefix);
        if (!attr.getNodeValue( ).equals(namespaceURI)) {
            printNamespaceDecl(prefix, namespaceURI,
                               namespaceStack, out);
        }
    }
catch (IllegalArgumentException e)
    {
        printNamespaceDecl(prefix,
                           attr.getNodeValue( ),
                           namespaceStack, out);
    }
}
else
    {
        out.print(' ' + attr.getNodeName( ) +"=\"" + normalize(attr.getValue( )) + '\"');
    }
```

Now add the new method in Example 7-3 to the DOM2Writer class.

Example 7-3. New method for the DOM2Writer class

```
private static void printNamespaceDecl(String prefix,
        String namespaceURI, ObjectRegistry namespaceStack,
        PrintWriter out)
{
    if (!(namespaceURI.equals(NS_URI_XMLNS) && prefix.equals("xmlns")))
    {
        out.print(" xmlns:" + prefix + "=\"" + namespaceURI + '\"');
    }
    namespaceStack.register(prefix, namespaceURI);
}
```

Next, compile the Apache SOAP package.

Compiling Apache SOAP

To build Apache SOAP, you need to use Ant, a Java build-management tool released by Apache. Ant is available from *http://jakarta.apache.org* and is officially a part of the Jakarta Tomcat project. Once downloaded, please follow the detailed instructions included with the package on how to install it.

Ant uses an XML-based script (*build.xml*) for defining how to compile the code. Apache SOAP's *build.xml* file is located in the *%SOAP_HOME%\java* directory.

Before you can build, you need to make sure that all of the prerequisites are in place. These are listed at the start of the *build.xml* file:

- Any JAXP-enabled XML Parser (Xerces is preferred)
- The JavaMail package, available from *http://java.sun.com/products/javamail/*
- The Java Activation Framework package, available from *http://java.sun.com/products/beans/glasgow/jaf.html*

These packages must all be in your classpath prior to attempting the build. Once there, start the build using the following command:

```
java org.apache.tools.ant.Main <target>
```

Where target is one of four options:

compile
Creates the *soap.jar* package

javadocs
Creates the *soap.jar* JavaDocs

dist
Creates the complete binary distribution

srcdist
Creates the complete source code distribution

For our purposes, use the compile target option. This will create a new *soap.jar* file with the modified DOM2Writer.java class included. Once built, replace all other *soap.jar* files that may be in your application servers classpath with the newly built *soap.jar*.

The Code Share Index

The source code shared through the CodeShare network is organized around a simple index structure that preserves the original directory-file hierarchy. Everybody wanting to share source code through the CodeShare must create an index. As an example, let's assume that we are sharing the following Java project:

```
HelloWorld
+---build.xml
+---lib
|   +---HelloWorld.jar
+---src
    +---oreilly
        +---samples
            +---HelloWorld
                +---HelloWorld.java
```

There are a total of six directories and three files being shared. Within the Code-Share index, we represent this project as Example 7-4.

Example 7-4. CodeShare index for sample project

```xml
<codeShare xmlns:dc="http://purl.org/dc/elements/1.1/">
  <project location="HelloWorld">
    <dc:Title>HelloWorld</dc:Title>
    <dc:Creator>James Snell, et al</dc:Creator>
    <dc:Date>2001-08-20</dc:Date>
    <dc:Subject>Hello World Web service example</dc:Subject>
    <dc:Description>
        Example Hello World Web service
    </dc:Description>
    <file location="build.xml">
      <dc:Title>Ant Build Script</dc:Title>
    </file>
    <directory location="lib">
      <dc:Title>Compiled libraries</dc:Title>
      <file location="HelloWorld.jar">
        <dc:Title>Compiled Hello World JAR</dc:Title>
      </file>
    </directory>
    <directory location="src">
      <dc:Title>Source Code</dc:Title>
      <directory location="oreilly">
        <dc:Title>oreilly</dc:title>
        <directory location="samples">
          <dc:Title>samples</dc:Title>
          <directory location="HelloWorld">
            <dc:Title>HelloWorld</dc:Title>
            <file location="HelloWorld.java">
              <dc:Title>HelloWorld.java</dc:Title>
            </file>
          </directory>
        </directory>
      </directory>
    </directory>
  </project>
</codeShare>
```

As you can see, the structure of the index is very basic. The codeShare element is the root for the entire index. The project element defines a shared project. The directory element defines a directory being shared within a project. The file element defines a file being shared.

The most interesting feature of the index is the use of Dublin Core metadata elements (dc:Title, for example) to add descriptive properties to each of the shared items.

The Dublin Core metadata project is an initiative to define standard types of metadata (data about data) capable of describing Internet content. We use it here to provide more flexible searching options when people are looking for particular types of code. Without these descriptive elements, the CodeShare searching capability would be limited to searches based only on the name of the file or directory being searched. Later, we'll see exactly how this additional data is used.

The Dublin Core specification (*http://www.dublincore.org/documents/dces/*) defines a set of 15 metadata elements, all of which may be used within the CodeShare index. The elements are described in Table 7-1.

Table 7-1. Dublin Core element set

Element name	Element description
Title	The name given to the resource
Creator	The entity responsible for creating the resource
Subject	A short topic that describes the resource
Description	A detailed, textual description of the resource
Publisher	The entity responsible for making the resource available
Contributor	An entity responsible for making contributions to the resource
Date	Typically, the date the resource was created
Type	The generic type of resource (not the MIME Content Type)
Format	The MIME Content Type or other physical format of the resource
Identifier	An unambiguous reference to the resource
Source	A reference to the resource from which this resource is derived
Language	The language (not programming language) in which the resource is presented
Relation	A reference to a related resource
Coverage	The extent or scope of the resource
Rights	Information about rights held in or over the resource

Web Services Security

What does it mean to add security to web services? In the case of the CodeShare example, our goal is to let the owners of the code specify access rights for particular individuals. If a user is not on the list of approved users, she will not be able to download the code.

Security in web services means adding basic security capabilities to the technologies that make web services happen. This means having the ability to encrypt SOAP messages, digitally sign WSDL service descriptions, add reliability to the protocol transports we use to carry this information around, assert a user's identity, define policies that govern how information is to be used, by whom it can be used, and for what purposes it can be used, and any number of a laundry list of other items. It could take almost an entire book by itself to describe how to implement all of these requirements. Unfortunately, while efforts are currently being made in each of these areas, we are still a long way from having defined standards (de facto or otherwise) on how all of this will happen in the web services environment. For the CodeShare example, we focus on only one: user authentication.

Authentication in SOAP-based web services can occur in a wide variety of ways. The service may choose to use traditional transport-layer authentication methods, such as HTTP Basic or Digest Authentication. Alternatively, the service may choose to implement a service-layer authentication mechanism that makes the service itself responsible for validating a user's identity.

The second approach is what we see emerging in the form of Microsoft's Passport authentication service, which provides Kerberos-based authentication over web service protocols. Kerberos is a popular Internet-standard authentication mechanism based on the exchange of *tickets*. These tickets are used in much the same way as a ticket to a movie. The bearer of the ticket presents it as a pass to get in to see the movie, or in our case, to access a service.

Chapter 8 discusses the Passport authentication scheme and several other alternative approaches in greater detail.

The Security Assertions Markup Language (SAML)

One of the many emerging web service technologies is specifically designed to be used as a method of implementing service-layer global sign-on for web services. The specification, called the Security Assertions Markup Language, or SAML, defines an XML syntax for expressing security-related facts. For example, SAML may be used to express the fact that Pavel Kulchenko authenticated at 10:00 a.m. and that the authentication expires at 2:00 p.m.

SAML assertions, as they are called, are created and digitally signed by the authentication authority who handles the actual authentication process. For example, when a user invokes the login operation on the CodeShare client interface, the CodeShare server (which validates the user ID and password) issues the SAML assertion stating that the login was successful. By digitally signing that assertion, anybody who receives it may validate that it was, in fact, created and issued by the CodeShare server.

Example 7-5 is a digitally signed SAML assertion returned by the login operation. The assertion itself is highlighted in bold type. The first part of this structure is the XML Digital Signature, which validates that the SAML assertion is authentic. XML Digital Signatures are being standardized through a joint effort by the W3C and the IETF. The structure of these signatures is too complex to explain here, so we've provided links to some supplemental information in Chapter 8. Luckily, we do not have to create these signatures manually. This particular example was created using IBM's XML Security suite.

Example 7-5. SAML assertion

```
<Signature xmlns="http://www.w3.org/2000/09/xmldsig#">
  <SignedInfo>
    <CanonicalizationMethod
          Algorithm="http://www.w3.org/TR/2000/WD-xml-c14n-20000119"/>
    <SignatureMethod
          Algorithm="http://www.w3.org/2000/09/xmldsig#dsa-sha1"/>
    <Reference URI="#999852828470">
      <DigestMethod
          Algorithm="http://www.w3.org/2000/09/xmldsig#sha1"/>
      <DigestValue>pCvvhLY/UdR7D8Jzja7kG2+finQ=</DigestValue>
    </Reference>
  </SignedInfo>
  <SignatureValue>
      T110Nd9tt4f1m9Ahoe82HoPXWrZOse/9ON9qUO1TRkZ4FrOg8DBg9g==
  </SignatureValue>
  <KeyInfo>
    <KeyValue>
      <DSAKeyValue>
        <P>
         /X9TgR11EilS3OqcLuzk5/YRt1I87OQAwx4/gLZRJmlFXUAiUftZPY1Y+r/F9bow9s
         ubVWzXgTuAHTRv8mZgt2uZUKWkn5/oBHsQIsJPu6nX/rfGG/g7V+fGqKYVDwT7g/bT
         xR7DAjVUE1oWkTL2dfOuK2HXKu/yIgMZndFIAcc=          </P>
        <Q>l2BQjxUjC8yykrmCouuEC/BYHPU=</Q>
        <G>
         9+GghdabPd7LvKtcNrhXuXmUr7v6OuqC+VdMCzOHgmdRWVeOutRZT+ZxBxCBgLRJFn
         Ej6EwoFhO3zwkyjMim4TwWeotUfIOo4KOuHiuzpnWRbqN/C/ohNWLx+2J6ASQ7zKTx
         vqhRkImog9/hWuWfBpKLZl6Ae1UlZAFMO/7PSSo=          </G>
        <Y>
         xbzyPw8CzjbnzxmoB9WDLnROEnw2/5CxHLsozIXNT+n/EtZpi3okfytFxjAcQVUuiZ
         Jwkf2/Eke7peA/R5dd9krb1jOEdlTVXd+eOcyWJOWplKEJuNYclrC4f+zy6FTcxGlq
         d/GqVEwud1kUiQ+5RPoAYsxpzaRDAVIeaarxXNO=          </Y>
      </DSAKeyValue>
    </KeyValue>
    <X509Data>
      <X509IssuerSerial>
        <X509IssuerName>CN=Codeshare</X509IssuerName>
        <X509SerialNumber>999849441</X509SerialNumber>
      </X509IssuerSerial>
      <X509SubjectName>CN=Codeshare</X509SubjectName>
      <X509Certificate>
MIICXjCCAhsCBDuYfeEwCwYHKoZIzjgEAwUAMBQxEjAQBgNVBAMTCUNvZGVzaGFyZTAeFwOwMTA5MDcwNzU3MjFaF
wOwMTEyMDYwNzU3MjFaMBQxEjAQBgNVBAMTCUNvZGVzaGFyZTCCAbgwggEsBgcqhkjOOAQBMIIBHwKBgQD9f1OBHX
USKVLfSpwu7OTn9hG3UjzvRADDHj+AtlEmaUVdQCJR+1k9jVj6v8X1ujD2y5tVbNeBO4AdNG/
yZmC3a5lQpaSfn+gEexAiwk+7qdf+t8Yb+DtX58aophUPBPuD9tPFHsMCNVQTWhaRMvZ1864rYdcq7/
IiAxmdOUgBxwIVAJdgUI8VIwvMspK5gqLrhAvwWBz1AoGBAPfhoIXWmz3ey7yrXDa4V7l5lK+7+jrqgvlXTAs9B4J
nUVlXjrrUWU/
mcQcQgYCOSRZxI+hMKBYTt88JMozIpuE8FnqLVHyNKOCjrh4rs6Z1kW6jfwv6ITVi8ftiegEkO8yk8b6oUZCJqIPf
4VrlnwaSi2ZegHtVJWQBTDv+zOkqA4GFAAKBgQDFvPI/DwLONufPGagH1YMudHQSfDb/
kLEcuyjMhc1P6f8S1mmLeiR/KOXGMBxBVS6JknCR/
b8SR7ul4D9Hl132StvWPQR2VNVd3545zJYk5amUoQm41hyWsLh/
7PLoVNzEaWp38apUTC53WRSJD7lE+gBizGnNpEMBUh5pqvFc3TALBgcqhkjOOAQDBQADMAAwLQIVAIyej/
xrPI4jpVCBUdHz/zz4nUY9AhRGb/VRBiqS2NKo+POOkbURVg2g5A==     </X509Certificate>
```

Example 7-5. SAML assertion (continued)

```
    </X509Data>
  </KeyInfo>
  <dsig:Object Id="999852828470" xmlns=""
                xmlns:dsig="http://www.w3.org/2000/09/xmldsig#">
    <AuthenticationAssertion AssertionID="999852828470"
                IssueInstant="Fri Sep 07 01:53:48 PDT 2001"
                Issuer="CodeShare.org" Version="1.0"
                xmlns="http://www.oasis-open.org/committees/security/docs/
                        draft-sstc-schema-assertion-15.xsd">

      <Subject>
        <NameIdentifier>
          <SecurityDomain>CodeShare.org</SecurityDomain>
          <Name>james</Name>
        </NameIdentifier>
      </Subject>
      <AuthenticationMethod>http://codeshare.org</AuthenticationMethod>
      <AuthenticationInstant>
          Fri Sep 07 01:53:48 PDT 2001
      </AuthenticationInstant>
      <AuthenticationLocale>
        <IP>123.123.123.123</IP>
        <DNS_Domain>codeshare.org</DNS_Domain>
      </AuthenticationLocale>
    </AuthenticationAssertion>
  </dsig:Object>
</Signature>
```

The purpose of this example SAML assertion is to state that the user james from the domain CodeShare.org authenticated on Friday, September 7, at 1:53 p.m. Pacific Daylight Time 2001, using CodeShare's default authentication method (the login operation). The authentication itself was provided by a server located at the 123.123.123.123 IP address with the DNS domain name codeshare.org. This statement is digitally signed using the CodeShare Servers X509 digital certificate, guaranteeing its authenticity.

When a user presents this token to a CodeShare owner, the owner can verify that it is authentic by asking the CodeShare server if it really did issue the statement. Figure 7-2 illustrates the flow of messages.

SAML assertions can be created and validated by anybody, making them a very good mechanism for implementing single sign-on functionality. Later in this chapter, we will demonstrate how this SAML assertion was created and signed.

Definitions and Descriptions

Because web services are all about the interfaces that tie applications together, the first thing we need to do is define what those interfaces look like.

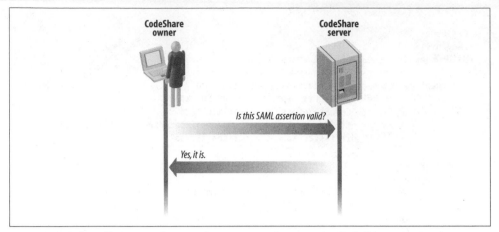

Figure 7-2. A flow illustrating the typical conversation between the CodeShare owner and CodeShare server

In this example there are four interfaces of interest:

- The owner interface implemented by CodeShare owners and the CodeShare server for allowing users to search for and retrieve source code.
- The client interface implemented by the CodeShare server for allowing users to register and login.
- The login verification interface implemented by the CodeShare server to allow CodeShare owners to ensure that users have logged on.
- The master index interface that allows CodeShare owners to update their entries in the master index maintained by the CodeShare server.

Each of these interfaces is expressed using WSDL service interface descriptions.

The Owner Interface

The owner interface consists of four fundamental operations:

search
> Searches the *index.xml* file for elements that match a given value. By default, this operation searches only the Dublin Core `Title` element, but other Dublin Core elements may be targeted instead.
>
> If this was a Java function, it would be something like:
> ```
> public List search(String value,
>                     String dcElement);
> ```
> In this example, `dcElement` equals the name of the Dublin Core element that you want to search.

list

Lists all of the projects and items being shared by the owner. Only basic information about the items is returned, including the location and title of the items. Filters may be applied that return only items that match a given value of a specified Dublin Core element. Like the search operation, the title is the default element upon which filters are applied.

Again looking at this from a Java perspective, the signature of this operation is:

```
public List list(String value,
                 String dcElement);
```

Unlike the search operation, however, both the value and dcElement parameters are optional.

info

Returns detailed information about each of the projects and items being shared. Like the list operation, filters may be applied to limit the number of items that are returned. The signature of this operation is exactly the same as the list operation.

get

Returns all of the files being shared for a specified project or projects. The exact directory structures will be recreated. The signature of this operation is also the same as the list operation.

All of these operations return a SOAP encoded array of item elements similar to Example 7-6.

Example 7-6. Sample array returned by owner operations

```
<env:Envelope xmlns:env="http://schemas.xmlsoap.org/soap/envelope/"
              xmlns:enc="http://schemas.xmlsoap.org/soap/encoding/">
  <env:Body>
    <env:listResponse>
      <Items enc:arrayType="csi:item[2]"
             xsi:type="csi:ArrayOfItems">
        <item xsi:type="namesp1:SOAPStruct">
          <path xsi:type="xsd:string">HelloWorld</path>
          <title xsi:type="xsd:string"> HelloWorld </title>
          <fullpath xsi:type="xsd:string">HelloWorld/</fullpath>
          <type xsi:type="xsd:string">project</type>
        </item>
        <item xsi:type="namesp1:SOAPStruct">
          <path xsi:type="xsd:string" />
          <title xsi:type="xsd:string">build.xml</title>
          <fullpath xsi:type="xsd:string">HelloWorld/</fullpath>
          <type xsi:type="xsd:string">file</type>
        </item>
      </enc:Array>
    </env:listResponse>
```

Example 7-6. Sample array returned by owner operations (continued)

```
  </env:Body>
</env:Envelope>
```

WSDL port type definition

The full WSDL port type definition is given in Appendix C. We'll cover the highlights here: the data types, the messages, the port type, and the protocol binding.

Data types

The data types are defined with an embedded XML schema. This schema defines two data types: an item, which, as we saw in the previous SOAP envelope, represents a project item within the CodeShare index, and an array of items.

The item definition, shown in Example 7-7, is straightforward. It is a complex type element with four children and a flag to include any Dublin Core elements that the CodeShare service may want to add.

Example 7-7. The item definition

```
<xsd:element name="item">
  <xsd:annotation>
    <xsd:documentation>
      CodeShare Indexed Item
    </xsd:documentation>
  </xsd:annotation>
  <xsd:complexType>
    <xsd:sequence>
      <xsd:all>
        <xsd:element name="path" type="xsd:string"
                     nullable="true" minOccurs="0"/>
        <xsd:element name="title" type="xsd:string"
                     nullable="true" minOccurs="0"/>
        <xsd:element name="fullpath" type="xsd:string"
                     nullable="true" minOccurs="0"/>
        <xsd:element name="type" type="xsd:string"
                     nullable="true" minOccurs="0"/>
      </xsd:all>
      <xsd:any namespace='xmlns:dc="http://purl.org/dc/elements/1.1/"'
               processContents="lax" minOccurs="0"
               maxOccurs="unbounded"/>
    </xsd:sequence>
  </xsd:complexType>
</xsd:element>
```

The ArrayOfItems data type, given in Example 7-8, is a derivative of the Array data type defined by the SOAP Section 5 encoding style. With this definition, we state this is an array of item elements as specified by the Section 5 encoding rules.

Example 7-8. The ArrayOfItems definition

```
<xsd:complexType name="ArrayOfItems">
  <xsd:annotation>
    <xsd:documentation>
      Array of CodeShare item elements
    </xsd:documentation>
  </xsd:annotation>
  <xsd:complexContent>
    <xsd:extension base="se:Array">
      <xsd:attribute ref="se:arrayType"
                     wsdl:arrayType="types:item[]" />
    </xsd:extension>
  </xsd:complexContent>
</xsd:complexType>
```

Messages

There are exactly two messages defined for each operation. A sample operation's messages are defined in Example 7-9. See the complete listing in Appendix C.

Example 7-9. Search message definitions

```
<wsdl:message name="search">
    <part name="p1" type="xsd:string" />
    <part name="p2" type="xsd:string" />
</wsdl:message>
<wsdl:message name="searchResponse">
    <part name="response" type="types:ArrayOfItems" />
</wsdl:message>
```

Port type

The owner interface port type is defined in terms of the messages we just created. Example 7-10 shows the portType element with a representative operation defined. See Appendix C for the complete listing. The parameterOrder attribute is a WSDL mechanism for specifying the order in which the parts of a message must appear within the body of the SOAP message.

Example 7-10. The portType definition

```
<wsdl:portType name="CodeShareOwnerInterface">
    <wsdl:operation name="search" parameterOrder="p1 p2">
        <wsdl:input name="search" message="tns:search" />
        <wsdl:output name="searchResponse"
                     message="tns:searchResponse" />
    </wsdl:operation>
    <!-- and so on for the other operations -->
</wsdl:portType>
```

Protocol binding

Example 7-11 specifies that the owner interface port type is accessed via SOAP messages transported over HTTP. Each of the SOAP messages will conform to the Section 5 encoding style (as indicated by the soap:body elements). As before, only one operation is shown here. For the full set, see the complete WSDL listing in Appendix C.

Example 7-11. Binding the interface to the portType

```
<wsdl:binding name="CodeShareOwner_SOAP_HTTP"
            type="tns:CodeShareOwnerInterface">
    <soap:binding style="rpc"
     transport="http://schemas.xmlsoap.org/soap/http" />
    <wsdl:operation name="search">
        <soap:operation soapAction="urn:CodeShareOwner#search" />
        <wsdl:input>
            <soap:body use="encoded" namespace="urn:CodeShareOwner"
             encodingStyle="http://schemas.xmlsoap.org/soap/encoding/" />
        </wsdl:input>
        <wsdl:output name="Name">
            <soap:body use="encoded" namespace="urn:CodeShareOwner"
             encodingStyle="http://schemas.xmlsoap.org/soap/encoding/" />
        </wsdl:output>
    </wsdl:operation>
    <!-- and so on for the other operations -->
/wsdl:binding>
```

The Client Interface

The client interface consists of two operations: register and login. Because the WSDL interface is similar in structure to the one defined for the owner interface, we will not show it here. It is printed in full in Appendix C.

register

    Takes a simple user ID and password pair to create a new user account on the CodeShare server.

login

    Receives a Base64 encoded string consisting of the user ID and password and returns a digitally signed SAML assertion indicating that the user logged in successfully. If login was not successful, a SOAP fault with the type "Client.Authentication" will be returned.

CodeShare login operation

The CodeShare login operation validates the user ID and password and generates a signed SAML assertion, as shown in Figure 7-3. It's not a perfect security solution—the SAML specification is missing some very significant pieces (for example, it is very

---

easy for somebody to intercept a signed SAML assertion and pretend to be the person for whom it is issued). It will be some time before all of these issues get worked out. For our purposes, we need only something simple, just to demonstrate the basic idea.

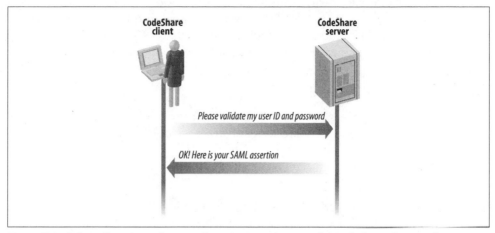

Figure 7-3. A flow illustrating the typical conversation between the CodeShare client and CodeShare server

The Login Verification Interface

The user presents the CodeShare server's SAML assertions to retrieve the code being shared. The assertion is given to the code owner who must validate that it did in fact come from the CodeShare service. The CodeShare login verification interface provides this functionality.

There is only a single verify operation defined by this interface. It takes the SAML assertion as an input and returns a simple true or false value indicating the validity of the assertion. See Appendix C for the full WSDL.

The Master Index Interface

Aside from providing the user management and authentication functions for the Code-Share network, the CodeShare service also provides a master index of all code being shared. Code owners update this master index through the master index interface.

This interface defines two operations. New code owners participate in the Code-Share network through register, and the update operation lets owners update their entries in the master index. The update operation receives the owner's user ID, password, and up-to-date project index.

Implementing the CodeShare Server

The CodeShare server is implemented as a set of Java classes that maintain a master index of every CodeShare owner who is sharing code and all of the registered users who may have access to that code. The server is divided into four distinct web services, each an implementation of the four interfaces that we've already defined: the master index service, the owner service, the client service, and the verification service.

The Master Index Service

The master index service allows CodeShare owners to update their entries in the index maintained by the Code Share server. The codeshare.OwnerService class implements the index service.

Operations

The list of registered owners is stored as an XML file. The register operation in Example 7-12 simply adds a new element to that XML file.

Example 7-12. The register operation

```
public static boolean register(String ownerid, String password, String url) {
    Element e = doc.getDocumentElement( );
    NodeList nl = e.getElementsByTagName("owner");
    for (int n = 0; n < nl.getLength( ); n++) {
        Element ex = (Element)nl.item(n);
        if (ex.getAttribute("id").equals(ownerid)) {
            throw new IllegalArgumentException(
                "An owner with that ID already exists!");
        }
    }
    Element u = doc.createElement("owner");
    u.setAttribute("id", ownerid);
    u.setAttribute("password", password);
    u.setAttribute("url", url);
    e.appendChild(u);
    XMLUtil.put(owners, doc);
    return true;
}
```

The master index itself (the list of all code being shared through the CodeShare network) is also maintained as an XML file. As with the register operation, the update operation shown in Example 7-13 does nothing more than update this XML file by either inserting the index passed in by the owner, or replacing an existing part of the index updated at a previous time.

Example 7-13. The update operation

```java
public static boolean update(String ownerid, String password, Element index) {
    Element el = doc.getDocumentElement();
    NodeList nl = el.getElementsByTagName("owner");
    for (int n = 0; n < nl.getLength(); n++) {
        Element e = (Element)nl.item(n);
        if (e.getAttribute("id").equals(ownerid) &&
            e.getAttribute("password").equals(password)) {
            Element i = (Element)doc.importNode(index, true);
            NodeList c = e.getElementsByTagName("index");
            if (c.getLength() > 0) {
                Node node = c.item(1);
                e.replaceChild(node, i);
            } else {
                e.appendChild(i);
            }
            XMLUtil.put(owners, doc);
            return true;
        }
    }
    return false;
}
```

Deployment

This service is deployed to the Apache SOAP engine using the process we described in Chapter 3. The deployment descriptor we'll use is shown in Example 7-14.

Example 7-14. The deployment descriptor for the master index service

```xml
<isd:service xmlns:isd="http://xml.apache.org/xml-soap/deployment"
             id="urn:CodeShareService-MasterIndex">
  <isd:provider type="java"
                scope="Application"
                methods="register update">
    <isd:java class="codeshare.IndexService"/>
  </isd:provider>
  <isd:faultListener>org.apache.soap.server.DOMFaultListener
  </isd:faultListener>
</isd:service>
```

The Owner Service

The owner service is a partial implementation of the CodeShare owner interface. This interface allows users to search the master index, but does not allow them to use the get or info operations—these must be performed directly against the CodeShare owner service that is providing the code. The CodeShare server will provide the information users need to find the owner services sharing the code they wish to access.

The operations implemented by the owner service (search and list) basically do the same thing: return an array of shared items that match the specified criteria. The search operation is shown in Example 7-15. This operation loops through all of the items in the master index looking for matching items.

Example 7-15. The owner service operations

```
public org.w3c.dom.Element search(String p1)
{
    return search(p1, "dc:Title");
}

public Element search(String p1, String p2)
{
  Element e = doc.getDocumentElement( );
  NodeList nl = e.getElementsByTagName(p2);

  Document d = SAMLUtil.newDocument( );
  Element list = doc.createElement("list");
  d.appendChild(list);

  for (int n = 0; n < nl.getLength( ); n++)
  {
    Element next = (Element)nl.item(n);
    try
      {
        RE targetRE = new RE(p1);
        if (targetRE.match(SAMLUtil.getInnerText(next.getText( )))
        {
          Element item = (Element)d.importNode(next);
          list.appendChild(item);
        }
      }
    catch (Exception exc)
      {
      }
  }
  return list;
}
```

The CodeShare server does not support the info and get operations, so we do not need to write any code to implement them at this point.

This service is deployed to the Apache SOAP engine using the same process we described in Chapter 3. The deployment descriptor we'll use is shown in Example 7-16.

Example 7-16. Deployment descriptor for the CodeShare server

```
<isd:service xmlns:isd="http://xml.apache.org/xml-soap/deployment"
             id="urn:CodeShareService-OwnerService">
  <isd:provider type="java"
                scope="Application"
```

Example 7-16. Deployment descriptor for the CodeShare server (continued)

```
                  methods="list search">
    <isd:java class="codeshare.OwnerService"/>
  </isd:provider>
  <isd:faultListener>org.apache.soap.server.DOMFaultListener
  </isd:faultListener>
</isd:service>
```

The Client Service

The client service is a Java implementation of the client interface that allows users to register and log in to the CodeShare service. This service keeps track of all the various user accounts and issues the digitally signed SAML assertions that users present to the CodeShare owners. Owners use those assertions to ensure that only authorized users can access the code they are sharing.

Creating SAML assertions

Creating a SAML assertion involves nothing more than creating an XML document that conforms to the SAML schema. Because SAML is still being developed, this application implements just a small subset of the most recent working draft being discussed within the SAML working group.

We create the SAML assertion by building an object model (which we created; there currently is no standard SAML API) that corresponds to each of the major parts of the SAML schema, then serializing that object model out to an XML document. The full code for this example is available in Appendix C. Here we just show the assertion being created.

We use the AssertionFactory class to create an instance of the object model. This class, given in full in Appendix C, is discussed next.

The first step is to set the various required properties, such as the assertion ID, the name of the issuer, and the data and time at which the assertion was created. Example 7-17 shows this step.

Example 7-17. Setting assertion properties

```
AuthenticationAssertion aa =
  new AuthenticationAssertion();

IDType aid = new IDType(id);
aa.setAssertionID(aid);
aa.setIssuer(issuerName);
aa.setIssueInstant(issueInstant);
```

Every SAML assertion has a subject that indicates what the assertion is about. In this case, the subject is a name identifier that states which user has been authenticated. Example 7-18 shows how to set the subject.

Example 7-18. Setting the SAML subject

```
Subject subject = new Subject();
{
    NameIdentifier ni = new NameIdentifier();
    ni.setName(name);
    ni.setSecurityDomain(domain);
    subject.setNameIdentifier(ni);
    aa.setSubject(subject);
}
```

Finally, we fill in additional details about the type of authentication that was used, and an indication of where the authentication occurred (Example 7-19).

Example 7-19. Completing the authentication assertion

```
aa.setAuthenticationMethod(
new AuthenticationMethod(method));
aa.setAuthenticationInstant(new AuthenticationInstant(authInstant));
AuthenticationLocale locale = new AuthenticationLocale();
locale.setIP(ip);
locale.setDNSDomain(dns);
aa.setAuthenticationLocale(locale);
```

The AssertionFactory provides a convenient wrapper to this dogwork. To create an assertion, simply pass in the various relevant pieces of information, and the authentication assertion is created, filled out, and returned.

Example 7-20 uses the AsssertionFactory class to generate a SAML assertion.

Example 7-20. Using the AssertionFactory class

```
AuthenticationAssertion aa = AssertionFactory.newInstance(
    new String( new Long(System.currentTimeMillis()).toString() ),
    "CodeShare.org",
    new java.util.Date(),
    userid,
    "CodeShare.org",
    "http://codeshare.org",
    java.net.InetAddress.getLocalHost().getHostAddress(),
    java.net.InetAddress.getLocalHost().getHostName()
  );
```

Example 7-21 shows the SAML assertion created by Example 7-20.

Example 7-21. The SAML assertion

```
<AuthenticationAssertion
     AssertionID="999852828470"
     IssueInstant="Fri Sep 07 01:53:48 PDT 2001"
     Issuer="CodeShare.org" Version="1.0"
     xmlns="http://www.oasis-open.org/committees/security/docs/draft-
            sstc-schema-assertion-15.xsd">
 <Subject>
```

Example 7-21. The SAML assertion (continued)

```
  <NameIdentifier>
    <SecurityDomain>CodeShare.org</SecurityDomain>
    <Name>james</Name>
  </NameIdentifier>
</Subject>
<AuthenticationMethod>
   http://codeshare.org
</AuthenticationMethod>
<AuthenticationInstant>
   Fri Sep 07 01:53:48 PDT 2001
</AuthenticationInstant>
<AuthenticationLocale>
  <IP>127.0.0.1</IP>
  <DNS_Domain>diamond</DNS_Domain>
</AuthenticationLocale>
</AuthenticationAssertion>
```

This is the assertion in Example 7-5.

Java keystores

Signing the assertion will use Java's support for public and private keys, which warrants a quick refresher. Somewhere on your computer is a Java keystore, a local database where all of your private keys are stored. You create a new key in this database by using the keytool utility that ships with Java. You can also use keytool to create new keystore databases.

This command creates the private key for the CodeShare server, which is used to sign all SAML assertions.

```
C:\book>keytool -genkey -dname "cn=CodeShare Server" -keypass CodeShare -alias
CodeShare -storepass CodeShare -keystore codeshare.db
```

This creates a new file called *codeshare.db* in the *C:\book* folder that contains the private key corresponding to the cn=CodeShare Server distinguished name.

Signing the SAML assertion

We use the IBM XML Security Suite's XML Digital Signature capability to sign the SAML assertion. The full source to the AssertionSigner class is given in Appendix C. The highlights are discussed in this section. At the time of writing, the programming interface of the IBM XML Security Suite was being redesigned. The code shown here was tested with Version XYZ of the XML Security Suite but may not work with other versions.

We can't sign an assertion object directly. Instead we have to serialize it to a DOM document and sign that. The serialization is handled by the code in Example 7-22.

Example 7-22. Serializing the assertion to a DOM document

```
Document doc = SAMLUtil.newDocument( );
Element root = doc.createElement("root");
assertion.serialize(root);
```

A `SignatureGenerator` object will make the signature for us. In the constructor, we indicate the encryption and signing protocols we want to use. This is shown in Example 7-23.

Example 7-23. Creating a SignatureGenerator

```
SignatureGenerator siggen =
  new SignatureGenerator(doc,
    DigestMethod.SHA1,
    Canonicalizer.W3C,
    SignatureMethod.DSA,
    null);
```

The XML signature document can include the message being signed, or the message might be linked as an external resource or another XML document. The most common approach is to include the message being signed—so that's what we'll do, as shown in Example 7-24.

Example 7-24. Embedding the message being signed

```
siggen.addReference(
  siggen.createReference(
    siggen.wrapWithObject(
      root.getFirstChild( ),
      assertion.getAssertionID( ).getText( ))
    )
  );
```

The code in Example 7-25 accesses the keystore and extracts the information it needs to prepare the key needed for signing the SAML assertion. Also prepared is an X509 digital certificate that includes the public key for the `cn=CodeShare Server`. This certificate is embedded into the signature so that it can be used later to validate the signature.

Example 7-25. Preparing the key

```
KeyStore keystore = KeyStore.getInstance("JKS");
keystore.load(
  new FileInputStream(keystorepath),
  storepass.toCharArray( ));
X509Certificate cert = (X509Certificate)keystore.getCertificate(alias);
Key key = keystore.getKey(alias, keypass.toCharArray( ));
if (key == null) {
  throw
  new IllegalArgumentException("Invalid Key Info");
}
```

Example 7-25. Preparing the key (continued)

```
KeyInfo keyInfo = new KeyInfo( );
KeyInfo.X509Data x5data = new KeyInfo.X509Data( );
x5data.setCertificate(cert);
x5data.setParameters(cert, true, true, true);
keyInfo.setX509Data(new KeyInfo.X509Data[] { x5data });
keyInfo.setKeyValue(cert.getPublicKey( ));
siggen.setKeyInfoGenerator(keyInfo);
```

Finally, we can use the prepared key to sign the assertion. The `sign` operation on the `SignatureContext` object handles the complex cryptographic processes to create the signature (see Example 7-26). Once the assertion has been signed, we return the DOM element that contains the signature just created.

Example 7-26. Signing the assertion

```
Element sig = siggen.getSignatureElement( );
SignatureContext context = new SignatureContext( );
context.sign(sig, key);
return sig;
```

The login operation

The encryption code is used in the `login` operation, shown in Example 7-27. It verifies the user's password, generates the SAML assertion, and signs it.

Example 7-27. The login operation

```
public static Element login(String userid,
                            String password) throws Exception {

    Element el = doc.getDocumentElement( );
    NodeList nl = el.getElementsByTagName("user");
    for (int n = 0; n < nl.getLength( ); n++) {
        Element e = (Element)nl.item(n);
        if (e.getAttribute("id").equals(userid) &&
            e.getAttribute("password").equals(password)) {

            AuthenticationAssertion aa =
                AssertionFactory.newInstance(new String(new
                        Long(System.currentTimeMillis()).toString( )),
                        "CodeShare.org",
                        new java.util.Date( ),
                        userid,
                        "CodeShare.org",
                        "http://codeshare.org",
                        new java.util.Date( ),
                        java.net.InetAddress.getLocalHost( ).
                            getHostAddress( ),
                        java.net.InetAddress.getLocalHost().getHostName( ));
```

Example 7-27. The login operation (continued)

```
        Element sa = AssertionSigner.sign(aa,
                            "CodeShare.db",
                            "CodeShare",
                            "CodeShareKeyPass",
                            "CodeShareStorePass");
        return sa;
    }
}
    return null;
}
```

The deployment descriptor we use to deploy the client service to Apache Axis is shown in Example 7-28.

Example 7-28. Deployment descriptor

```
<isd:service xmlns:isd="http://xml.apache.org/xml-soap/deployment"
            id="urn:CodeShareService-ClientService">
  <isd:provider type="java"
                scope="Application"
                methods="register login">
    <isd:java class="codeshare.AuthenticationService"/>
  </isd:provider>
  <isd:faultListener>org.apache.soap.server.DOMFaultListener
  </isd:faultListener>
</isd:service>
```

The Verification Service

The task of the verification service is to validate the signed SAML assertion on behalf of the CodeShare owner. The CodeShare server handles this validation for the owner, so the owner doesn't have to worry about the complexities of implementing the full XML digital signature specification. Granted, it's not a very secure approach, but it works for our purposes here.

The verification service exposes a single operation, verify, which receives the signature and returns a Boolean response indicating whether that signature is valid (see Example 7-29). A real verification of the SAML assertion would include a number of checks, such as ensuring that all of the fields contain valid data. We have omitted those checks in the interest of brevity.

Example 7-29. The verify operation

```
public static boolean verify(Element signature) throws Exception {

    Key key = null;
    Element keyInfoElement = KeyInfo.searchForKeyInfo(signature);
    if (keyInfoElement != null) {
        KeyInfo keyInfo = new KeyInfo(keyInfoElement);
```

Example 7-29. The verify operation (continued)

```
        key = keyInfo.getKeyValue( );
    }
    SignatureContext context = new SignatureContext( );
    Validity validity = context.verify(signature, key);
    return validity.getCoreValidity( );
}
```

Deploy this service using the deployment descriptor in Example 7-30.

Example 7-30. Deployment descriptor for the verification service

```
<isd:service xmlns:isd="http://xml.apache.org/xml-soap/deployment"
             id="urn:CodeShareService-Verification">
  <isd:provider type="java"
                scope="Application"
                methods="verify">
    <isd:java class="codeshare.VerificationService"/>
  </isd:provider>
  <isd:faultListener>org.apache.soap.server.DOMFaultListener
  </isd:faultListener>
</isd:service>
```

Implementing the CodeShare Owner

The CodeShare owner server is a lightweight Perl application that consists of two parts: the owner module and a SOAP-enabled HTTP daemon. The server builds on top of SOAP::Lite.

The Owner Module

The CodeShare::Owner module works with the owner's *index.xml* to allow users to search for and retrieve shared code. The owner service also interacts with the Code-Share service to update the master index and validate the identities of users who submit SAML assertions.

This code, written in Perl, implements the same owner interface as the Java Code-Share owner service seen in the previous example. The same WSDL interface description applies to both. The operations have the same effect and return the same types of data.

The init method shown in Example 7-31 turns the owner's *index.xml* into a data structure, stored in the variable $index.

Example 7-31. The init method

```
sub init {
  my($class, $root) = @_;
  open(F, $root) or die "$root: $!\n";
  $index = SOAP::Custom::XML::Deserializer
```

Example 7-31. The init method (continued)

```
              ->deserialize(join '', <F>)->root;
  close(F) or die "$root: $!\n";
}
```

To interact with the CodeShare server master index and validation services, we create a SOAP::Lite proxy to the CodeShare server (shown in Example 7-32).

Example 7-32. Constructing a SOAP::Lite proxy to the server

```
my $codeshare_server;

sub codeshare_server {
  return $codeshare_server ||=
        SOAP::Lite
          ->proxy($SERVER_ENDPOINT)
          ->uri("urn:Services:CodeShareServer");
}
```

The update operation shown in Example 7-33 updates this owner's entry in the master index with the information given as arguments to the method.

Example 7-33. The update operation

```
sub update {
  shift->codeshare_server->update(@_)->result;
}
```

When a user submits a SAML assertion, it must be validated by the owner service. The code in Example 7-34 uses the CodeShare service proxy created in Example 7-32 to do just that. Once the assertion is validated, it is cached so the owner doesn't have to validate it again.

Example 7-34. Validating an assertion

```
sub is_valid_signature {
  my($self, $username, $signature) = @_;

  my $key = join "\0", $username, $signature;

  # already cached?
  return $cache{$key} if exists $cache{$key};

  my $response = eval { $self->codeshare_server
    ->isValid(SOAP::Data->type(xml => $signature)) };
  die "CodeShare server is unavailable. Can't validate credentials\n" if $@;
  die "CodeShare server is unavailable. ",
      $response->faultstring, "\n" if $response->fault;
  die "Invalid credentials\n"
      unless $cache{$key} = $response->result;

  return $cache{$key};
}
```

The traverse procedure shown in Example 7-35 navigates the *index.xml*, checking whether the items in the index match the criteria requested by the user in the search, info, list, or get operations.

Example 7-35. The traverse method

```
sub traverse {
  my($self, %params) = @_;

  my $start = $params{start};

  my $type = $start->SOAP::Data::name; # file|project|directory
  my $location = ref $start->location ? $start->location->value : '';

  # path to current structure. Empty for projects
  my $path = $type eq 'directory' ||
             $type eq 'file' ? join('/', $params{path} || (), $location)
               : '';
  my $prefix = $type eq 'project' ? $location : $params{prefix} || '';
  my $fullpath = join '/', $prefix, $path; # full path. Used to GET files

  my $where = $params{where};
  my $matched =
    $params{get} && $params{matched} ||
    $params{what} &&
    # check only subelements in Dublin Core namespace
    $start->$where() =~ /$params{what}/ && $start->$where()->uri eq $DC_NS;

  return
    # current element
    ($matched
       ? +{ type => $type,
            path => $path,
            ($params{get} ? (fullpath => $fullpath) : ()),
            map { ref $start->$_() ? ($_ => $start->$_()->value) : ()
                } @ELEMENTS
         }
       : ()
    ),

    # and everything below
    map { $self->traverse(start => $_, where => $where,
          what    => $params{what},
          path => $path,
          prefix  => $prefix,
      get => ($params{get} || 0),
          matched => $matched) }
        $start->project, $start->directory,
        ($type eq 'file' ? () : $start->file)
  ;
}
```

The list operation provides a simple listing of all shared items, and is shown in Example 7-36.

Example 7-36. The list method

```
sub list {
  pop;
  my($self, $what) = @_;
  return [ map { my $e = $_; +{ map {$_ => $e->{$_}}
                          qw(type path Title file fullpath) } }
    $self->traverse(start => $index, where => 'Title',
                    what  => $what,  get    => 1)
  ];
}
```

The get operation shown in Example 7-38 retrieves the requested set of items; before it can do so, however, it must check to see if the user is authorized to access those items. It does so by validating the SAML assertion of the user and checking to see if the owner has explicitly allowed the user to access.

The owner specifies access permissions for a specific item in the index by adding a Dublin Core dc:Rights element to it. The value of this element is the list of users allowed to access it. If the element is missing, it is assumed that everyone is allowed to access it. Example 7-37 shows a sample index file.

Example 7-37. Sample index file

```
<codeshare>
  <project location="HelloWorld">
    <dc:Title>Hello World</dc:Title>
    <dc:Rights>james paul doug</dc:Rights>
  </project>
</codeshare>
```

The index in Example 7-37 indicates that the users james, paul, and doug are allowed to get the HelloWorld project item. The get operation shown in Example 7-38 retrieves the requested set of items.

Example 7-38. The get operation

```
sub get {
  my $self = shift;
  my $envelope = $_[-1];
  my $username = $envelope->valueof('//{http://www.oasis-open.org/committees/security/
docs/draft-sstc-schema-assertion-15.xsd}Name');
  my $results = $self->list(@_);
  [ map { # return file
      $_->{type} eq 'file' && open(F, delete $_->{fullpath})
        ? ($_->{file} = join('', <F>), close F) : (); $_
    }
    grep { # check rights
```

Example 7-38. The get operation (continued)

```
    ($_->{Rights} || '') =~ /^\s*$/ || # public access if empty
     $username && $_->{Rights} =~ /\b$username\b/ &&
       $self->is_valid_signature($username, get_signature($envelope))
  }
    @$results
];
}
```

The Server Daemon

To deploy this code as a web service, simply create and run the HTTP server daemon given in Example 7-39.

Example 7-39. The HTTP server daemon

```
use SOAP::Transport::HTTP;
use CodeShare::Owner;

print "\n\nWelcome to CodeShare! The Open source code sharing network!";
print "\nCopyright(c) 2001, James Snell, Paul Kulchenko, Doug Tidwell\n";

CodeShare::Owner->init(shift or die "Usage: $0 <path/to/index.xml>\n");

my $daemon = SOAP::Transport::HTTP::Daemon
  -> new (LocalPort => 8080)
  -> dispatch_to('CodeShare::Owner::(?:get|search|info|list)')
;
print "CodeShare Owner Server started at ", $daemon->url, "\n";
print "Waiting for a request...\n";
$daemon->handle;
```

Launch the daemon with the following command line:

```
C:\book>start perl cs_server.pl index.xml
```

The running program is shown in Figure 7-4.

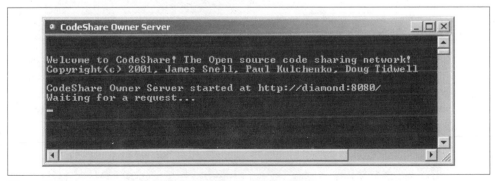

Figure 7-4. Screenshot of the CodeShare owner server running

Implementing the CodeShare Client

The CodeShare client, like the owner server, is a Perl application that implements a simple shell for interacting with the CodeShare server and owner services. It also uses SOAP::Lite. The full source to the client is given in Appendix C. We discuss the highlights here.

First we create a proxy, shown in Example 7-40, to the CodeShare server to authenticate the user.

Example 7-40. Creating the proxy

```
my($server, $uri) =
  $ownerserver ? ($ownerserver      => 'http://namespaces.soaplite.com/CodeShare/Owner')
               : ($codeshareserver => 'urn:Services:CodeShareServer');
my $soap = SOAP::Lite
 ->proxy($server)
 ->uri($uri);
```

If the user logs in (doing so is completely optional), the client invokes the login operation exposed by the CodeShare service client interface. This returns a SAML assertion, which the client caches. We can tell whether the user is logging in based on whether he provides a username and password. Example 7-41 demonstrates this.

Example 7-41. Logging in

```
my $signature;
if ($username || $password) {
  my $response = $soap->login(
    SOAP::Data->name(credential => join ':', $username, $password)->type('base64')
  );
  die $response->faultstring if $response->fault;
  $signature = SOAP::Data->type(xml => get_signature($response));
}
```

The client is implemented as a simple shell interface, shown in Figure 7-5.

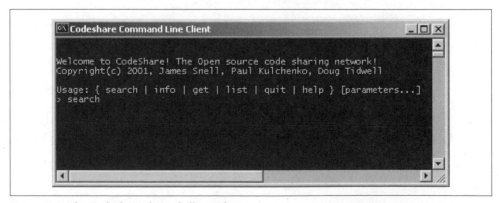

Figure 7-5. The CodeShare client shell interface

We create this shell using a while loop (shown in Example 7-42) to read input, work out what to do, and do it. The loop:

1. Waits for the user to enter a command (search, info, get, list, quit, or help).

2. Checks to see which command was entered.

3. Invokes the SOAP operation.

4. If the get command was issued, the resulting list of items is looped through and the items are returned using a simple HTTP-GET operation to the CodeShare owner server.

Example 7-42. The loop at the heart of the client

```perl
while (defined($_ = shift || <>)) {
  next unless /\w/;# must have a command
  my($method, $modifier, $parameters) =# split input
    m!^\s*(\w+)(?:\s*/(\w*)\s)?\s*(.*)!;

  last if $method =~ /^q(?:uit)?$/i;       # handle quit command
  help(), next if $method =~ /^h(?:elp)?$/i; # handle help comma


  # call the SOAP method

  my $res = eval "\$soap->$method('$parameters', '$modifier',
                  \$signature || ())";

  # check for errors
  $@                        and print(STDERR join "\n", $@, ''), next;
  defined($res) && $res->fault  and print(STDERR join "\n",
                                $res->faultstring, ''), next;
  !$soap->transport->is_success and print(STDERR join "\n",
                                $soap->transport->status, ''), next;

  # check for result
  my @result = @{$res->result} or print(STDERR "No matches\n"), next;

  foreach (@result) {
    print STDERR "$_->{type}: ",
        join(', ', $_->{Title} || (), $_->{path} || ()), "\n";
    if ($method eq 'get') {
      if ($_->{type} eq 'directory') { File::Path::mkpath($_->{path}) }
      if ($_->{type} eq 'file') {
        open(F, '>'. $_->{path}) or warn "$_->{path}: $!\n";
        print F $_->{file};
        close(F) or warn "$_->{path}: $!\n";
      }
    } elsif ($method eq 'info') {
      foreach my $key (grep {$_ !~ /^(?:type|path)/} keys %$_) {
        print "  $key: $_->{$key}\n";
      }
    }
  }
}
```

Example 7-42. The loop at the heart of the client (continued)

```
} continue {
  print STDERR "\n> ";
}
```

Seeing It in Action

You can download an archive of the code from the O'Reilly web site (*http://www. oreilly.com/catalog/progwebsoap/*), and run the CodeShare service yourself. First make sure that you have properly installed Apache SOAP, Perl, and SOAP::Lite. Then run the `codeshare.bat` script for Windows or the `codeshare.sh` shell script for Unix. These scripts deploy the CodeShare services and launch the various components, allowing you to experiment with the shell client.

What's Missing from This Picture?

That was a lot of code, but even with all the programs we've written for the Code-Share server, we still haven't used all the web services components. There's no UDDI, and we haven't used the features of many P2P services, such as presence and asynchronous messaging.

Where Is UDDI?

One piece that is conspicuously missing is UDDI. Nowhere in the CodeShare example we've laid out so far is there any mention of how UDDI fits into the picture. This shows that none of these web services technologies are overly dependent upon one another. If UDDI is not useful in a given situation, leave it out. If SAML hadn't been useful, we would have left that out also.

In COM, CORBA, J2EE, etc., there are parts that just aren't useful, but that you still have to deal with, or at least deploy along with your sample. In web services, you are not locked into a monolithic set of technologies, but instead have a loosely coupled conglomeration of standards that make writing code easier.

UDDI could be used in this example. For instance, the CodeShare server could be listed in a public UDDI registry so that it can be more readily discovered. Additionally, since each CodeShare owner is itself a web service, owners themselves could be listed in a UDDI registry.

Presence and Asynchronous Messaging

Even though the CodeShare service implements a peer-to-peer architecture, there are two aspects of P2P that are missing: the concept of presence and the ability to have peers communicate with each other asynchronously.

Presence boils down to the ability of one peer to see if another peer (in this case an owner server) is currently online. The owner's HTTP daemon could very easily tell the CodeShare server when it is starting up and when it is shutting down, allowing the CodeShare server to pass that information on to users who are looking for code. This would work just like the buddy list in your Instant Messaging application.

Even if your buddies are offline, you should still be able to send messages to be delivered when they do come online. If a CodeShare user wants to get some code, and the owner of that code is currently offline, it would be nice if the owner could still get that request and handle it later. CodeShare does not yet support asynchronous communication like this.

Developing CodeShare

CodeShare has been registered as an open source project at SourceForge, a leading open source development portal. If this example has inspired you to add features to the application, you can take an active role in developing the CodeShare Service Network into a real-life infrastructure for sharing code.

To access the project at SourceForge, visit *http://www.sourceforge.com*, create a user account, and search for the "CodeShare" project. To be an active contributor, you'll need to become familiar with the source code control system, called CVS. Details are available at the SourceForge web site.

CHAPTER 8
Web Services Security

Security is one of the key issues that developers of web services face, particularly in the enterprise. Without a comprehensive security infrastructure, web services will simply not reach their highest potential. It is no surprise that we are starting to see new battles emerge in the marketplace as companies vie for the dominant security position.

Authentication is one of the key components that has emerged. Currently, there are three widely known, competing (and unfortunately, incompatible) web service authentication infrastructures jockeying for position in the marketplace:

Passport
> Microsoft's proprietary single sign-on service that provides authentication and digital wallet services for millions of users.

Magic Carpet
> AOL's own single sign-on service and digital wallet for use by AOL members.

Sun's Liberty Project
> A collaborative effort among Java and open source development communities to develop an alternative to Passport.

Of the three, Passport is the best known and understood architecture. We discuss that architecture in this chapter, but first we will look more closely at web services security in general, including a look at the XML digital signature and XML encryption specifications.

What Is a "Secure" Web Service?

Web services are all about moving information; it doesn't really matter what type of information is being moved. A "secure" web service is one in which the information sender trusts that the recipient of that information is really who he claims to be and vice versa. Also, a "secure" web service is one in which the information can be received and accessed only by the intended recipient. This definition implies two things:

1. There must be some type of authentication.
2. There must be some type of privacy and integrity protection, such as encryption and authorization.

Authentication

Authentication asks questions like:

- Who am I?
- How do I prove who I am?
- Why should you trust me when I tell you who I am?
- Who are you?
- How can I prove that you are who you say you are?
- Why should I trust you when you tell me who you are?

In the web services world, answering these questions is vitally important. Of equal importance is coming up with a standard *method* to ask and answer these questions.

That's where protocols like the Security Assertions Markup Language (SAML) come into play. In Chapter 5 we briefly discussed SAML and demonstrated in a very simple way how it can be used to provide single sign-on capabilities, but there is more to it than that.

SAML assertions can provide a standard machine-readable expression of a person, application, or device's identity. This identity can be validated, passed around, and used as proof that you really are who you say you are. Because the assertion is digitally signed, we can establish some sort of trust based not on my word that I am who I say I am, but on the word of a trusted third party (the issuer of the assertion).

Even though SAML still has hurdles to jump through on its way to completion, there is a huge amount of potential to provide a very comprehensive, standard framework for implementing global sign-on.

Microsoft recently proposed an alternative approach to authentication based on embedding structures such as Kerberos tickets within the SOAP header. This approach, defined by two related specifications called WS-Security and WS-License, is used extensively by Microsoft's .NET My Services project (formerly known as Hailstorm).

There are no standards (real or de facto) that define how to carry authentication information within a SOAP Envelope.

Privacy

There are two important issues involved in ensuring privacy; both address the protection of assets. The first issue is the protection of an individual's personal information. For example, if I give you my home address and credit card number, I expect that you will protect that information and not send it out over the Internet unguarded. The second issue deals with how you would actually go about protecting that data; this aspect of protection implies authorization policies that detail who is allowed access to the information and what they are allowed to do with it, and encryption methods that ensure unauthorized parties cannot access it.

Currently, there is little Internet privacy infrastructure. While there are simple mechanisms in place to obscure information as it passes from one point to the next (SSL, for example), there is no way to ensure that your personal information is used only for the specific purpose you intended it for once it is sent out over the wire.

The closest thing we have to a privacy infrastructure is the W3C Platform for Privacy Preferences (P3P), which specifies an XML-based language for creating privacy profiles. Service providers create these profiles to tell service consumers how they intend to use the personal information provided by the consumer. While it is a valuable first step, these profiles are not legally binding, can change at any time, and often do. So if a company decides to use your information in a way that violates the original terms of the profile, there are no laws to stop them. This is changing, though, and hopefully laws will be passed in the very near future to make privacy policies legally binding.

Another problem with privacy on the Internet is that people conflate authentication with authorization. This is seen in the version of Microsoft's Passport service currently being used at a wide range of e-commerce sites. When a user authenticates with Passport, almost all of the personal information contained in his Passport profile is shared automatically with the Passport-enabled web sites the user visits. The problem of authenticating users is solved, but the authorization of companies allowed to access your information is not.

Authentication of a user's identity and management of a user's personal information need to be completely separated from one another. Services like Passport, Magic Carpet, and Liberty blur these lines.

Microsoft Passport, Version 1.x and 2.x

The current version of Microsoft Passport is designed around providing single sign-on and digital wallet services for web browser-based services. It is easy to understand:

1. A user, Jane, visits a Passport-enabled web site (*MSN.com*, for instance).
2. She is presented with a "Passport Sign-on" link that redirects her web browser to *http://www.passport.com*, where she types her Passport user ID and password.

3. Upon validating the username and password, *Passport.com* creates a cookie on Jane's computer that contains her encrypted user profile (all of her personal information).

4. Passport then redirects her back to the original site, which checks for the existence of the cookie, accesses it, and extracts the information it needs about Jane to provide more personalized service.

Drawbacks

There are several problems with this architecture. First, it would be very simple for a malicious person to fool Jane into voluntarily compromising her user ID and password, by simply creating a fake Passport login page. The average user, redirected to the fake page rather than the authentic *Passport.com* page, would not be able to tell the difference. She would enter her login information, press Submit, and never know that she never actually logged in. Meanwhile, the bad guy now has Jane's password and can access all of her personal information and even pretend to be Jane at real Passport-enabled sites.

A second problem is that there is nothing to stop a malicious person from setting up a real Passport-enabled site and taking advantage of Passport, freely dispersing Jane's personal information when she happens to visit the site.

In either situation, it is likely that neither Jane nor Passport will ever know that her information has been compromised because Passport does not include any auditing capabilities that would let Jane go back and monitor the activity of her account.

Another big problem is the natural insecurity of using cookies to store profile information—even if it is encrypted. All it would take is a simple worm virus targeted at locating and decrypting these encrypted Passport cookies to cause a very serious security issue for the millions of Passport users.

In fact, Microsoft's Passport service has recently come under heavy criticism due to a very serious security flaw that allowed credit card numbers and other personal information stored by Passport to be read by a malicious hacker.

Microsoft Passport, Version 3.x

While the details are still sketchy, Microsoft is busy working to implement the next generation of their Passport service—this time basing it on the much more secure Kerberos authentication scheme and providing more robust privacy controls.

Overview of Kerberos

Kerberos is an authentication protocol that's been around for quite some time. Originally developed by a university, many large companies, such as Microsoft and IBM, have picked up Kerberos and incorporated support for it into their product lines. Microsoft is by far the largest proponent of Kerberos in the industry today.

Kerberos is too complex to explain in detail. Here's a very abbreviated rundown of how it works:

- First, the user (we'll use Jane again) asks the Kerberos authentication server to validate her credentials. Jane does this by encrypting a packet of information using her private key. The Kerberos server decrypts this packet using her public key. If the decryption was successful, the Kerberos service rules that Jane really is Jane, and sends her an authentication ticket.

- Whenever Jane wants to use some network resource, she must go to the Kerberos Ticket Granting Service (TGS) and explicitly ask permission to use that specific service. The TGS will validate her authentication ticket and issue, as appropriate a one-time use ticket for the service she is requesting.

- Jane presents that one-time use ticket to the service when she submits her request. Also included in the request is an authenticator that proves the one-time use ticket is authentic and really did come from Jane, not some malicious bad guy trying to impersonate her.

That, while being a gross oversimplification, is all that Kerberos does. Passport 3.0 will implement this model, allowing (hopefully) a more robust and secure authentication model that will offer better protection to the services' 160 million plus users. This process protects the user from the impersonation and spoofing attacks that are possible in the current version of Passport. It is a huge advantage.

The Passport privacy management is also improved. Passport users will be able to establish policies that dictate how their information is shared, and who is allowed to access it. The details have not been fleshed out yet, but it will use P3P privacy policies. This doesn't change the fact that P3P policies are not yet legally binding, but it is a huge leap forward for Passport.

Give Me Liberty or Give Me . . .

A new arrival in the web services security battle is a collaborative project called Liberty. Sponsored by Sun and a handful of significant industry players, this project seeks to achieve three main objectives:

1. To allow individual consumers and businesses to maintain personal information securely by enabling a decentralized approach to garnering personal or proprietary information, and promoting interoperability or service delivery across networks.

2. To provide a universal, open standard for "single sign-on," which users and service providers can rely upon, and leverage to interoperate.

3. To provide an open standard for network identity spanning all network-connected devices, allowing the providers of network services and the infrastructure that

enables those services to adopt a neutral, open standard, available wherever the Internet is available, securing reliable identity authentication across handsets, automobiles, credit cards—literally any device attached to the Internet.

No technical details have been released on how these goals will be met. At the time of this writing, the Liberty project is essentially vaporware.

A Magic Carpet

There is as little information about AOL's Magic Carpet proposal as there is about Liberty. The little that is available points to Magic Carpet being an extension of AOL's Screen Name service. Screen Name attempts to provide a single sign-on that can give access to many different web sites across the Web. You can create a profile for the web sites you visit, and you can limit the web sites' access to various parts of your profile. At the time of this writing, AOL's Magic Carpet is still in stealth mode, and should be considered vaporware like Sun's Liberty.

The Need for Standards

Microsoft is not the only company working on this problem. Unfortunately, those who are working on it are not necessarily working together. To date, we have three incompatible solutions being proposed for web services. In a battle that is starting to resemble the Great Browser Wars of old, traditional enemies are drawing lines and duking it out over who is going to control web services security.

A better approach (the approach that developers need to demand) is for standards to be developed and adopted by all the different players. While it will probably be a long time coming, what we don't need is to develop a great new open interoperability and integration-focused architecture only to have interoperability break down once we actually try to do something really interesting, like global sign-on.

XML Digital Signatures and Encryption

Two positive examples of standardization efforts currently going on the XML and web services arena are the XML Digital Signature and XML Encryption activities being conducted primarily through the W3C (the IETF is also involved heavily in the XML Digital Signature effort). Providing comprehensive digital signature and encryption support will be by far a more important issue than the choice of authentication services.

The XML Digital Signature project is working to define a standard syntax for digitally signing data (including XML data) and for encoding that signature as XML. Digital Signatures are critical to protecting the integrity of business transactions on the Internet and will be a key piece of the overall web services infrastructure.

The XML Encryption project is working to define how encrypted data (including XML data) and the metainformation necessary to decrypt that data can be encoded as XML. Encryption of XML data is critical to ensuring the confidentiality of information exchanged between web service participants.

Currently, only IBMs Web Services ToolKit and Microsofts .NET web services implementations include support for digitally signing and encrypting SOAP messages. While they both support the same XML Encryption and Digital Signature standards, they have different ideas as to how exactly signatures and encrypted data should be placed within a SOAP Envelope. So while each set of tools supports encryption and signing, they are not compatible with one another.

Expect these interoperability differences to be worked out soon, leading to compatible implementations. A key issue will be getting other web service tool vendors to support these security standards within their products.

## CHAPTER 9

The Future of Web Services

Throughout this book, we've maintained a fairly narrow focus on what web services are and how to go about creating them. To finish up, we will spend some time discussing the future of web services from both the point of view of the technologies, and from the point of view of the architecture as a whole. Specifically, we'll discuss the futures of SOAP, WSDL, and UDDI, as well as the next generation of even more useful and powerful services.

The Future of Web Development

Before we get into where the technologies are going in the future, let's take a moment to highlight exactly how web services are most likely to impact web development.

We've spent a great deal of time talking about interoperability. With web services, we're concerned about how to find information and move it across the Web. Issues that used to be important, such as the programming language in which the code was written, the operating system on which the code is running, the object model on which the code is based, or the vendor of the underlying database system, don't matter that much anymore.

Now that's a strong statement. Some may even say that it is too strong. Here's the reasoning.

First, prior to web services, the vast majority of enterprise-scale development platforms were rather inbred. Java applications worked best with Java applications; COM applications worked best with COM applications; CORBA applications worked best with CORBA applications, and so on. To make the most of each environment, you had to standardize and focus on the technology platform itself. You could get Java and COM to work together, but it was painful.

Web services, however, opened an integration channel between Java and COM, and COM and CORBA, etc., that did not exist before. Because this channel is built with open standards that any platform can implement, for the first time we have a situation where one can *easily* invoke functionality written in one programming language on one platform from any other programming language on any other platform. This allows us to look beyond programming languages and focus on the applications themselves.

This point was demonstrated in the Hello World example in Chapter 3. We created the same type of web service with three different programming languages. Barring minor interoperability bugs that exist in the web services tools, we could easily switch between the three service implementations without paying attention to how they were actually written. If we were to go looking for a Hello World service somewhere out on the Internet, it would be of no importance to me whether it is written in Java, Perl, .NET, or even COBOL or ADA. (There is an implementation of SOAP for ADA, by the way. And Microsoft's Visual Studio.NET will support writing assemblies with COBOL.)

Web Services and Existing Technologies

A critical insight is that web services *do not replace existing technology infrastructures*. Rather, they help to integrate existing technologies. In other words, if you need a J2EE application to talk to a COM application, web services makes it easier. Web services won't completely replace that 30-year-old mainframe system in the back closet that nobody ever thinks about anymore. But web services might provide cross-platform automated access to the mainframe's applications, thus opening new channels of business.

The Future of SOAP

The SOAP protocol is already a couple of years old. One of the original versions became what is now called XML-RPC, a simple, popular alternative to SOAP championed by Userland Software. (Userland's CEO, Dave Winer, is one of the coauthors of the original SOAP specification.) To learn more about XML-RPC, read *Programming Web Services with XML-RPC* by Simon St. Laurent, Joe Johnston, and Edd Dumbill (O'Reilly).

XML-RPC split from SOAP in 1998. The first version of the SOAP protocol was announced in 1999, and since then there have been four revisions with a fifth now being worked on by the W3C. The two versions we've discussed in this book (Version 1.1 and Version 1.2) are those currently being used in production environments, even though they are not official W3C standards.

In the not-too-distant future, the SOAP 1.2 working draft specification will evolve into the W3C XML Protocol Version 1.0 recommendation, which will be the first *standardized* version of the protocol.

There should not be many changes between SOAP 1.2 and XML Protocol Version 1.0, because the W3C working group has committed to using SOAP as the basis for their work and to ensuring that backwards compatibility is maintained at least on a fundamental level. Unfortunately, it is still far too early in the process to know about any differences between the XML Protocol and SOAP 1.2. If you're curious, monitor the XML Protocol development discussion through the *xml-dist-app* mailing list (see the W3C XML Protocol home page at *http://www.w3.org/2000/xp* for subscription details).

The Future of WSDL

Like SOAP, the Web Service Description Language is not yet an official Internet standard, but it is well on the road to becoming one. It has been submitted to the W3C and a working group is being formed to manage it. Unlike SOAP, which has a fairly stable direction within the W3C, standardized WSDL may be different from the version being widely used in web services today. It's too early to know how different, or when the W3C-blessed standard will be released.

Missing Pieces

There are several important things missing from WSDL that will have to be addressed by the W3C working group. For example, there is no standardized mechanism for extending the WSDL description to include information about security requirements, quality of service attributes, sequencing of operations, and so on. While not a strict requirement when WSDL is used to describe simple, basic RPC-style services, such standard extensions become critical when applying web services technology to enterprise e-business scenarios.

An Alternative to WSDL

Another key issue that the WSDL working group will need to address is the reconciliation of WSDL to other, alternative service description mechanisms, such as the DARPA Agent Markup Language (DAML) based DAML-S (S stands for "services"). DAML-S is focused on the task of building a formal semantic data model for web services. In other words, they're formalizing the language we use to describe web services. While DAML-S has no solid corporate backing, much of the work being done will have an impact on the future direction of WSDL standardization.

The concepts involved in DAML-S are really not all that different from WSDL, but the syntax is much more complex. For instance, Example 9-1 shows a partial description of the Hello World service from Chapter 3, in DAML-S instead of WSDL.

Example 9-1. Sample DAML-S description of the WSDL service

```
<rdf:RDF xmlns:rdf="http://www.w3.org/1999/02/22-rdf-syntax-ns#"
         xmlns:daml="http://www.daml.org/2001/03/daml+oil#"
```

Example 9-1. Sample DAML-S description of the WSDL service (continued)

```
      xmlns:service="http://www.daml.org/services/daml-s/2001/05/Service#"
      xmlns:process="http://www.daml.org/services/daml-s/2001/05/Process#"
          xmlns:profile="http://www.daml.org/services/daml-s/2001/05/Profile#">

<daml:Ontology about="">

    <daml:versionInfo>HelloWorld</daml:versionInfo>
    <daml:imports
        rdf:resource="http://www.w3.org/1999/02/22-rdf-syntax-ns" />
    <daml:imports
        rdf:resource="http://www.w3.org/2000/01/rdf-schema" />
    <daml:imports
        rdf:resource="http://www.w3.org/2000/10/XMLschema" />
    <daml:imports
        rdf:resource="http://www.daml.org/2001/03/daml+oil" />
    <daml:imports
        rdf:resource="http://www.daml.org/services/daml-s/2001/05/Service" />
    <daml:imports
        rdf:resource="http://www.daml.org/services/daml-s/2001/05/Process" />
    <daml:imports
        rdf:resource="http://www.daml.org/services/daml-s/2001/05/Profile" />
</daml:Ontology>

<rdf:Service rdf:ID="StockQuoteService">
   <service:presents>
      <profile:Advertisement rdf:about="#StockQuote_Advertisement" />
   </service:presents>
   <service:implements>
      <process:ProcessModel rdf:about="#StockQuote_ProcessModel" />
   </service:implements>
</rdf:Service>

<process:ProcessModel rdf:ID="StockQuote_ProcessModel">
   <service:topLevelEvent rdf:resource="#GetStockQuote" />
</process>

<rdfs:Class rdf:ID="GetStockQuote">
   <rdfs:subClassOf
   rdf:resource="http://www.daml.org/services/daml-s/2001/05/Process#Process" />
</rdfs:Class>

<rdf:Property rdf:id="symbol">
    <rdfs:domain rdf:resource="#GetStockQuote" />
    <rdfs:subPropertyOf
    rdf:resource="http://www.daml.org/services/daml-s/2001/05/Profile#input" />
    <rdfs:range
        rdf:resource="http://www.w3.org/2000/10/XMLschema#string" />
</rdf:Property>

<rdf:Property rdf:id="value">
    <rdfs:domain rdf:resource="#GetStockQuote" />
    <rdfs:subPropertyOf
```

Example 9-1. Sample DAML-S description of the WSDL service (continued)

```
        rdf:resource="http://www.daml.org/services/daml-s/2001/05/Profile#output" />
      <rdfs:range
          rdf:resource="http://www.w3.org/2001/10/XMLSchema#float" />
    </rdf:Property>

    <profile:Advertisement rdf:ID="StockQuote_Advertisement">
      <profile:serviceName>StockQuoteService</profile:serviceName>
      <!-- elements removed for brevity -->
    </profile:Advertisement>
</rdf:RDF>
```

DAML-S is based on the Resource Description Framework (RDF) standard. This tends to make it more complex, verbose, and difficult to use than WSDL.

That said, there are several lessons WSDL can learn from DAML-S:

1. DAML-S naturally supports the ability to extend service descriptions to include a wide variety of semantic and functional information such as security, quality of service, etc.

2. DAML-S naturally supports inheritance throughout the entire description.

3. DAML-S provides a rich mechanism for describing web service processes (logical sequences of operations). WSDL does not support sequencing operations at all.

4. DAML-S allows a service to implement multiple processes (the DAML-S equivalent to a WSDL port type).

5. DAML-S supports a rich service advertisement description that provides information about who is providing the service, what the provider's capabilities are, and so on. WSDL does not include any advertisement information at all.

These features of DAML-S are likely to be a part of the next generation WSDL.

Standard Extensions

One key component of the success of web services will be the ability to describe not only the service itself, but also all of the services' capabilities, requirements, assumptions, and processes in a standard, consistent way.

For example, consider how to describe a web service that uses a SAML-based single sign-on like the one we discussed in Chapter 5. There is no way to declare the type of authentication a service supports in WSDL. For that matter, there is no way to declare that a service supports any type of authentication.

How might the WSDL of the future let you express what type of authentication mechanism is used? One way would be to define a standard extension to the WSDL binding element, as in Example 9-2.

Example 9-2. Hypothetical extension to WSDL bindings

```
<binding name="HelloWorldBinding" type="HelloWorldPortType">
    <soap:binding transport="http://schemas.xmlsoap.org/soap/http" />
    <s:authentication method="http://schemas.xmlsoap.org/security/saml" />
</binding>
```

WSDL-enabled web services tools that understand the authentication extension would then know that SAML could be used for authentication.

Currently, though, there are no standard extensions to WSDL, nor is there a broad industry effort to define them. This also may become part of the W3C-standardized WSDL.

The Future of UDDI

Chapter 4 introduced UDDI as a web service for discovering other web services. Through the definition of a standardized registry format and port type interface, UDDI allows service providers and service consumers to dynamically discover and integrate with one another.

UDDI was originally developed by Microsoft, IBM, and Ariba, and is now managed by a broad industry consortium of companies. The plan is to submit UDDI for standardization once Version 3.0 of the specification is finished (the current version is 2.0).

One of the key requirements for future versions of UDDI is a security infrastructure that would allow service consumers to validate the identity of service providers publishing their services—allowing for a much more robust trust relationship to be established.

Problems with UDDI

There are some problems with UDDI that will need to be addressed in future versions of the specification. Weak security is one of the most significant issues. Currently, it is possible for anybody to create an entry in a UDDI registry, pretending to be somebody else. For example, I can easily create an entry in a UDDI registry pretending to be Microsoft. Needless to say, this is not good.

Another major problem is the proliferation of "bad links" in public UDDI registries. These links point to companies or services that don't exist or are no longer available.

There is a lack of understanding in companies about what UDDI is for and how it may be useful. This might hamper its adoption in future. Even among companies who understand it, there have been some doubts raised about whether public UDDI registries will be useful in the long term.

Web Services Battlegrounds

Over the last few decades, we've seen companies go to war to establish their operating systems, component models, programming languages, browsers, and so on. One refreshing aspect of the web services world is that most of these battles become irrelevant. Consider the SOAP services and clients we've discussed in this book. When we deploy a SOAP service, we define the methods we want to expose across the network. In the past, we'd have defined those methods with CORBA IDL or something similar, generated language bindings for various programming languages and platforms, then hoped we could get enough of the marketplace to use our service. If your platform or your development tools weren't compatible with your infrastructure (maybe they didn't support the correct level of CORBA, for example), you would probably be out of luck.

With SOAP, we can describe everything in terms of platform-independent XML Schema data types. If your development platform has XML parsing tools (and these days you're hard-pressed to find a platform that doesn't, from mobile phones to mainframes), you can start developing applications that use the service.

Don't think for a moment that the fierce competitors of today's marketplace will suddenly get along swimmingly, though. As companies discover that the old battles no longer matter, everyone will try to get an edge on their competitors in some other way. We'll take a look at a couple of the battlegrounds of the future.

Development Tools

One of the reasons for the dominance of the Windows platforms is Microsoft's success in courting developers. Whatever the benefits of your technology, if you can convince hundreds of thousands of clever people to start building products with them, you gain an overwhelming advantage in the market. You don't have to come up with the killer app yourself; third-party developers can do that for you.

With that in mind, you'll see the major software vendors working very aggressively to differentiate their web services development tools. If I can convince you that my tools will make you infinitely more productive and successful, the task of locking you into my development tools becomes much easier. And once you're comfortable with my development tools, I can integrate my proprietary technology initiatives with those tools, slowly removing your ability to use other tools.

Vendors must appear to be standards-compliant, yet also seem somehow superior. A lot of the differentiating features will be nonstandard add-ons, a form of "embracing and extending" that has the potential to weaken web services interoperability while locking in developers to one vendor's products.

Killer Services

If millions of developers can access web services with free tools, one obvious business model is to provide web services so cool that developers will be willing to tie themselves to those services. This is similar to the Web, in which millions of customers can access web sites with a free browser.

One early contestant in the race for killer services is the online wallet. A next-generation online wallet is a web service that allows customers to store passwords, credit card numbers, and other sensitive information. The online wallet provider becomes a clearinghouse for e-commerce. If we want to set up an online store, we can use the service to process credit card transactions. A customer gives us some information (username and password, for example), and we access the online clearinghouse to get an approval code for the transaction.

We might have to pay the clearinghouse a fee (a percentage of the total, perhaps) for each transaction, but if this service is easy to use and access, provides a high level of service, is secure, and is widely accepted by consumers, we could save ourselves a great deal of time and headache in operating and managing our online store. If development tools make it very easy to use a particular online wallet, the vendor behind the development tools and the online wallet is in a very good position. This is widely thought to be part of Microsoft's .NET and .Net My Services (formerly known as Hailstorm) strategies.

As web services take hold in the marketplace, we'll see lots of providers try to come up with other killer services to bring the world to their online doorsteps.

Lucrative Marketplaces

The EDI industry has worked for decades to automate the exchange of purchase orders, invoices, and similar documents. Unfortunately, these systems have traditionally been very expensive to create and maintain. With the lower startup costs of web services (you can build, deploy, and access web services with the technologies you already have), many smaller firms can now participate in these online business communities, just as the advent of the Web introduced many new companies that gave established merchants a run for their money.

As the web services revolution takes off, we'll see the industry try once again to establish business-to-business (B2B) marketplaces. In the past, these have failed for two reasons:

- Buyers wanted more control over their buying decisions; they didn't want a machine to make a buy decision based on which company came up first on the alphabetized list of search results.

- Providers wanted more control over pricing. A marketplace in which a seller's prices are shopped around online might be good for an agent trying to find the lowest online price, but it's not good for the providers, particularly when an agent might not take into account such things as a provider's ability to handle large orders, how other buyers have rated a particular provider, etc.

As web services mature, these concerns will be addressed. Through SOAP method calls to a UDDI registry, an online buyer can find all of the providers that claim to meet the buyer's needs. New web services built on top of UDDI will allow agents to get more information about providers, including their credit ratings, how quickly they've delivered orders in the past, etc. Other services can reassure providers that buyers will be able to compare different providers fairly. For example, my company may have slightly higher prices, but we don't claim to have products in stock when our warehouses are empty.

Web services promise to create an environment in which agents can evaluate various factors the way a human would, allowing those human users to focus on things more important to their businesses.

The Enterprise

Perhaps one of the most significant battles yet to emerge will be the one for dominance in the market for enterprise web services. These are the infrastructure services that will provide the foundation for delivering on the promise of agents, and more dynamic forms of e-business. These services include such things as distributed trust management and negotiation; metering, accounting, and billing; content and information management; privacy enforcement and auditing; intelligent and dynamic sourcing and materials procurement; and any number of other services that provide the bedrock of enterprise business development. It is still unclear what effect basing such core pieces of the infrastructure on web services technology will have on the marketplace, and at this point, far too early to offer any real insight. Whatever the impact, expect to see much more activity in this area in the very near future, as Internet technology companies (both old and new) vie for position in a burgeoning new market.

Web services are a young approach to writing distributed applications. As such, they are nowhere near as mature and feature-rich as mechanisms like J2EE, CORBA, and .NET. Particularly needed is functionality that enables web services to operate in the enterprise environment: security, transactions, database integration, etc. This is similar to the early days of Java—it took until Java 2 Enterprise Edition for programmers to have a set of standard extensions to Java for security, transactions, messaging, server support, databases, etc.

With web services, we see a parallel evolution. Currently, we have the technologies (e.g., SOAP, WSDL, and UDDI) for allowing web services to function. By themselves, these technologies hold great promise, but they are not quite enough for the enterprise environment.

Technologies

Although many web services standards are already defined, there are also many technologies that aren't quite there yet. We'll discuss those missing pieces, and speculate about how and when those missing pieces will be filled in.

Agents

An agent is a program that can act on your behalf. For example, I'd like to have an agent make flight, rental car, and hotel reservations for an upcoming business trip. My ideal agent would know which airlines and hotels I prefer, possibly based on previous trips to the same region. If we assume that all of the relevant data our agent might use is in a richly structured XML document, an agent might be programmed to take advantage of all sorts of information when planning a trip. For example, when flying coast to coast, Chicago is more likely to have weather delays in the winter, while Dallas is more likely to have weather delays in the summer. An agent could find out that there is a frequent-flyer promotion that would give me 10,000 extra frequent-flyer miles if I fly through Toronto. Maybe an agent could automatically check my calendar to see what time I'm free to leave the day of my flight.

Agents have been an AI pipedream for years. XML and web services have the potential to make them real, though. Here's what's needed:

- All the data involved must be encoded in XML, using well-understood vocabularies. That means we need standard tag sets for calendars, flights, airports, weather forecasts, etc. A few of those vocabularies exist, but most of them will need to be created.

- All of the various airlines, hotels, rental car companies, and other vendors must provide web services that make it easy for my agent to create, change, and cancel reservations.

- Most importantly, the agent technology must be powerful, reliable, secure, and easy to use. That's not exactly the easiest task in the world of software development. People won't use agents if they are untrustworthy, can't do much, or are too complicated for anyone without a Ph.D. in Computer Science.

Quality of Service

Web services make it possible to build applications from multiple components spread out across the Web. That's a very powerful notion, but for some applications, developers need assurance that those components will be available constantly with acceptable speeds. That means Quality of Service contracts will become even more important, simply because the Web will become a vital part of more and more applications.

Privacy

If the devices and agents in my life have been entrusted with sensitive personal data, it's crucial that they understand my wishes about privacy. It's also crucial that those devices and agents understand how various entities around the network will handle that data.

The Platform for Privacy Preferences (P3P) work done by the W3C will become increasingly important. P3P documents are machine readable, meaning that agents and other pieces of code can examine a site's privacy policy and determine whether it is acceptable.

As the importance of privacy grows (as well as the public's awareness of how little the Web actually has), other privacy technologies may be needed. For example, an agent could get a digitally signed and encrypted P3P document from a provider, obtaining a legally binding agreement that data supplied to the provider by the agent will be protected and handled a particular way.

The first step is relatively simple: create a P3P policy and associate it with your web service through links provided in the WSDL description of that service. However, this is only part of the solution. What is needed is a more comprehensive, *standardized* infrastructure for protecting information as it travels across the Web. Until such a framework is in place, the impact and usefulness of web services geared at handling personal information will be limited at best. Currently, there are no proposals on the table for doing this.

Example 9-3 shows what a P3P policy reference might look like from within a WSDL document. Here, we are stating that the *Privacy.xml* P3P policy applies to every operation defined by the HelloWorldBinding.

Example 9-3. P3P within WSDL

```
<definitions xmlns="http://schemas.xmlsoap.org/wsdl/">
   <binding name="HelloWorldBinding" type="HelloWorldPortType">
      <P3P:POLICY-REFERENCES>
         <P3P:POLICY-REF about="Privacy.xml">
            <INCLUDE>*</INCLUDE>
         </P3P:POLICY-REF>
      </P3P:POLICY-REFERENCES>
   </binding>
</definitions>
```

Security

Beyond everything else, security is paramount. It doesn't matter what a given web service can do—if it's likely to give away my credit card number, I don't want to use it. Although the base SOAP specification itself was not designed with security in mind, that doesn't mean security is impossible.

One of the examples we've discussed in this book uses IBM's XML Security Suite to encrypt the contents of SOAP envelopes as they move across a network. As web services take hold, we'll see more technologies like this, with the end result being that secure SOAP envelopes will become as common as HTML documents transmitted across the Secure Socket Layer.

The question of security demands a complex answer—one that always comes back around to point not at the technology, but at how that technology is implemented, deployed, and used. Technology companies can only do so much in the way of providing methods of expressing trust or asserting facts. Security happens only when businesses take the time to make it a priority.

Trust Management

Trust is the paramount requirement for conducting business over the Internet and will be a key component to the success of the web services architecture. Already technologies are emerging that help companies express and establish trust relationships within the context of web services. One example of such a technology is the XML Key Management Service, a standard mechanism for managing public and private keys.

Online Contracts

We've talked about contracts and other legally binding documents throughout this section, emphasizing the point that if web services are commonplace, the impact of a particular service being unavailable or providing incorrect data could be catastrophic. How will those contracts be negotiated or enforced? Clearly, having the attorneys for the service provider meet with the attorneys for the service requestor won't work in a world of applications built from conglomerations of services.

Several attempts have been made to create XML-based languages capable of describing agreements and contracts. The Collaboration Profile Protocol and Collaboration Profile Agreement (CPP-CPA) from ebXML is one such technology. Unfortunately, none of these attempts have been widely adopted and the ultimate winner is yet to emerge.

Reliable Messaging

Reliable messaging involves ensuring that both the sender and recipient of a message know whether a message was actually sent and received, and ensuring that the message was sent once and only once to the intended recipient. It is a problem that has plagued Internet application development since its inception.

The Internet is, by its very nature, unreliable. Servers that were up and running one moment may be down the next. The protocols used to connect senders and receivers have not been designed to support reliable messaging constructs, such as message identifiers and acknowledgments. Recipients of messages must be able to acknowledge that they did in fact receive a message. Senders of messages must be able to cache those messages in the event that an acknowledgment is not received and the message needs to be sent again. The fundamental technology that drives the Internet today does not support such mechanisms. Therefore, we are forced to implement new protocols and technologies that address these needs.

The importance of reliable messaging within the enterprise cannot be understated, especially when we are discussing the implementation of web services that may span across firewalls to integrate with customers, suppliers, and partners.

Within the enterprise, reliable messaging has typically been provided by proprietary solutions such as IBM's MQ Series or Microsoft Message Queue, neither of which are capable of integrating easily with each other (there are ways to make them work together, but they are painful at best).

From the context of web services, there are two ways to approach the implementation of reliable messaging:

1. You can implement reliable messaging on the application layer, meaning that the tenets of reliable messaging must be incorporated directly into the implementation of the web service.

2. You can implement reliable messaging on the transport layer, meaning that web services don't have to do anything to support the use of reliable messaging.

The first approach is implemented by products such as Microsoft's BizTalk, which uses web services technologies such as SOAP to exchange business documents (e.g., purchase orders and requests for quotes) in a reliable way.

The second approach is implemented by protocols such as IBM's Reliable HTTP (HTTP-R). HTTP-R is an implementation of standard HTTP with the addition of "endpoint managers" that ensure the reliability of the connection between the HTTP requester and the HTTP server.

A full discussion of HTTP-R and BizTalk are out of the scope of this discussion. For more information on them, see the online references in Appendix A.

Transactions

One of the key requirements for applications deployed within an enterprise is the support of transactions. Multiple operations that need to be executed in a batch must either all succeed or all fail in order for any of the operations to be valid. Currently, there is no standard (or even proposed) method for implementing and managing transactions in the web service environment.

There is a long-running debate as to whether web services require a method for doing two-phase commit style transactions. A two-phase commit transaction is one in which all of the operations in a batch must be invoked, but not finalized. Once all operations report successful invocation, they may all go back and finalize their operations. The classic example of a two-phase commit is when an application needs to write data to two different tables in a database. Both tables must be updated or neither of the tables can be updated. If the write operation on one table succeeds, but the write operation on the second table fails, the first write must be undone and an error reported back to the user.

The primary problem with two-phase commit on the Web is that when each of the participants in the transaction (for example, the two database tables in the previous example), is waiting for the final confirmation that all of the operations have been completed successfully, they must hold a lock on the resource being modified within the transaction. This lock prevents anybody else from making changes to the resource that otherwise may have caused the transactions to fail. These locks are fine when all of the resources are being managed by the same computer, but cause performance, scalability, and reliability problems in a distributed computing environment.

This problem goes back to the discussion of reliable messaging. With web services, by far the most amount of traffic will be over HTTP. Without the promise of absolute reliability, if the connection between two participants in a transaction is broken while the transaction is being carried out, neither participant can finalize their operations because neither can figure out if the other's operation completed successfully. The locks placed on the resources in question could be held indefinitely, and processing would grind to a halt.

One promising IBM research project in the transaction area is something called a *Dependency Sphere*. A Dependency Sphere, or D-Sphere for short, is a new way of looking at transactions from a distributed computing, messaging-based viewpoint. In a two-phase commit, a transaction is successful if all of the operations executed within the context of that transaction perform without generating any errors. In the D-Sphere approach, the transaction is successful if all messages sent are reliably received and acknowledged by the intended recipient of those messages.

D-Spheres applied to web services introduce a new type of web service for managing the D-Sphere transaction context. It is the job of this management service to ensure that the transaction either succeeds or fails. If it fails, a notice will be sent to the participants of the transaction so that they can make the appropriate compensating actions. The advantage to this approach is that reliable messaging is assumed (so temporary disconnections between participants are no longer a factor) and resource locks are not necessary, stopping the types of deadlocks that could occur with a two-phase commit approach.

An example of how D-Spheres might come into play within an enterprise web services environment is when a service requester must perform multiple operations on multiple services—for instance, creating a new user in CRM and ERP services at the same time. The D-Sphere could ensure that both services successfully receive and acknowledge the request to add a new user. Appendix A has pointers to more information on D-Spheres.

Licensing and Accounting Services

Part of the web services vision is the idea that software can be sold as a service. That is, companies will pay to lease access to applications rather than take on the cost of purchasing and maintaining the applications themselves. This concept can ease maintenance costs, but requires standard web services for managing licenses and monitoring the use of services.

Within the enterprise, these services will have to integrate with existing accounting and billing solutions, authentication and authorization solutions, and event and notification services in order to be meaningful and useful.

Web Services Rollout

How are web services likely to be rolled out in the marketplace? We think the most likely scenario is that customers will build web services internally, then move on to applications built with more broadly distributed web services.

We've already discussed the technologies that must be built on top of SOAP and related technologies for web services to bear more of the weight of business. Given that issues like security, authentication, and nonrepudiation are difficult to address on the Web of today, we feel that many early adopters will start by implementing web services internally. As a network administrator, I can control access to internal servers much more easily than I can control access to a public web site.

As an example, say I build a SOAP-based application for processing expense accounts. Whenever a user returns from a business trip, she uses the SOAP client application to fill out her expense report. The SOAP client sends a query to the local UDDI registry, which points the client to a WSDL document, which provides the information the client needs to access the expense account application. The head of the accounting department can move the location of the expense account application at any time, and the client will still be able to find it and access it.

Because the application is built on SOAP, it's possible (it might even be easy) to write client applications that work on almost any platform I support. Because all the clients are internal to my network, I'm less concerned about security and privacy than I would be otherwise. Because the metadata about the application is described with WSDL and stored in a UDDI registry, I can change the location, host platform, host language, etc., of the application without affecting the clients. This gives system administrators a tremendous amount of flexibility.

As more and more internal applications are built with web services, we'll see early adopters start to bring in their vendors and business partners. It's great that I can do an inter-company requisition for supplies; the obvious next step is to do requisitions from outside suppliers. That next step requires that my suppliers use SOAP (and WSDL and UDDI and . . .) as well. Applications based on web services will become commonplace, and a component architecture based on SOAP will become the dominant development paradigm.

Web Service Standardization

This appendix contains a listing of many of the better known standardization efforts (by category) currently being pursued that relate to web services in some way. A brief description is offered, but complete information is available through the information links provided.

Packaging Protocols

SOAP/XML Protocol

Originally an acronym for the "Simple Object Access Protocol," now the basis for the W3C XML Protocol effort.

Version 1.1 of the specification is available at *http://www.w3.org/tr/soap*. The Version 1.2 working draft is available at *http://www.w3.org/tr/soap12*.

More information about SOAP and the W3C XML Protocol effort can be found by visiting the W3C XML Protocol working group home page at *http://www.w3. org/2000/xp/*.

XML-RPC

The original manifestation of SOAP invented by Dave Winer of Userland software. This simple, popular protocol—while not officially a standard—has a significant, vocal user base in the open source community. Information is available at *http://www.xmlrpc.org/*.

Jabber

Jabber is both a transport protocol and a simple packaging protocol that can be used in asynchronous peer-to-peer style web services. It too is not an official standard but is building a significant user and developer base. Information can be found by visiting the Jabber home page at *http://www.jabber.org*.

DIME

The Direct Internet Message Encapsulation (DIME) protocol is "a lightweight, binary encapsulation format that can be used to encapsulate multiple application defined entities or payloads of arbitrary type as well as to provide efficient message delimiting." More information is available at *http://www.gotdotnet.com/team/xml_wsspecs/default.aspx*.

Description Protocols

WSDL

The Web Service Description Language is the de facto standard language for describing web services. It has been submitted to the W3C for standardization and a working group is being organized. WSDL replaces the previous description proposals put forth by IBM and Microsoft (NASSL and SDL respectively).

Version 1.1 of the WSDL specification can be found at *http://www.w3.org/tr/wsdl*.

DAML-S

The DARPA Agent Markup Language Ontology for web services is an academic research project for semantically describing web services. Information can be found by visiting the DAML-S home page at *http://daml.semanticweb.org*.

RDF

There has been some discussion around the fact that RDF could have "very easily" been used as a method of describing web services. Several examples have cropped up, including a demonstration of how WSDL could be modified to conform to RDF syntax. DAML-S is another example that is built completely on top of RDF. Information is available at *http://www.w3.org/rdf*.

Discovery Protocols

UDDI

The Universal Description, Discovery, and Integration initiative promises to define a standard service registry. Information can be accessed at *http://www.uddi.org*.

WS-Inspection

The Web Service Inspection Language provides an XML index for discovering the services available at a given network location. See *http://www-106.ibm.com/developerworks/webservices/library/ws-wsilspec.html*.

ebXML Registry

Part of the ebXML effort (*http://www.ebxml.org*) was to define a standard registry model for discovering business services. The approach is somewhat different, but not incompatible with UDDI, and includes many more types of information than UDDI does.

JXTA Search

The Sun-sponsored JXTA peer-to-peer services infrastructure defines a distributed search protocol for discovering content and services in a peer-to-peer architecture. Information is available by visiting *http://www.jxta.org/project/www/white_papers.html*.

Security Protocols

XML Digital Signatures

A joint W3C and IETF effort to define a standard method of representing digital signatures as XML content (*http://www.w3.org/Signature/*).

XML Encryption

A W3C effort to define a standard way of both encrypting XML content and representing encrypted data as XML content (*http://www.w3.org/Encryption/2001/*).

SAML

The Security Assertions Markup Language, being developed under the auspices of Oasis (*http://www.oasis-open.org/committees/security/*).

XKMS

The XML Key Management Service is a web service specification submitted to the W3C for implementing a service-based public key infrastructure. The XKMS specification is available at *http://www.w3.org/tr/xkms*, and additional information is at *http://www.xkms.org*.

XACML

An effort to define a standard access control mechanism for XML documents (*http://www.oasis-open.org/committees/xacml/*).

WS-Security and WS-License

These are two proposals from Microsoft defining how to carry authentication, encryption, and digital signatures within a SOAP Envelope. These specifications are used primarily by in Microsoft .NET and the .NET My Services (Hailstorm). As they have not yet been submitted to a standards body, they should be considered proprietary to Microsoft.

SOAP Security Extensions

Initially worked on as a joint effort between IBM and Microsoft, these specifications define how to carry authentication, encryption, and digital signatures within a SOAP Envelope. The Digital Signatures portion of the specification has already been submitted to the W3C with the encryption and authentication parts soon to be released and submitted. Currently, IBM's Web Services ToolKit is the only known available implementation of the SOAP Security Extensions.

Transport Protocols

HTTP

The most common transport used for web services.

Jabber

A new, XML-based asynchronous transport protocol used most frequently in peer-to-peer style applications (*http://www.jabber.org*).

BEEP

A new XML-based transport protocol being worked on by the IETF that claims a duplexed connection and asynchronous transport (*http://www.bxxp.org/*).

Reliable HTTP (HTTPr)

A new version of HTTP proposed by IBM for adding reliable messaging support to the venerable HTTP protocol. An overview and link to the specification is available at *http://www-106.ibm.com/developerworks/webservices/library/ws-phtt*.

Routing and Workflow

WSFL

The Web Services Flow Language provides a WSDL-based grammar for scripting business processes out of web services (*http://www.ibm.com/developerWorks/webservices*).

XLANG

Microsoft's own workflow scripting language for web services (*http://msdn.microsoft.com/webservices*).

WS-Routing

A Microsoft proposed mechanism for defining the route that a SOAP message must take through various intermediaries (*http://msdn.microsoft.com/library/en-us/dnsrvspec/html/ws-routing.asp*).

Programming Languages/Platforms

JAXP

Java API for XML Parsing is the Java Community Process (JCP) effort to standardized XML API's in Java (*http://java.sun.com/xml/jaxp.html*).

JAX-RPC

Java API for XML RPC is the JCP effort to standardized Java API's for using web services (*http://java.sun.com/xml/jaxrpc.html*).

JAXR

Java API for XML Registries is the JCP effort to define Java API's for discovery registries such as UDDI (*http://java.sun.com/xml/jaxr/index.html*).

JAXM

Java API for XML Messaging is the JCP effort to define Java API's for XML messaging (*http://java.sun.com/xml/jaxm/index.html*).

JSR-109

JCP effort to define how web services are to be integrated into the Java 2 Enterprise Edition architecture.

JSR-105

JCP effort to create standard Java API's for XML digital signatures (*http://www. jcp.org/jsr/detail/105.jsp*).

JSR-106

JCP effort to create standard Java API's for XML encryption (*http://www.jcp.org/ jsr/detail/106.jsp*).

JSR-110

JCP effort to define a standard Java API for WSDL (*http://www.jcp.org/jsr/detail/ 110.jsp*).

Any relevant efforts that may be missing from this list are an oversight on the authors' part, and not a reflection on the merit or importance of the work.

XML Schema Basics

The XML Schema specification is long and complex. To create SOAP and WSDL XML, you must know how XML Schema specify data types. This appendix is a quick introduction to the topic, with examples. You won't come away a Schema guru; you will be able to follow WSDL.

Simple and Complex Types

In an XML Schema, all data types are either *primitive* or *derived*. A primitive data type is one that cannot be expressed in terms of any other data type. The XML Schema specification gives the example of a *float*, "a well-defined mathematical concept that cannot be defined in terms of other data types," where an *integer* is a derivative of *decimal* data type. In this case, a float is primitive and an integer is derived.

All *primitive* data types are *atomic*. That is, the value of the data type cannot be broken down any more than it already is. For example, the number 1 is an atomic value. *Derived* data types may or may not be atomic. For example, an integer as we have already seen is a derived data type that has an atomic value. A telephone number, however, is also a derived data type whose value is not atomic; it is actually a collection of three individual atomic values.

Data types are mainly derived through *restriction* or *extension* (there are other ways, but these are the most common). In derivation through restriction, the value of the data type is restricted in some way. For example, an integer is a derivation of the decimal data type that allows for a narrower range of values than does a decimal; an integer, in other words, is allowed to contain a restricted subset of decimal values. Derivation through extension means that various restrictions on the base data type are being lifted to allow additional values that otherwise wouldn't be allowed. For example, a telephone number data type may be extended to include a country code field.

This is somewhat analogous to Java classes and objects. All Java classes are types of Java objects. All Java objects are of type `java.lang.Object`. When I create a new Java class that derives from java.lang.Object, most of the time I am adding new functionality (a new operation, a new property, etc). This is *derivation by extension*. When I override an existing operation (such as the toString( ) operation), I am *deriving by restriction*. This analogy obviously doesn't bear close examination, but may be useful nonetheless.

The authors of the XML Schema specification realized that while they had a simple and extensible data typing mechanism, they still needed to define a handful of built-in data types that reflect common use scenarios. That way, application developers wouldn't have to keep reinventing the same common data types time and time again, which would just end with the same confusion that interferes with interoperability between programming platforms. So the built-in XML Schema data types were born and we now have things like string, integer, float, boolean, URI, and time finally defined in a common way that all application platforms are capable of understanding.

These data types form a hierarchy that can be traced back to a single primitive atomic data type called anyType. All other data types used in XML Schemas derive from this single primitive type.

There are two kinds of data types that can be derived from anyType: simple types and complex types. Simple types represent all derived, atomic data types built into XML Schema. This includes things like string, integer, and boolean. Complex types represent all derived, nonatomic data types—the telephone number, for instance.

Figure B-1, adapted from the one used in the XML Schema data type specification, illustrates the hierarchy of built-in data types.

Be sure to notice that every built-in "simple type" does not derive directly from anyType, but from the anySimpleType data type, which is itself a derivative of anyType. As a rule, the XML Schema specification dictates that any derivative of anySimpleType cannot be derived by *extension*. Basically, this means the element cannot contain any attributes or child elements, in terms of expressing the data type as XML. Again, if this isn't making much sense, it will soon as we look at a few simple examples.

A quick review: we introduced the fact that there are essentially two types of data defined by an XML Schema. These include simple types, which are atomic. Single value data types that may or may not be derived through restriction from other simple types. The other type of data defined by an XML Schema is complex types, which are composed of collections of simple types and must be derived either from other complex types or simple types.

Some Examples

While the XML Schema data typing mechanism is actually quite easy to use, we have found that it is often a difficult thing to explain. Let's walk through some simple examples to clear things up.

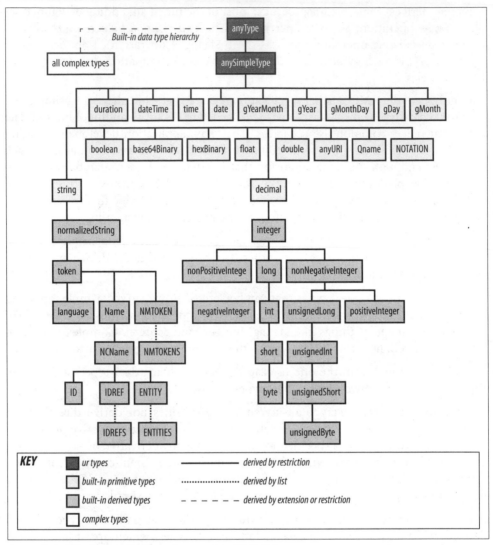

Figure B-1. Hierarchy of built-in data types in XML Schemas

Simple Types

Let's practice defining a simple data type. Say we have a productCode data type. This product code must start with two numbers followed by a dash and five more numbers. Example B-1 illustrates how to express this data type within an XML Schema.

Example B-1. productCode

```
<xsd:simpleType name="productCode">
  <xsd:restriction base="xsd:string">
```

```
    <xsd:pattern value="\d{2}-\d{5}"/>
  </xsd:restriction>
</xsd:simpleType>
```

Here, we see that productCode is a derivative of the XML Schema built-in data type string that has been restricted to only allow values that match the regular expression \d{2}-\d{5}. If we were to express an instance of this data type in XML, it would look something like Example B-2.

Example B-2. Instance of productCode

```
<pCode xsi:type="abc:productCode">12-12345</pCode>
```

In this simple example, we demonstrate several things: the productCode is a derived simple type with an atomic value, and we derive the productCode by restricting the possible set of values that its base data type (in this case string) can contain.

Now let's create an extended product code that may or may not have an additional -[a-z] (a dash followed by any lowercase letter). We could do this by deriving a new productCodeEx simpleType and changing the pattern to \d{2}-\d{5}(-[a-z]){0,1}, as in Example B-3.

Example B-3. Extended productCode

```
<xsd:simpleType name="productCodeEx">
  <xsd:restriction base="productCode">
    <xsd:pattern value="\d{2}-\d{5}(-[a-z]){0,1}"/>
  </xsd:restriction>
</xsd:simpleType>
```

Complex Types

Now you've probably got the hang of simple types and are itching to look at complex types. A complex type is any data type that contains a collection of other primitive data types. A telephone number is an example. It contains three distinct pieces of information. A telephone number complex type in XML Schema looks like Example B-4.

Example B-4. telephoneNumber type

```
<xsd:complexType name="telephoneNumber">
  <xsd:sequence>
    <xsd:element name="area">
      <xsd:simpleType>
        <xsd:restriction base="xsd:string">
          <xsd:pattern value="\d{3}"/>
        </xsd:restriction>
      </xsd:simpleType>
    </xsd:element>
    <xsd:element name="exchange">
      <xsd:simpleType>
```

Example B-4. telephoneNumber type (continued)

```
          <xsd:restriction base="xsd:string">
            <xsd:pattern value="\d{3}"/>
          </xsd:restriction>
        </xsd:simpleType>
      </xsd:element>
      <xsd:element name="number">
        <xsd:simpleType>
          <xsd:restriction base="xsd:string">
            <xsd:pattern value="\d{4}"/>
          </xsd:restriction>
        </xsd:simpleType>
      </xsd:element>
    </xsd:sequence>
</xsd:complexType>
```

The `telephoneNumber` data type consists of a sequence of three data elements, each of which are restricted derivatives of the XML Schema `string` data type. An instance of this data type would look something like Example B-5.

Example B-5. Instance of telephoneNumber

```
<telephone xsi:type="abc:telephoneNumber">
    <area>123</area>
    <exchange>123</exchange>
    <number>1234</number>
</telephone>
```

If I were to go back and create an extended version of this data type that includes a country code, I would do so by creating a new `complexType` derived by extension. This is shown in Example B-6.

Example B-6. Extending telephoneNumber to include a country code

```
<xsd:complexType name="telephoneNumberEx">
  <xsd:complexContent>
    <xsd:extension base="telephoneNumber">
      <xsd:sequence>
        <xsd:element name="countryCode">
          <xsd:simpleType>
            <xsd:restriction base="xsd:string">
              <xsd:pattern value="\d{2}"/>
            </xsd:restriction>
          </xsd:simpleType>
        </xsd:element>
      </xsd:sequence>
    </xsd:extension>
  </xsd:complexContent>
</xsd:complexType>
```

An instance of the extended telephone number would look like Example B-7.

Example B-7. Instance of extended telephoneNumber

```
<telephone xsi:type="abc:telephoneNumber">
   <area>123</area>
   <exchange>123</exchange>
   <number>1234</number>
   <countryCode>01</countryCode>
</telephone>
```

Notice that the countryCode element is at the end of the sequence of data elements. This is due to the way that XML Schema enforces element ordering within data types. Because we are deriving by extension, all new elements defined in the telephoneNumberEx data type have to appear after the elements defined in its base telephoneNumber data type. If we wanted countryCode to appear first in the sequence, we would actually have to derive by restriction and redeclare each of the data elements, as in Example B-8.

Example B-8. restricted telephoneNumber

```
<xsd:complexType name="telephoneNumberEx">
    <xsd:complexContent>
      <xsd:restriction base="telephoneNumber">
        <xsd:sequence>
          <xsd:element name="countryCode">
            <xsd:simpleType>
              <xsd:restriction base="xsd:string">
                <xsd:pattern value="\d{2}"/>
              </xsd:restriction>
            </xsd:simpleType>
          </xsd:element>
          <xsd:element name="area">
            <xsd:simpleType>
              <xsd:restriction base="xsd:string">
                <xsd:pattern value="\d{3}"/>
              </xsd:restriction>
            </xsd:simpleType>
          </xsd:element>
          <xsd:element name="exchange">
            <xsd:simpleType>
              <xsd:restriction base="xsd:string">
                <xsd:pattern value="\d{3}"/>
              </xsd:restriction>
            </xsd:simpleType>
          </xsd:element>
          <xsd:element name="number">
            <xsd:simpleType>
              <xsd:restriction base="xsd:string">
                <xsd:pattern value="\d{4}"/>
              </xsd:restriction>
            </xsd:simpleType>
          </xsd:element>
        </xsd:sequence>
      </xsd:restriction>
```

Example B-8. restricted telephoneNumber (continued)

```
    </xsd:complexContent>
  </xsd:complexType>
```

And that's the basics of defining data types with XML Schemas. There are plenty of details that we are leaving out. It's worthwhile taking the time to learn more about XML Schemas.

XML Spy

XML Spy is perhaps the best product available for working with XML Schemas. Its XML development environment allows you to visually design XML Schemas quickly and easily, hiding away the syntactic complexity that normally trips people up. Figure B-2 shows a screenshot of XML Spy's visual schema editor.

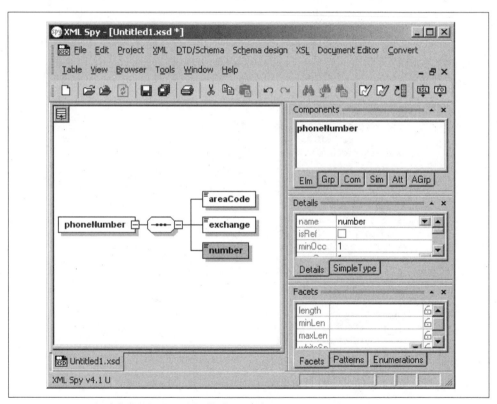

Figure B-2. A view of the XML Spy visual schema editor

XML Spy is a commercial product available from *http://www.xmlspy.com*. Though it's not cheap (a few hundred U.S. dollars at the time of this writing), it is well worth the price for serious developers.

Code Listings

This appendix contains the source code to the many example programs developed throughout the book. To explain the programs, we often presented them piece by piece, sometimes omitting repetitive sections. Examples C-1 through C-54 are the full programs: intact, unabridged, in all their glory. You can also download them from the web at *http://www.oreilly.com/catalog/progwebsoap/*.

Hello World in Perl

Example C-1. HelloWorld.pm (server)

```
package Hello;
sub sayHello {
  shift;
  my $self = "Hello " . shift;
}
1;
```

Example C-2. HelloWorld.cgi (server)

```
use SOAP::Transport::HTTP;
SOAP::Transport::HTTP::CGI
 -> dispatch_to('Hello::(?:sayHello)')
 -> handle
;
```

Example C-3. HelloWorldClient.pm (client)

```
use SOAP::Lite;
my $name = shift;
print "\n\nCalling the SOAP Server to say hello\n\n";
print "The SOAP Server says: ";
print SOAP::Lite
  -> uri('urn:Example1')
  -> proxy('http://localhost/cgi-bin/helloworld.cgi')
  -> sayHello($name)
  -> result . "\n\n";
```

Hello World Client in Visual Basic

Example C-4. Helloworld.vbs (client)

```
Dim x, h
Set x = CreateObject("MSXML2.DOMDocument")

x.loadXML "<s:Envelope   8
  xmlns:s='http://schemas.xmlsoap.org/soap/envelope/'8
  xmlns:xsi='http://www.w3.org/1999/XMLSchema-instance'    8
  xmlns:xsd='http://www.w3.org/1999/XMLSchema'><s:Body><m:sayHello 8
  xmlns:m='urn:Example1'><name xsi:type='xsd:string'>James</name> 8
  </m:sayHello></s:Body></s:Envelope>"8

msgbox x.xml, , "Input SOAP Message"
Set h = CreateObject("Microsoft.XMLHTTP")
h.open "POST", "http://localhost/cgi-bin/helloworld.cgi"
h.send (x)
while h.readyState <> 4
wend
msgbox h.responseText,,"Output SOAP Message"
```

Hello World over Jabber

Example C-5. HelloWorldJabber.pm (server)

```
use SOAP::Transport::JABBER;
my $server = SOAP::Transport::JABBER::Server
  -> new('jabber://soaplite_server:soapliteserver@jabber.org:5222')
  -> dispatch_to('Hello')
;
print "SOAP Jabber Server Started\n";
do { $server->handle } while sleep 1;
```

Example C-6. HelloWorldJabberClient.pm (client)

```
use SOAP::Lite;
my $name = shift;
print "\n\nCalling the SOAP Server to say hello\n\n";
print "The SOAP Server says: ";
print SOAP::Lite
  -> uri('urn:Example1')
  -> proxy('jabber://soaplite_client:soapliteclient@jabber.org:5222/' .
           'soaplite_server@jabber.org/')
  -> sayHello($name)
  -> result . "\n\n";
```

Hello World in Java

Example C-7. Hello.java (server)

```
package samples;
public class Hello {
```

Example C-7. Hello.java (server) (continued)

```java
   public String sayHello(String name) {
       return "Hello " + name;
   }
}
```

Example C-8. Hello.java Deployment Descriptor (server)

```xml
<dd:service xmlns:dd="http://xml.apache.org/xml-soap/deployment" id="urn:Example1">
 <dd:provider type="java"
              scope="Application"
              methods="sayHello">
   <dd:java class="samples.Hello"
            static="false" />
 </dd:provider>
 <dd:faultListener>
  org.apache.soap.server.DOMFaultListener
 </dd:faultListener>
 <dd:mappings />
</dd:service>
```

Example C-9. Hello_Client.java (client)

```java
import java.io.*;
import java.net.*;
import java.util.*;
import org.apache.soap.*;
import org.apache.soap.rpc.*;

public class Hello_client {

  public static void main (String[] args)
       throws Exception {

    System.out.println("\n\nCalling the SOAP Server to say hello\n\n");
    URL url = new URL (args[0]);
    String name = args[1];

    Call call = new Call ();
    call.setTargetObjectURI("urn:Example1");
    call.setMethodName("sayHello");
    call.setEncodingStyleURI(Constants.NS_URI_SOAP_ENC;);
    Vector params = new Vector ();
    params.addElement (new Parameter("name", String.class, name, null));
    call.setParams (params);

    System.out.print("The SOAP Server says: ");

    Response resp = call.invoke(url, "");

    if (resp.generatedFault ()) {
      Fault fault = resp.getFault ();
      System.out.println ("\nOuch, the call failed: ");
      System.out.println ("  Fault Code   = " + fault.getFaultCode ());
      System.out.println ("  Fault String = " + fault.getFaultString ());
```

Example C-9. Hello_Client.java (client) (continued)

```
    } else {
      Parameter result = resp.getReturnValue ();
      System.out.print(result.getValue ());
      System.out.println();
    }
  }
}
```

Hello, World in C# on .NET

Example C-10. Helloworld.asmx (server)

```
<%@ WebService Language="C#" Class="Example1" %>

using System.Web.Services;

[WebService(Namespace="urn:Example1")]
public class Example1 {

    [ WebMethod ]
    public string sayHello(string name) {
        return "Hello " + name;
    }

}
```

Example C-11. Helloworld.cs (client)

```
// HelloWorld.cs

using System.Diagnostics;
using System.Xml.Serialization;
using System;
using System.Web.Services.Protocols;
using System.Web.Services;

[System.Web.Services.WebServiceBindingAttribute(
     Name="Example1Soap",
     Namespace="urn:Example1")]
public class Example1 :
            System.Web.Services.Protocols.SoapHttpClientProtocol {

    public Example1() {
        this.Url = "http://localhost/helloworld.asmx ";
    }

    [System.Web.Services.Protocols.SoapDocumentMethodAttribute(
        "urn:Example1/sayHello",
        RequestNamespace="urn:Example1",
        ResponseNamespace="urn:Example1",
        Use=System.Web.Services.Description.SoapBindingUse.Literal,
```

Example C-11. Helloworld.cs (client) (continued)

```
        ParameterStyle=System.Web.Services.Protocols.SoapParameterStyle.Wrapped)]
    public string sayHello(string name) {
        object[] results = this.Invoke("sayHello",
                                    new object[] {name});
        return ((string)(results[0]));
    }

    public static void Main(string[] args) {
        Console.WriteLine("Calling the SOAP Server to say hello");
        Example1 example1 = new Example1();
        Console.WriteLine("The SOAP Server says: " +
                        example1.sayHello(args[0]));
    }
}
```

Example C-12. Modified Perl HelloWorld_Client.pm for use with .NET (client)

```
use SOAP::Lite;

my $name = shift;

print "\n\nCalling the SOAP Server to say hello\n\n";

print "The SOAP Server says: ";

print SOAP::Lite
  -> uri('urn:Example1')
  -> on_action(sub{sprintf '%s/%s', @_ })
  -> proxy('http://localhost:8080/helloworld/example1.asmx')
  -> sayHello(SOAP::Data->name(name => $name->type->('string')->uri('urn:Example1'))
  -> result . "\n\n";
```

Publisher Service

Example C-13. Publisher.pm (server)

```
package Publisher;

use strict;

package Publisher::DB;

use DBI;
use vars qw($CONNECT);

$CONNECT = "DBI:CSV:f_dir=/home/soaplite/book;csv_sep_char=\0";

my $dbh;

sub dbh {
  shift;
```

Example C-13. Publisher.pm (server) (continued)

```perl
  unless ($dbh) {
    $dbh = DBI->connect(shift || $CONNECT);
    $dbh->{'RaiseError'} = 1;
  }
  return $dbh;
}

END { $dbh->disconnect if $dbh; }

sub create {
  my $dbh = shift->dbh;

  $dbh->do($_) foreach split /;/, '

  CREATE TABLE members (
    memberID   integer,
    email      char(100),
    password   char(25),
    firstName  char(50),
    lastName   char(50),
    title      char(50),
    company    char(50),
    url        char(255),
    subscribed integer
  );

  CREATE TABLE items (
    itemIDinteger,
    memberIDinteger,
    type          integer,
    title  char(255),
    description char(512),
    postStampinteger
  )

';

}

sub insert_member {
  my $dbh = shift->dbh;
  my $newMemberID = 1 + $dbh->selectrow_array(
        "SELECT memberID FROM members ORDER BY memberID DESC");

  my %parameters = (@_, memberID => $newMemberID, subscribed => 0);
  my $names = join ', ', keys %parameters;
  my $placeholders = join ', ', ('?') x keys %parameters;

  $dbh->do("INSERT INTO members ($names) VALUES ($placeholders)", {},
          values %parameters);
  return $newMemberID;
}
```

Example C-13. Publisher.pm (server) (continued)

```perl
sub select_member {
  my $dbh = shift->dbh;
  my %parameters = @_;

  my $where = join ' AND ', map {"$_ = ?"} keys %parameters;
  $where = "WHERE $where" if $where;

  # returns row in array context and first element (memberID) in scalar
  return $dbh->selectrow_array("SELECT * FROM members $where", {},
                               values %parameters);
}

sub update_member {
  my $dbh = shift->dbh;
  my($memberID, %parameters) = @_;

  my $set = join ', ', map {"$_ = ?"} keys %parameters;

  $dbh->do("UPDATE members SET $set WHERE memberID = ?", {},
           values %parameters, $memberID);
  return $memberID;
}

sub insert_item {
  my $dbh = shift->dbh;
  my $newItemID = 1 + $dbh->selectrow_array(
           "SELECT itemID FROM items ORDER BY itemID DESC");

  my %parameters = (@_, itemID => $newItemID, postStamp => time());
  my $names = join ', ', keys %parameters;
  my $placeholders = join ', ', ('?') x keys %parameters;

  $dbh->do("INSERT INTO items ($names) VALUES ($placeholders)", {},
           values %parameters);

  return $newItemID;
}

sub select_item {
  my $dbh = shift->dbh;
  my %parameters = @_;

  my $where = join ' AND ', map {"$_ = ?"} keys %parameters;

  return $dbh->selectrow_array("SELECT * FROM items WHERE $where", {},
                               values %parameters);
}

sub select_all_items {
  my $dbh = shift->dbh;
  my %parameters = @_;
```

Example C-13. Publisher.pm (server) (continued)

```perl
  my $where = join ' AND ', map {"$_ = ?"} keys %parameters;
  $where = "WHERE $where" if $where;

  return $dbh->selectall_arrayref("SELECT type, title, description,
      postStamp, memberID FROM items $where", {}, values %parameters);
}

sub delete_item {
  my $dbh = shift->dbh;
  my $itemID = shift;

  $dbh->do('DELETE FROM items WHERE itemID = ?', {}, $itemID);
  return $itemID;
}


# ========================================================================

package Publisher;

use POSIX qw(strftime);

@Publisher::ISA = qw(SOAP::Server::Parameters);

# ------------------------------------------------------------------------
# private functions
# ------------------------------------------------------------------------

use Digest::MD5 qw(md5);

my $calculateAuthInfo = sub {
  return md5(join '', 'unique (yet persistent) string', @_);
};

my $checkAuthInfo = sub {
  my $authInfo = shift;
  my $signature = $calculateAuthInfo->(@{$authInfo}{qw(memberID email
                                       time)});
  die "Authentication information is not valid\n" if $signature ne
        $authInfo->{signature};
  die "Authentication information is expired\n"
  if time() > $authInfo->{time};
  return $authInfo->{memberID};
};

my $makeAuthInfo = sub {
  my($memberID, $email) = @_;
  my $time = time()+20*60;
  my $signature = $calculateAuthInfo->($memberID, $email, $time);
  return +{memberID => $memberID, time => $time, email => $email,
        signature => $signature};
};
```

Example C-13. Publisher.pm (server) (continued)

```perl
# -----------------------------------------------------------------------
# public functions
# -----------------------------------------------------------------------

sub register {
  my $self = shift;
  my $envelope = pop;
  my %parameters = %{$envelope->method() || {}};

  die "Wrong parameters: register(email, password, firstName, lastName [,
       title][, company][, url])\n"
    unless 4 == map {defined} @parameters{qw(email password firstName
               lastName)};

  my $email = $parameters{email};
  die "Member with email ($email) already registered\n"
    if Publisher::DB->select_member(email => $email);
  return Publisher::DB->insert_member(%parameters);
}

sub modify {
  my $self = shift;
  my $envelope = pop;
  my %parameters = %{$envelope->method() || {}};

  my $memberID = $checkAuthInfo->($envelope->valueof('//authInfo'));
  Publisher::DB->update_member($memberID, %parameters);
  return;
}

sub login {
  my $self = shift;
  my %parameters = %{pop->method() || {}};

  my $email = $parameters{email};
  my $memberID = Publisher::DB->select_member(email => $email,
                                              password => $parameters{password});
  die "Credentials are wrong\n" unless $memberID;
  return bless $makeAuthInfo->($memberID, $email) => 'authInfo';
}

sub subscribe {
  my $self = shift;
  my $memberID = $checkAuthInfo->(pop->valueof('//authInfo'));

  Publisher::DB->update_member($memberID, subscribed => 1);
  return;
}

sub unsubscribe {
  my $self = shift;
  my $memberID = $checkAuthInfo->(pop->valueof('//authInfo'));
```

Example C-13. Publisher.pm (server) (continued)

```perl
  Publisher::DB->update_member($memberID, subscribed => 0);
  return;
}

my %type2code = (news => 1, article => 2, resource => 3);
my %code2type = reverse %type2code;

sub postItem {
  my $self = shift;
  my $envelope = pop;
  my $memberID = $checkAuthInfo->($envelope->valueof('//authInfo'));
  my %parameters = %{$envelope->method() || {}};

  die "Wrong parameter(s): postItem(type, title, description)\n"
    unless 3 == map {defined} @parameters{qw(type title description)};

  $parameters{type} = $type2code{lc $parameters{type}}
                                or die "Wrong type of item ($parameters{type})\n";
  return Publisher::DB->insert_item(memberID => $memberID, %parameters);
}

sub removeItem {
  my $self = shift;
  my $memberID = $checkAuthInfo->(pop->valueof('//authInfo'));
  die "Wrong parameter(s): removeItem(itemID)\n" unless @_ == 1;

  my $itemID = shift;
  die "Specified item ($itemID) can't be found or removed\n"
    unless Publisher::DB->select_item(memberID => $memberID, itemID => $itemID);
  Publisher::DB->delete_item($itemID);
  return;
}

my $browse = sub {
  my $envelope = pop;
  my %parameters = %{$envelope->method() || {}};

  my($type, $format, $maxRows, $query) = @parameters{qw(type format maxRows query)};
  $type = {all => 'all', %type2code}->{lc($type) || 'all'} or
    die "Wrong type of item ($type)\n";

  $maxRows ||= 25;
  $format ||= 'XML';
  my $items = Publisher::DB->select_all_items($type ne 'all' ? (type => $type) : ());
  my %members;
  my @items = map {
    my($type, $title, $description, $date, $memberID) = @$_;
    my($email, $firstName, $lastName) = @{
      $members{$memberID} ||= [Publisher::DB->select_member(memberID => $memberID)]
    }[1,3,4];
    +{
      $format =~ /^XML/ ? (
```

Example C-13. Publisher.pm (server) (continued)

```
        type        => $code2type{$type},
        title       => $title,
        description => $description,
        date        => strftime("%Y-%m-%d", gmtime($date)),
        creator     => "$firstName $lastName ($email)"
    ) : (
        category    => $code2type{$type},
        title       => "$title by $firstName $lastName ($email) on "
                       . strftime("%Y-%m-%d", gmtime($date)),
        description => $description,
    )
  }
  } @{$items}[0..(!$query && $maxRows <= $#$items ? $maxRows-1 : $#$items)];
  if ($query) {
    my $regexp = join '', map {
      /\s+and\s+/io ? '&&' : /\s+or\s+/io ? '||' : /[()]/ ? $_ : $_ ? '/' . quotemeta($_)
. '/o' : ''
    } split /(\(|\))|\s+and\s+|\s+or\s+)/io, $query;
    eval "*checkfor = sub { for (\@_) { return 1 if $regexp; } return }" or die;
    @items = grep {checkfor(values %$_)} @items;
    splice(@items, $maxRows <= $#items ? $maxRows : $#items+1);
  }
  return $format =~ /^(XML|RSS)str$/
    ? SOAP::Serializer
        -> autotype(0)
        -> readable(1)
        -> serialize(SOAP::Data->name(($1 eq 'XML' ? 'itemList' : 'channel')
                     => \SOAP::Data->name(item => @items)))
    : [@items];
};

sub browse {
  my $self = shift;
  return SOAP::Data->name(browse => $browse->(@_));
}

sub search {
  my $self = shift;
  return SOAP::Data->name(search => $browse->(@_));
}

# =================================================================

1;
```

Example C-14. Publisher.daemon (server)

```
#!/bin/perl

use SOAP::Transport::HTTP;

use Publisher;
```

Example C-14. Publisher.daemon (server) (continued)

```
$Publisher::DB::CONNECT =
   "DBI:CSV:f_dir=d:/book;csv_sep_char=\0";
$authinfo = 'http://www.soaplite.com/authInfo';

my $server = SOAP::Transport::HTTP::CGI
  -> dispatch_to('Publisher');

$server->serializer->maptype({authInfo => $authinfo});
$server->handle;
```

Example C-15. Client.java (client)

```java
import java.io.*;
import java.net.*;
import java.util.*;

import javax.xml.parsers.DocumentBuilderFactory;
import javax.xml.parsers.DocumentBuilder;
import org.w3c.dom.*;

import org.apache.soap.util.xml.*;
import org.apache.soap.*;
import org.apache.soap.encoding.*;
import org.apache.soap.encoding.soapenc.*;
import org.apache.soap.rpc.*;


public class Client {

  private URL url;
  private String uri;
  private authInfo authInfo;

  public Client (String url, String uri) throws Exception {
    try {
      this.uri = uri;
      this.url = new URL(url);
    } catch (Exception e) {
      throw new Exception(e.getMessage());
    }
  }

  public Header makeAuthHeader (authInfo auth) throws Exception {
    if (auth == null) {
        throw new Exception(
            "Oops, you are not logged in. Please login first"); }
    DocumentBuilderFactory dbf = DocumentBuilderFactory.newInstance();
    dbf.setNamespaceAware(true);
    dbf.setValidating(false);
    DocumentBuilder db = dbf.newDocumentBuilder();
```

Example C-15. Client.java (client) (continued)

```java
    Document doc = db.newDocument();
    Element authEl =
        doc.createElementNS("http://www.soaplite.com/authInfo",
                            "auth:authInfo");
    Element emailEl = doc.createElement("email");
    emailEl.appendChild(doc.createTextNode(auth.getEmail()));
    Element signatureEl = doc.createElement("signature");
    signatureEl.setAttribute("xmlns:enc", Constants.NS_URI_SOAP_ENC);
    signatureEl.setAttribute("xsi:type", "enc:base64");
    signatureEl.appendChild(doc.createTextNode(
        Base64.encode(auth.getSignature())));
    Element memberIdEl = doc.createElement("memberID");
    memberIdEl.appendChild(doc.createTextNode(String.valueOf(
        auth.getMemberID())));
    Element timeEl = doc.createElement("time");
    timeEl.appendChild(doc.createTextNode(String.valueOf(
        auth.getTime())));
    authEl.appendChild(emailEl);
    authEl.appendChild(signatureEl);
    authEl.appendChild(memberIdEl);
    authEl.appendChild(timeEl);
    Vector headerEntries = new Vector();
    headerEntries.add(authEl);
    Header header = new Header();
    header.setHeaderEntries(headerEntries);
    return header;
}

private Call initCall () {
  Call call = new Call();
  call.setEncodingStyleURI(Constants.NS_URI_SOAP_ENC);
  call.setTargetObjectURI(uri);
  return call;
}

private Object invokeCall (Call call) throws Exception {
  try {
    Response response = call.invoke(url, "");

    if (!response.generatedFault()) {
      return response.getReturnValue() == null
        ? null : response.getReturnValue().getValue();
    } else {
      Fault f = response.getFault();
      throw new Exception("Fault = " + f.getFaultCode() + ", " +
                          f.getFaultString());
    }
  } catch (SOAPException e) {
    throw new Exception("SOAPException = " + e.getFaultCode() + ", " +
                        e.getMessage());
  }
}
```

Example C-15. Client.java (client) (continued)

```java
public void login (String email, String password) throws Exception {
  Call call = initCall();

  SOAPMappingRegistry smr = new SOAPMappingRegistry();
  BeanSerializer beanSer = new BeanSerializer();
  smr.mapTypes(Constants.NS_URI_SOAP_ENC,
               new QName("http://www.soaplite.com/Publisher",
                         "authInfo"),
               authInfo.class, beanSer, beanSer);

  Vector params = new Vector ();
  params.add(new Parameter("email", String.class, email, null));
  params.add(new Parameter("password", String.class, password, null));
  call.setParams(params);
  call.setMethodName("login");
  call.setSOAPMappingRegistry(smr);

  authInfo = (authInfo) invokeCall(call);

  System.out.println(authInfo.getEmail() + " logged in.");
}

public void register (String email, String password,
                      String firstName, String lastName,
                      String title, String company, String url)
                      throws Exception {
  Call call = initCall();

  Vector params = new Vector ();
  params.add(new Parameter("email", String.class, email, null));
  params.add(new Parameter("password", String.class, password, null));
  params.add(new Parameter("firstName", String.class, firstName, null));
  params.add(new Parameter("lastName", String.class, lastName, null));
  if (url != null)
      params.add(new Parameter("url", String.class, url, null));
  if (title != null)
      params.add(new Parameter("title", String.class, title, null));
  if (company != null)
      params.add(new Parameter("company", String.class, company, null));
  call.setParams(params);
  call.setMethodName("register");
  invokeCall(call);
  System.out.println("Registered.");
}

public void postItem (String type, String title,
                      String description)
                      throws Exception {
  Call call = initCall();
  Vector params = new Vector ();
  params.add(new Parameter("type", String.class, type, null));
```

Example C-15. Client.java (client) (continued)

```
    params.add(new Parameter("title", String.class, title, null));
    params.add(new Parameter("description", String.class, description,
                             null));
    call.setParams(params);
    call.setMethodName("postItem");
    call.setHeader(makeAuthHeader(authInfo));
    Integer itemID = (Integer)invokeCall(call);
    System.out.println("Posted item " + itemID + ".");
  }

  public void removeItem (Integer itemID) throws Exception {
    Call call = initCall();
    Vector params = new Vector ();
    params.add(new Parameter("itemID", Integer.class, itemID, null));
    call.setParams(params);
    call.setMethodName("removeItem");
    call.setHeader(makeAuthHeader(authInfo));
    invokeCall(call);
    System.out.println("Removed item " + itemID + ".");
  }

  public void browse (String type, String format,
                      Integer maxRows)
                      throws Exception {
    Call call = initCall();
    Vector params = new Vector ();
    params.add(new Parameter("format", String.class, format != null ?
               format : "XMLstr", null));
    if (type != null)    params.add(new Parameter("type", String.class,
               type, null));
    if (maxRows != null) params.add(new Parameter("maxRows",
               Integer.class, maxRows, null));
    call.setParams(params);
    call.setMethodName("browse");
    System.out.println((String)invokeCall(call));
  }

  public static void main(String[] args) {

    String myname = Client.class.getName();

    if (args.length < 1) {
      System.err.println("Usage:\n  java " + myname +
        " SOAP-router-URL");
      System.exit (1);
    }

    try {
      Client client = new Client(args[0],
                      "http://www.soaplite.com/Publisher");

      InputStream in = System.in;
      InputStreamReader isr = new InputStreamReader(in);
```

Example C-15. Client.java (client) (continued)

```java
      BufferedReader br = new BufferedReader(isr);
      String action = null;
      while (!("quit".equals(action))) {
         System.out.print("> ");
         action = br.readLine();


         if ("register".equals(action)) {

            String email = null;
            String password = null;
            String firstName = null;
            String lastName = null;
            String title = null;
            String company = null;
            String url = null;

            System.out.print("\n\nIn order to register, you must answer the following
questions.");
            System.out.print("\n\nWhat is your email address: ");
            email = br.readLine();
            System.out.print("\nWhat is your first name: ");
            firstName = br.readLine();
            System.out.print("\nWhat is your last name: ");
            lastName = br.readLine();
            System.out.print("\nWhat is your job title: ");
            title = br.readLine();
            System.out.print("\nWhat company do you work for: ");
            company = br.readLine();
            System.out.print("\nWhat is your company or personal URL: ");
            url = br.readLine();
            System.out.print("\nFinally, what password do you want to use: ");
            password = br.readLine();

            System.out.println("\nAttempting to register....");
            client.register(email, password, firstName,
                           lastName, title, company, url);
            System.out.println();
         }

         if ("login".equals(action)) {
            String id = null;
            String pwd = null;

            System.out.print("\n\nWhat is your user id: ");
            id = br.readLine();
            System.out.print("\nWhat is your password: ");
            pwd = br.readLine();

            System.out.println("\nAttempting to login....");
            client.login(id,pwd);
            System.out.println();
         }
```

Example C-15. Client.java (client) (continued)

```java
if ("post".equals(action)) {

    String type = null;
    String title = null;
    String desc = null;

    System.out.print("\n\nWhat type of item [1 = News, 2 = Article,
    3 = Resource]: ");
    type = br.readLine();
    if (type.equals("1")) type = "news";
    if (type.equals("2")) type = "article";
    if (type.equals("3")) type = "resource";
    System.out.println("\nWhat is the title: ");
    title = br.readLine();
    System.out.println("\nWhat is the description: ");
    desc = br.readLine();

    System.out.println("\nAttempting to post item....");
    client.postItem(type, title, desc);
    System.out.println();
}

if ("remove".equals(action)) {
    System.out.print("\n\nPlease enter the numeric ID of the item to remove: ");
    String id = br.readLine();
    try {
        System.out.println("\nAttempting to remove item....");
        client.removeItem(Integer.valueOf(id));
    } catch (Exception ex) {
        System.out.println("\nCould not remove item!");
    }
    System.out.println();
}

if ("browse".equals(action)) {
    System.out.print("\n\nWhat is the maximum number of rows to return (blank to
return all): ");
    String mRows = br.readLine();
    System.out.print("\nType of resource to browse ([0] = All, [1] = News,
    [2] = Article, [3] = Resource): ");
    String type = br.readLine();
    if (type.equals("0")) type = "all";
    if (type.equals("1")) type = "news";
    if (type.equals("2")) type = "article";
    if (type.equals("3")) type = "resource";
    System.out.print("\nHow would you like to see the results ([1] = XML,
    [2] = RSS): ");
    String format = br.readLine();
    if (format.equals("1")) format = "XMLstr";
    if (format.equals("2")) format = "RSSstr";
```

Example C-15. Client.java (client) (continued)

```
            System.out.println("\nAttempting to browse....");
            try {
                Integer ival = null;
                if (!("".equals(mRows))) {
                    ival = Integer.valueOf(mRows);
                }
                client.browse(type, format, ival);
            } catch (Exception ex) {
              System.out.println(ex);
              System.out.println("\nCould not browse!");
            }
        }

        if ("help".equals(action)) {
            System.out.println("\nActions: register | login | post | remove | browse");
        }
      }
    } catch (Exception e) {
      System.err.println("Caught Exception: " + e.getMessage());
    }
  }
}
```

This is WSDL for the Hello World service.

Example C-16. WSDL for the Hello World service

```
<?xml version="1.0" encoding="UTF-8"?>
<wsdl:definitions    name="HelloWorld"
          targetNamespace="urn:HelloWorld"
          xmlns:tns="urn:HelloWorld"
          xmlns:soap="http://schemas.xmlsoap.org/wsdl/soap/"
          xmlns:wsdl="http://schemas.xmlsoap.org/wsdl/">
  <wsdl:message name="sayHello_IN">
    <part name="name" type="xsd:string" />
  </wsdl:message>
  <wsdl:message name="sayHello_OUT">
    <part name="greeting" type="xsd:string" />
  </wsdl:message>
  <wsdl:portType name="HelloWorldInterface">
    <wsdl:operation name="sayHello" >
      <wsdl:input message="tns:sayHello_IN" />
      <wsdl:output message="tns:sayHello_OUT" />
    </wsdl:operation>
  </wsdl:portType>
  <wsdl:binding name="HelloWorldBinding"
    type="tns:HelloWorldInterface">
    <soap:binding style="rpc"
      transport="http://schemas.xmlsoap.org/soap/http" />
    <wsdl:operation name="sayHello">
     <soap:operation soapAction="urn:Hello" />
     <wsdl:input>
      <soap:body use="encoded"
```

Example C-16. WSDL for the Hello World service (continued)

```
        namespace="urn:Hello"
        encodingStyle="http://schemas.xmlsoap.org/soap/encoding/" />
    </wsdl:input>
    <wsdl:output>
     <soap:body use="encoded"
       namespace="urn:Hello"
       encodingStyle="http://schemas.xmlsoap.org/soap/encoding/" />
    </wsdl:output>
   </wsdl:operation>
  </wsdl:binding>
  <wsdl:service name="HelloWorldService">
    <wsdl:port name="Perl_HelloWorld" binding="tns:Binding_Name">
      <soap:address
        location="http://localhost/cgi-bin/hello.cgi" />
    </wsdl:port>
    <wsdl:port name="Java_HelloWorld" binding="tns:Binding_Name">
      <soap:address
        location="http://localhost:8080/soap/servlet/rpcrouter" />
    </wsdl:port>
    <wsdl:port name="NET_HelloWorld" binding="tns:Binding_Name">
      <soap:address
        location="http://localhost/helloworld.asmx" />
    </wsdl:port>
  </wsdl:service>
</wsdl:definitions>
```

Example C-17. Authinfo.java (client)

```
public class authInfo {
  private int memberID;
  private long time;
  private String email;
  private byte [] signature;

  public authInfo() { }

  public authInfo(int memberID, long time, String email, byte[] signature) {
    this.memberID = memberID;
    this.time = time;
    this.email = email;
    this.signature = signature;
  }

  public void setMemberID(int memberID) {
    this.memberID = memberID;
  }

  public int getMemberID() {
    return memberID;
  }

  public void setTime(long time) {
    this.time = time;
  }
```

Example C-17. Authinfo.java (client) (continued)

```java
  public long getTime() {
    return time;
  }

  public void setEmail(String email) {
    this.email = email;
  }

  public String getEmail() {
    return email;
  }

  public void setSignature(byte [] signature) {
    this.signature = signature;
  }

  public byte [] getSignature() {
    return signature;
  }

  public String toString() {
    return "[" + memberID + "] " + email;
  }
}
```

SAML Generation

Example C-18. Assertion.java

```java
package saml;

import java.util.Date;
import org.w3c.dom.Element;
import org.w3c.dom.Document;

public abstract class Assertion implements AssertionAbstractType {

    private IDType assertionID;
    private String issuer;
    private Date issueInstant;

    public String getVersion() {
        return "1.0";
    }

    public IDType getAssertionID() {
        return this.assertionID;
    }

    public void setAssertionID(IDType assertionID) {
        this.assertionID = assertionID;
    }
```

Example C-18. Assertion.java (continued)

```java
    public String getIssuer() {
        return this.issuer;
    }

    public void setIssuer(String issuer) {
        this.issuer = issuer;
    }

    public Date getIssueInstant() {
        return this.issueInstant;
    }

    public void setIssueInstant(Date issueInstant) {
        this.issueInstant = issueInstant;
    }

    protected void serializeAttributes(Element e) {
        e.setAttribute("Version", getVersion());
        if (assertionID != null)
            e.setAttribute("AssertionID", assertionID.getText());
        if (issuer != null)
            e.setAttribute("Issuer", issuer);
        if (issueInstant != null)
            e.setAttribute("IssueInstant", issueInstant.toString());
    }

    protected void deserializeAttributes(Element source) {
        String s1 = source.getAttribute("AssertionID");
        String s2 = source.getAttribute("Issuer");
        String s3 = source.getAttribute("IssueInstant");
        if (s1 != null) setAssertionID(new IDType(s1));
        if (s2 != null) setIssuer(s2);
        if (s3 != null) setIssueInstant(new Date(s3));
    }

    public abstract void serialize(Element parent);
}
```

Example C-19. AssertionAbstractType.java

```java
package saml;

import java.util.Date;

public interface AssertionAbstractType {

    public String getVersion();
    public IDType getAssertionID();
    public void setAssertionID(IDType assertionID);
    public String getIssuer();
    public void setIssuer(String issuer);
    public Date getIssueInstant();
    public void setIssueInstant(Date issueInstant);
}
```

Example C-20. AssertionFactory.java

```java
package saml;

import java.util.Date;

public class AssertionFactory {

    public static AuthenticationAssertion newInstance(String id,
                                                      String issuerName,
                                                      Date issueInstant,
                                                      String name,
                                                      String domain,
                                                      String method,
                                                      Date authInstant,
                                                      String ip,
                                                      String dns) {

        AuthenticationAssertion aa = new AuthenticationAssertion();
        IDType aid = new IDType(id);
        aa.setAssertionID(aid);
        aa.setIssuer(issuerName);
        aa.setIssueInstant(issueInstant);
        Subject subject = new Subject();
        {
            NameIdentifier ni = new NameIdentifier();
            ni.setName(name);
            ni.setSecurityDomain(domain);
            subject.setNameIdentifier(ni);
            aa.setSubject(subject);
        }
        aa.setAuthenticationMethod(new AuthenticationMethod(method));
        aa.setAuthenticationInstant(
            new AuthenticationInstant(authInstant));
        AuthenticationLocale locale = new AuthenticationLocale();
        locale.setIP(ip);
        locale.setDNSDomain(dns);
        aa.setAuthenticationLocale(locale);
        return aa;
    }

}
```

Example C-21. AssertionID.java

```java
package saml;

import org.w3c.dom.Element;
import org.w3c.dom.Document;

public class AssertionID extends IDType {

    public AssertionID() {}

    public AssertionID(String value) { super(value); }
```

Example C-21. AssertionID.java (continued)

```java
    public void serialize(Element parent) {
        Document doc = parent.getOwnerDocument();
        Element e = doc.createElementNS(SAMLUtil.NS, "AssertionID");
        e.appendChild(doc.createTextNode(getText()));
        parent.appendChild(e);
    }

    public void deserialize(Element source) {
        String id = SAMLUtil.getInnerText(source);
        setText(id);
    }
}
```

Example C-22. AssertionSigner.java

```java
package saml;

import java.io.FileInputStream;
import java.security.InvalidKeyException;
import java.security.Key;
import java.security.KeyStore;
import java.security.KeyStoreException;
import java.security.NoSuchAlgorithmException;
import java.security.NoSuchProviderException;
import java.security.SignatureException;
import java.security.UnrecoverableKeyException;
import java.security.cert.CertificateException;
import java.security.cert.X509Certificate;
import com.ibm.xml.dsig.*;
import org.w3c.dom.*;

public class AssertionSigner {

    public static Element sign(AuthenticationAssertion assertion,
                               String keystorepath,
                               String alias,
                               String storepass,
                               String keypass)
                               throws Exception {

        Document doc = SAMLUtil.newDocument();
        Element root = doc.createElement("root");
        assertion.serialize(root);

        //** Prepare the signature **//
        SignatureGenerator siggen = new SignatureGenerator(doc,
                                    DigestMethod.SHA1,
                                    Canonicalizer.W3C,
                                    SignatureMethod.DSA, null);
        siggen.addReference(
            siggen.createReference(
                siggen.wrapWithObject(root.getFirstChild(),
                    assertion.getAssertionID().getText())
```

Example C-22. AssertionSigner.java (continued)

```
            )
        );


        //** Prepare the key **//
        KeyStore keystore = KeyStore.getInstance("JKS");
        keystore.load(new FileInputStream(keystorepath),
                      storepass.toCharArray());
        X509Certificate cert =
            (X509Certificate)keystore.getCertificate(alias);
        Key key = keystore.getKey(alias, keypass.toCharArray());
        if (key == null) {
            throw new IllegalArgumentException("Invalid Key Info");
        }
        KeyInfo keyInfo = new KeyInfo();
        KeyInfo.X509Data x5data = new KeyInfo.X509Data();
        x5data.setCertificate(cert);
        x5data.setParameters(cert, true, true, true);
        keyInfo.setX509Data(new KeyInfo.X509Data[] { x5data });
        keyInfo.setKeyValue(cert.getPublicKey());
        siggen.setKeyInfoGenerator(keyInfo);

        //** Sign it **//
        Element sig = siggen.getSignatureElement();
        SignatureContext context = new SignatureContext();
        context.sign(sig, key);
        return sig;
    }

}
```

Example C-23. AssertionSpecifier.java

```
package saml;

import org.w3c.dom.Element;
import org.w3c.dom.Document;
import org.w3c.dom.NodeList;
import org.w3c.dom.Node;

public class AssertionSpecifier implements AssertionSpecifierType {

    private AssertionID assertionID;
    private Assertion assertion;

    public AssertionID getAssertionID() {
        return this.assertionID;
    }

    public void setAssertionID(AssertionID assertionID) {
        this.assertionID = assertionID;
    }
```

Example C-23. AssertionSpecifier.java (continued)

```java
    public Assertion getAssertion() {
        return this.assertion;
    }

    public void setAssertion(Assertion assertion) {
        this.assertion = assertion;
    }

    public void serialize(Element parent) {
        Document doc = parent.getOwnerDocument();
        Element e = doc.createElementNS(SAMLUtil.NS, "AssertionSpecifier");
        if (assertionID != null) assertionID.serialize(e);
        if (assertion != null) assertion.serialize(e);
        parent.appendChild(e);
    }

    public void deserialize(Element source) {
        NodeList nl = source.getChildNodes();
        for (int n = 0; n < nl.getLength(); n++) {
            Node node = nl.item(n);
            if (node.getNodeType() == Node.ELEMENT_NODE) {
                Element e = (Element)node;
                if ("AssertionID".equals(e.getLocalName())) {
                    AssertionID aid = new AssertionID();
                    aid.deserialize(e);
                    setAssertionID(aid);
                }
                if ("AuthenticationAssertion".equals(e.getLocalName())) {
                    AuthenticationAssertion aa = new AuthenticationAssertion();
                    aa.deserialize(e);
                    setAssertion(aa);
                }
            }
        }
    }
}
```

Example C-24. AssertionSpecifierType.java

```java
package saml;

public interface AssertionSpecifierType {

    public AssertionID getAssertionID();
    public void setAssertionID(AssertionID assertionID);
    public Assertion getAssertion();
    public void setAssertion(Assertion assertion);

}
```

Example C-25. AuthenticationAssertion.java

```java
package saml;

import java.util.Date;
import org.w3c.dom.Element;
import org.w3c.dom.Document;
import org.w3c.dom.NodeList;
import org.w3c.dom.Node;

public class AuthenticationAssertion
    extends SubjectAssertion implements AuthenticationAssertionType {

    private AuthenticationMethod method;
    private AuthenticationInstant instant;
    private AuthenticationLocale locale;

    public AuthenticationMethod getAuthenticationMethod() {
        return this.method;
    }

    public void setAuthenticationMethod(AuthenticationMethod method) {
        this.method = method;
    }

    public AuthenticationInstant getAuthenticationInstant() {
        return this.instant;
    }

    public void setAuthenticationInstant(AuthenticationInstant instant) {
        this.instant = instant;
    }

    public AuthenticationLocale getAuthenticationLocale() {
        return this.locale;
    }

    public void setAuthenticationLocale(AuthenticationLocale locale) {
        this.locale = locale;
    }

    public void serialize(Element parent) {
        Document doc = parent.getOwnerDocument();
        Element e = doc.createElementNS(SAMLUtil.NS, "AuthenticationAssertion");
        e.setAttribute("xmlns", SAMLUtil.NS);
        serializeAttributes(e);
        serializeSubject(e);
        if (method != null) method.serialize(e);
        if (instant != null) instant.serialize(e);
        if (locale != null) locale.serialize(e);
        parent.appendChild(e);
    }

    public void deserialize(Element source) {
        deserializeAttributes(source);
```

Example C-25. AuthenticationAssertion.java (continued)

```java
        NodeList nl = source.getChildNodes();
        for (int n = 0; n < nl.getLength(); n++) {
            Node node = nl.item(n);
            if (node.getNodeType() == Node.ELEMENT_NODE) {
                Element e = (Element)node;
                if ("Subject".equals(e.getLocalName())) {
                    Subject subject = new Subject();
                    subject.deserialize(e);
                    setSubject(subject);
                }
                if ("AuthenticationMethod".equals(e.getLocalName())) {
                    AuthenticationMethod method = new AuthenticationMethod();
                    method.deserialize(e);
                    setAuthenticationMethod(method);
                }
                if ("AuthenticationInstant".equals(e.getLocalName())) {
                    AuthenticationInstant instant = new AuthenticationInstant();
                    instant.deserialize(e);
                    setAuthenticationInstant(instant);
                }
                if ("AuthenticationLocale".equals(e.getLocalName())) {
                    AuthenticationLocale locale = new AuthenticationLocale();
                    locale.deserialize(e);
                    setAuthenticationLocale(locale);
                }
            }
        }
    }
}
```

Example C-26. AuthenticationAssertionType.java

```java
package saml;

import java.util.Date;

public interface AuthenticationAssertionType extends SubjectAssertionAbstractType {

    public AuthenticationMethod getAuthenticationMethod();
    public void setAuthenticationMethod(AuthenticationMethod method);
    public AuthenticationInstant getAuthenticationInstant();
    public void setAuthenticationInstant(AuthenticationInstant instant);
    public AuthenticationLocale getAuthenticationLocale();
    public void setAuthenticationLocale(AuthenticationLocale locale);

}
```

Example C-27. AuthenticationInstant.java

```java
package saml;

import java.util.Date;
import org.w3c.dom.Element;
import org.w3c.dom.Document;
```

Example C-27. AuthenticationInstant.java (continued)

```java
public class AuthenticationInstant {

    private Date instant;

    public AuthenticationInstant() {}

    public AuthenticationInstant(Date instant) {
        setValue(instant);
    }

    public Date getValue() {
        return this.instant;
    }

    public void setValue(Date value) {
        this.instant = value;
    }

    public void serialize(Element parent) {
        Document doc = parent.getOwnerDocument();
        Element e = doc.createElement("AuthenticationInstant");
        e.appendChild(doc.createTextNode(instant.toString()));
        parent.appendChild(e);
    }

    public void deserialize(Element source) {
        String value = SAMLUtil.getInnerText(source);
        instant = new Date(value);
    }
}
```

Example C-28. AuthenticationLocale.java

```java
package saml;

import org.w3c.dom.Element;
import org.w3c.dom.Document;
import org.w3c.dom.NodeList;
import org.w3c.dom.Node;

public class AuthenticationLocale implements AuthenticationLocaleType {

    private String ip;
    private String domain;


    public String getIP() {
        return this.ip;
    }

    public void setIP(String ip) {
        this.ip = ip;
```

Example C-28. AuthenticationLocale.java (continued)

```java
    }

    public String getDNSDomain() {
        return this.domain;
    }

    public void setDNSDomain(String domain) {
        this.domain = domain;
    }

    public void serialize(Element parent) {
        Document doc = parent.getOwnerDocument();
        Element e = doc.createElementNS(SAMLUtil.NS, "AuthenticationLocale");
        if (ip != null) {
            Element e1 = doc.createElement("IP");
            e1.appendChild(doc.createTextNode(ip));
            e.appendChild(e1);
        }
        if (domain != null) {
            Element e2 = doc.createElement("DNS_Domain");
            e2.appendChild(doc.createTextNode(domain));
            e.appendChild(e2);
        }
        parent.appendChild(e);
    }

    public void deserialize(Element source) {
        NodeList nl = source.getChildNodes();
        for (int n = 0; n < nl.getLength(); n++) {
            Node node = nl.item(n);
            if (node.getNodeType() == Node.ELEMENT_NODE) {
                Element e = (Element)node;
                if ("IP".equals(e.getLocalName())) {
                    String ip = SAMLUtil.getInnerText(e);
                    setIP(ip);
                }
                if ("DNS_Domain".equals(e.getLocalName())) {
                    String dns = SAMLUtil.getInnerText(e);
                    setDNSDomain(dns);
                }
            }
        }
    }
}
```

Example C-29. AuthenticationLocaleType.java

```java
package saml;

public interface AuthenticationLocaleType {
```

Example C-29. AuthenticationLocaleType.java (continued)

```
    public String getIP();
    public void setIP(String ip);
    public String getDNSDomain();
    public void setDNSDomain(String domain);

}
```

Example C-30. AuthenticationMethod.java

```
package saml;

import org.w3c.dom.Element;
import org.w3c.dom.Document;

public class AuthenticationMethod {

    private String value;

    public AuthenticationMethod() {}

    public AuthenticationMethod(String value) {
        setText(value);
    }

    public String getText() {
        return this.value;
    }

    public void setText(String value) {
        this.value = value;
    }

    public void serialize(Element parent) {
        Document doc = parent.getOwnerDocument();
        Element e = doc.createElementNS(SAMLUtil.NS, "AuthenticationMethod");
        e.appendChild(doc.createTextNode(value));
        parent.appendChild(e);
    }

    public void deserialize(Element source) {
        String s = SAMLUtil.getInnerText(source);
        setText(s);
    }
}
```

Example C-31. IDType.java

```
package saml;

public class IDType {

    private String value;
```

Example C-31. IDType.java (continued)

```java
    public IDType() {}

    public IDType(String value) {
        setText(value);
    }

    public String getText() {
        return this.value;
    }

    public void setText(String value) {
        this.value = value;
    }

}
```

Example C-32. NameIdentifier.java

```java
package saml;

import org.w3c.dom.Element;
import org.w3c.dom.Document;
import org.w3c.dom.NodeList;
import org.w3c.dom.Node;

public class NameIdentifier implements NameIdentifierType {

    private String domain;
    private String name;

    public String getSecurityDomain() {
        return this.domain;
    }

    public void setSecurityDomain(String securityDomain) {
        this.domain = securityDomain;
    }

    public String getName() {
        return this.name;
    }

    public void setName(String name) {
        this.name = name;
    }

    public void serialize(Element parent) {
        Document doc = parent.getOwnerDocument();
        Element e = doc.createElementNS(SAMLUtil.NS, "NameIdentifier");
        Element e1 = doc.createElement("SecurityDomain");
        e1.appendChild(doc.createTextNode(domain));
        e.appendChild(e1);
```

Example C-32. NameIdentifier.java (continued)

```java
        Element e2 = doc.createElement("Name");
        e2.appendChild(doc.createTextNode(name));
        e.appendChild(e2);
        parent.appendChild(e);
    }

    public void deserialize(Element source) {
        NodeList nl = source.getChildNodes();
        for (int n = 0; n < nl.getLength(); n++) {
            Node node = nl.item(n);
            if (node.getNodeType() == Node.ELEMENT_NODE) {
                Element e = (Element)node;
                if ("SecurityDomain".equals(e.getLocalName())) {
                    String sd = SAMLUtil.getInnerText(e);
                    setSecurityDomain(sd);
                }
                if ("Name".equals(e.getLocalName())) {
                    String name = SAMLUtil.getInnerText(e);
                    setName(name);
                }
            }
        }
    }
}
```

Example C-33. NameIdentifierType.java

```java
package saml;

public interface NameIdentifierType {

    public String getSecurityDomain();
    public void setSecurityDomain(String securityDomain);
    public String getName();
    public void setName(String name);

}
```

Example C-34. SAMLUtil.java

```java
package saml;

import javax.xml.parsers.DocumentBuilder;
import javax.xml.parsers.DocumentBuilderFactory;
import org.w3c.dom.Element;
import org.w3c.dom.NodeList;
import org.w3c.dom.Document;
import org.w3c.dom.Node;

public class SAMLUtil {

    public static final String NS =
```

Example C-34. SAMLUtil.java (continued)

```
        "http://www.oasis-open.org/committees/security/docs/draft-sstc-schema-assertion-15.
xsd";

    public static String getInnerText(Node e) {
        NodeList nl = e.getChildNodes();
        StringBuffer strbuf = new StringBuffer();
        for (int n = 0; n < nl.getLength(); n++) {
            Node node = nl.item(n);
            if (node.getNodeType() == Node.TEXT_NODE) {
                strbuf.append(node.getNodeValue());
            } else {
                strbuf.append(getInnerText(node));
            }
        }
        return strbuf.toString();
    }

    public static Document newDocument() {
        try {
            DocumentBuilderFactory dbf = DocumentBuilderFactory.newInstance();
            dbf.setValidating(false);
            dbf.setNamespaceAware(true);
            DocumentBuilder db = dbf.newDocumentBuilder();
            return db.newDocument();
        } catch (Exception e) {
            return null;
        }
    }

}
```

Example C-35. Subject.java

```
package saml;

import java.util.List;
import java.util.Vector;
import java.util.Iterator;
import org.w3c.dom.Element;
import org.w3c.dom.Document;
import org.w3c.dom.NodeList;
import org.w3c.dom.Node;

public class Subject implements SubjectType {

    private List nameid = new Vector();

    public NameIdentifier getNameIdentifier(int index) {
        return (NameIdentifier)this.nameid.get(index);
    }

    public void setNameIdentifier(NameIdentifier nameIdentifier) {
```

Example C-35. Subject.java (continued)

```
        this.nameid.add(nameIdentifier);
    }

    public void serialize(Element parent) {
        Document doc = parent.getOwnerDocument();
        Element e = doc.createElementNS(SAMLUtil.NS, "Subject");
        for (Iterator i = nameid.iterator(); i.hasNext();) {
            NameIdentifier ni = (NameIdentifier)i.next();
            ni.serialize(e);
        }
        parent.appendChild(e);
    }

    public void deserialize(Element source) {
        NodeList nl = source.getElementsByTagName("NameIdentifier");
        for (int n = 0; n < nl.getLength(); n++) {
            Element e = (Element)nl.item(n);
            NameIdentifier ni = new NameIdentifier();
            ni.deserialize(e);
            setNameIdentifier(ni);
        }
    }
}
```

Example C-36. SubjectAssertion.java

```
package saml;

import org.w3c.dom.Element;

public abstract class SubjectAssertion
    extends Assertion implements SubjectAssertionAbstractType {

    private Subject subject;

    public Subject getSubject() {
        return this.subject;
    }

    public void setSubject(Subject subject) {
        this.subject = subject;
    }

    protected void serializeSubject(Element e) {
        subject.serialize(e);
    }
}
```

Example C-37. SubjectAssertionAbstractType.java

```
package saml;

public interface SubjectAssertionAbstractType extends AssertionAbstractType {
```

Example C-37. SubjectAssertionAbstractType.java (continued)

```
    public Subject getSubject();
    public void setSubject(Subject subject);

}
```

Example C-38. SubjectType.java

```
package saml;

public interface SubjectType {

    public NameIdentifier getNameIdentifier(int index);
    public void setNameIdentifier(NameIdentifier nameIdentifier);

}
```

Codeshare

Example C-39<. CodeShareOwner.wsdl

```
<?xml version="1.0" encoding="UTF-8"?>
<wsdl:definitions name="CodeShare_Interfaces"
                          targetNamespace="urn:CodeShare_Interfaces"
                          xmlns:tns="urn:CodeShare_Interfaces"
                          xmlns:types="urn:CodeShare_Interfaces:DataTypes"
                          xmlns:wsdl="http://schemas.xmlsoap.org/wsdl/">

    <wsdl:types>
     <xsd:schema version="1.0"
              targetNamespace="urn:CodeShare_Interfaces:DataTypes"
              elementFormDefault="qualified"
              attributeFormDefault="unqualified"
              xmlns:se="http://schemas.xmlsoap.org/soap/encoding/"
              xmlns:xsd="http://www.w3.org/2000/10/XMLSchema" >
       <xsd:import  namespace="http://schemas.xmlsoap.org/soap/encoding/"
            schemaLocation="http://schemas.xmlsoap.org/soap/encoding/"/>
       <xsd:element name="item">
        <xsd:complexType>
         <xsd:sequence>
          <xsd:all>
           <xsd:element name="path" type="xsd:string"
                nullable="true" minOccurs="0"/>
           <xsd:element name="title" type="xsd:string"
                nullable="true" minOccurs="0"/>
           <xsd:element name="fullpath" type="xsd:string"
                nullable="true" minOccurs="0"/>
           <xsd:element name="type" type="xsd:string"
                nullable="true" minOccurs="0"/>
          </xsd:all>
          <xsd:any namespace='xmlns:dc="http://purl.org/dc/elements/1.1/"'
                processContents="lax" minOccurs="0"
                maxOccurs="unbounded"/>
```

Example C-39<. CodeShareOwner.wsdl (continued)

```
      </xsd:sequence>
     </xsd:complexType>
    </xsd:element>
    <xsd:complexType name="ArrayOfItems">
     <xsd:annotation>
      <xsd:documentation>
        Array of CodeShare item elements
      </xsd:documentation>
     </xsd:annotation>
     <xsd:complexContent>
      <xsd:extension base="se:Array">
       <xsd:attribute ref="se:arrayType"
                      wsdl:arrayType="types:item[]" />
      </xsd:extension>
     </xsd:complexContent>
    </xsd:complexType>
   </xsd:schema>
</wsdl:types>

<wsdl:message name="search">
    <part name="p1" type="xsd:string" />
    <part name="p2" type="xsd:string" />
</wsdl:message>
<wsdl:message name="searchResponse">
    <part name="response" type="types:ArrayOfItems" />
</wsdl:message>

<wsdl:message name="get">
    <part name="p1" type="xsd:string" />
    <part name="p2" type="xsd:string" />
</wsdl:message>
<wsdl:message name="getResponse">
    <part name="response" type="types:ArrayOfItems" />
</wsdl:message>

<wsdl:message name="info">
    <part name="p1" type="xsd:string" />
    <part name="p2" type="xsd:string" />
</wsdl:message>
<wsdl:message name="infoResponse">
    <part name="response" type="types:ArrayOfItems" />
</wsdl:message>

<wsdl:message name="list">
    <part name="p1" type="xsd:string" />
    <part name="p2" type="xsd:string" />
</wsdl:message>
<wsdl:message name="listResponse">
    <part name="response" type="types:ArrayOfItems" />
</wsdl:message>
```

Example C-39<. CodeShareOwner.wsdl (continued)

```
<wsdl:portType name="CodeShareOwnerInterface">
    <wsdl:operation name="search" parameterOrder="p1 p2">
        <wsdl:input name="search" message="tns:search" />
        <wsdl:output name="searchResponse"
                     message="tns:searchResponse" />
    </wsdl:operation>
    <wsdl:operation name="get" parameterOrder="p1 p2">
        <wsdl:input name="search" message="tns:search" />
        <wsdl:output name="searchResponse"
                     message="tns:searchResponse" />
    </wsdl:operation>
    <wsdl:operation name="info" parameterOrder="p1 p2">
        <wsdl:input name="search" message="tns:search" />
        <wsdl:output name="searchResponse"
                     message="tns:searchResponse" />
    </wsdl:operation>
    <wsdl:operation name="list" parameterOrder="p1 p2">
        <wsdl:input name="search" message="tns:search" />
        <wsdl:output name="searchResponse"
                     message="tns:searchResponse" />
    </wsdl:operation>
</wsdl:portType>

<wsdl:binding name="CodeShareOwner_SOAP_HTTP"
              type="tns:CodeShareOwnerInterface">

  <soap:binding style="rpc"
                transport="http://schemas.xmlsoap.org/soap/http" />

  <wsdl:operation name="search">
   <soap:operation soapAction="urn:CodeShareOwner#search" />
   <wsdl:input>
    <soap:body use="encoded" namespace="urn:CodeShareOwner"
               encodingStyle="http://schemas.xmlsoap.org/soap/encoding/" />
   </wsdl:input>
   <wsdl:output name="Name">
    <soap:body use="encoded" namespace="urn:CodeShareOwner"
          encodingStyle="http://schemas.xmlsoap.org/soap/encoding/" />
   </wsdl:output>
  </wsdl:operation>

  <wsdl:operation name="get">
   <soap:operation soapAction="urn:CodeShareOwner#get" />
   <wsdl:input>
    <soap:body use="encoded" namespace="urn:CodeShareOwner"
               encodingStyle="http://schemas.xmlsoap.org/soap/encoding/" />
   </wsdl:input>
   <wsdl:output>
    <soap:body use="encoded" namespace="urn:CodeShareOwner"
               encodingStyle="http://schemas.xmlsoap.org/soap/encoding/" />
   </wsdl:output>
  </wsdl:operation>
  <wsdl:operation name="info">
```

Example C-39<. CodeShareOwner.wsdl (continued)

```
      <soap:operation soapAction="urn:CodeShareOwner#info" />
      <wsdl:input>
        <soap:body use="encoded" namespace="urn:CodeShareOwner"
                   encodingStyle="http://schemas.xmlsoap.org/soap/encoding/" />
      </wsdl:input>
      <wsdl:output>
       <soap:body use="encoded" namespace="urn:CodeShareOwner"
                   encodingStyle="http://schemas.xmlsoap.org/soap/encoding/" />
      </wsdl:output>
    </wsdl:operation>
    <wsdl:operation name="list">
     <soap:operation soapAction="urn:CodeShareOwner#list"/>
     <wsdl:input>
      <soap:body use="encoded" namespace="urn:CodeShareOwner"
                   encodingStyle="http://schemas.xmlsoap.org/soap/encoding/" />
     </wsdl:input>
     <wsdl:output>
      <soap:body use="encoded" namespace="urn:CodeShareOwner"
                   encodingStyle="http://schemas.xmlsoap.org/soap/encoding/" />
     </wsdl:output>
    </wsdl:operation>
  </wsdl:binding>
</wsdl:definitions>


</wsdl:definitions>
```

Example C-40. AuthenticationService.java

```java
package codeshare;

import org.w3c.dom.Element;
import org.w3c.dom.Document;
import org.w3c.dom.NodeList;
import saml.*;

public class AuthenticationService {

    private static String users = "users.xml";
    private static Document doc;
    static {
        doc = XMLUtil.get(users);
        if (doc == null) {
            doc = SAMLUtil.newDocument();
            Element u = doc.createElement("users");
            doc.appendChild(u);
            XMLUtil.put(users, doc);
        }
    }

    public static boolean register(String userid, String password) {
        Element e = doc.getDocumentElement();
```

Example C-40. AuthenticationService.java (continued)

```java
        NodeList nl = e.getElementsByTagName("user");
        for (int n = 0; n < nl.getLength(); n++) {
            Element ex = (Element)nl.item(n);
            if (ex.getAttribute("id").equals(userid)) {
                throw new IllegalArgumentException("A user with that ID already exists!");
            }
        }
        Element u = doc.createElement("user");
        u.setAttribute("id", userid);
        u.setAttribute("password", password);
        e.appendChild(u);
        XMLUtil.put(users, doc);
        return true;
    }

    public static Element login(String userid, String password)
        throws Exception {
        Element el = doc.getDocumentElement();
        NodeList nl = el.getElementsByTagName("user");
        for (int n = 0; n < nl.getLength(); n++) {
            Element e = (Element)nl.item(n);
            if (e.getAttribute("id").equals(userid) &&
                e.getAttribute("password").equals(password)) {

                AuthenticationAssertion aa = AssertionFactory.newInstance(
                    new String(new Long(
                        System.currentTimeMillis()).toString()),
                        "CodeShare.org",
                        new java.util.Date(),
                        userid,
                        "CodeShare.org",
                        "http://codeshare.org",
                        new java.util.Date(),
                        java.net.InetAddress.
                            getLocalHost().getHostAddress(),
                            java.net.InetAddress.
                                getLocalHost().getHostName());

                Element sa = AssertionSigner.sign(aa, "CodeShare.db",
                            "CodeShare", "CodeShare", "CodeShare");
                return sa;
            }
        }
        return null;
    }
}
```

Example C-41. Authentication Service Deployment Descriptor

```xml
<isd:service xmlns:isd="http://xml.apache.org/xml-soap/deployment"
            id="urn:CodeShareService-ClientService">
  <isd:provider type="java"
                scope="Application"
```

Example C-41. Authentication Service Deployment Descriptor (continued)

```
                methods="register login">
    <isd:java class="codeshare.AuthenticationService"/>
  </isd:provider>
  <isd:faultListener>org.apache.soap.server.DOMFaultListener
  </isd:faultListener>
</isd:service>
```

Example C-42. VerificationService.java

```java
package codeshare;

import org.w3c.dom.Element;
import com.ibm.xml.dsig.*;
import java.security.Key;

public class VerificationService {

    public static boolean isValid(Element signature) throws Exception {

        Key key = null;
        Element keyInfoElement = KeyInfo.searchForKeyInfo(signature);
        if (keyInfoElement != null) {
            KeyInfo keyInfo = new KeyInfo(keyInfoElement);
            key = keyInfo.getKeyValue();
        }
        SignatureContext context = new SignatureContext();
        Validity validity = context.verify(signature, key);
        return validity.getCoreValidity();
    }

}
```

Example C-43. Verification Service Deployment Descriptor

```
<isd:service xmlns:isd="http://xml.apache.org/xml-soap/deployment"
             id="urn:CodeShareService-Verification">
  <isd:provider type="java"
                scope="Application"
                methods="verify">
    <isd:java class="codeshare.VerificationService"/>
  </isd:provider>
  <isd:faultListener>org.apache.soap.server.DOMFaultListener
  </isd:faultListener>
</isd:service>
```

Example C-44. MasterIndexService.java

```java
package codeshare;

import org.w3c.dom.Element;
import org.w3c.dom.Document;
import org.w3c.dom.NodeList;
import org.w3c.dom.Node;
```

Example C-44. MasterIndexService.java (continued)

```java
import saml.*;

/**
 * Master Index Service
 */

public class MasterIndexService {

    private static String owners = "owners.xml";
    private static Document doc;
    static {
        doc = XMLUtil.get(owners);
        if (doc == null) {
            doc = SAMLUtil.newDocument();
            Element u = doc.createElement("owners");
            doc.appendChild(u);
            XMLUtil.put(owners, doc);
        }
    }

    public static boolean register(String ownerid, String password, String url) {
        Element e = doc.getDocumentElement();
        NodeList nl = e.getElementsByTagName("owner");
        for (int n = 0; n < nl.getLength(); n++) {
            Element ex = (Element)nl.item(n);
            if (ex.getAttribute("id").equals(ownerid)) {
                throw new IllegalArgumentException("An owner with that ID already
exists!");
            }
        }
        Element u = doc.createElement("owner");
        u.setAttribute("id", ownerid);
        u.setAttribute("password", password);
        u.setAttribute("url", url);
        e.appendChild(u);
        XMLUtil.put(owners, doc);
        return true;
    }

    public static boolean login(String ownerid, String password, Element index) {
        Element el = doc.getDocumentElement();
        NodeList nl = el.getElementsByTagName("owner");
        for (int n = 0; n < nl.getLength(); n++) {
            Element e = (Element)nl.item(n);
            if (e.getAttribute("id").equals(ownerid) &&
                e.getAttribute("password").equals(password)) {
                Element i = (Element)doc.importNode(index, true);
                NodeList c = e.getElementsByTagName("index");
                if (c.getLength() > 0) {
                    Node node = c.item(1);
                    e.replaceChild(node, i);
                } else {
```

Example C-44. MasterIndexService.java (continued)

```java
                    e.appendChild(i);
                }
                XMLUtil.put(owners, doc);
                return true;
            }
        }
        return false;
    }

    public static boolean update(String ownerid, String password,
                                 Element index) {
        Element el = doc.getDocumentElement();
        NodeList nl = el.getElementsByTagName("owner");
        for (int n = 0; n < nl.getLength(); n++) {
            Element e = (Element)nl.item(n);
            if (e.getAttribute("id").equals(ownerid) &&
                e.getAttribute("password").equals(password)) {
                Element i = (Element)doc.importNode(index, true);
                NodeList c = e.getElementsByTagName("index");
                if (c.getLength() > 0) {
                    Node node = c.item(1);
                    e.replaceChild(node, i);
                } else {
                    e.appendChild(i);
                }
                XMLUtil.put(owners, doc);
                return true;
            }
        }
        return false;
    }

}
```

Example C-45. Master Index Service Deployment Descriptor

```xml
<isd:service xmlns:isd="http://xml.apache.org/xml-soap/deployment"
             id="urn:CodeShareService-MasterIndex">
  <isd:provider type="java"
                scope="Application"
                methods="register update">
    <isd:java class="codeshare.IndexService"/>
  </isd:provider>
  <isd:faultListener>org.apache.soap.server.DOMFaultListener
  </isd:faultListener>
</isd:service>
```

Example C-46. OwnerService.java

```java
package codeshare;

import org.apache.regexp.RE;
import org.w3c.dom.Document;
import org.w3c.dom.Element;
```

Example C-46. OwnerService.java (continued)

```java
import org.w3c.dom.NodeList;
import saml.SAMLUtil;

public class OwnerService {
  private static String index = "index.xml";
  private static org.w3c.dom.Document doc;
  static {
    doc = XMLUtil.get(index);
    if (doc == null)
    {
      doc = SAMLUtil.newDocument();
      Element e = doc.createElement("index");
      doc.appendChild(e);
      XMLUtil.put(index, doc);
    }
  }

  public org.w3c.dom.Element search(String p1) {
    return search(p1, "dc:Title");
  }

  public Element search(String p1, String p2)
  {
    Element e = doc.getDocumentElement();
    NodeList nl = e.getElementsByTagName(p2);

    Document d = SAMLUtil.newDocument();
    Element list = doc.createElement("list");
    d.appendChild(list);

    for (int n = 0; n < nl.getLength(); n++)
    {
      Element next = (Element)nl.item(n);
      try
      {
        RE targetRE = new RE(p1);
        if (targetRE.match(SAMLUtil.getInnerText(next.getText())))
        {
          Element item = (Element)d.importNode(next);
          list.appendChild(item);
        }
      }
      catch (Exception exc) {}
    }
    return list;
  }


  public Element list(String p1)
  {
    return search(p1, "dc:Title");
  }
```

Example C-46. OwnerService.java (continued)

```
  public Element list(String p1, String p2)
  {
    Element e = doc.getDocumentElement();
    NodeList nl = e.getElementsByTagName(p2);

    Document d = SAMLUtil.newDocument();
    Element list = doc.createElement("list");
    d.appendChild(list);

    for (int n = 0; n < nl.getLength(); n++)
    {
      Element next = (Element)nl.item(n);
      try
      {
        RE targetRE = new RE(p1);
        if (targetRE.match(SAMLUtil.getInnerText(next.getText())))
        {
          Element item = (Element)d.importNode(next);
          list.appendChild(item);
        }
      }
      catch (Exception exc) {}
    }
    return list;
  }

  public Element info(String p1) {
    throw new IllegalArgumentException("Not Implemented");
  }

  public Element get(String p1) {
    throw new IllegalArgumentException("Not Implemented");
  }
}
```

Example C-47. Owner Service Deployment Descriptor

```
<isd:service xmlns:isd="http://xml.apache.org/xml-soap/deployment"
             id="urn:CodeShareService-OwnerService">
  <isd:provider type="java"
                scope="Application"
                methods="list search">
    <isd:java class="codeshare.OwnerService"/>
  </isd:provider>
  <isd:faultListener>org.apache.soap.server.DOMFaultListener
  </isd:faultListener>
</isd:service>
```

Example C-48. XMLUtil.java

```
package codeshare;

import java.io.FileWriter;
import javax.xml.parsers.*;
```

Example C-48. XMLUtil.java (continued)

```java
import org.w3c.dom.*;
import org.apache.xml.serialize.*;

public class XMLUtil {

    public static Document get(String path) {
        try {
            DocumentBuilderFactory dbf = DocumentBuilderFactory.newInstance();
            dbf.setValidating(false);
            dbf.setNamespaceAware(true);
            DocumentBuilder db = dbf.newDocumentBuilder();
            return db.parse(path);
        } catch (Exception e) {
            return null;
        }
    }

    public synchronized static boolean put(String path, Document doc) {
        try {
            FileWriter fw = new FileWriter(path);
            OutputFormat of = new OutputFormat();
            of.setIndenting(true);
            XMLSerializer x = new XMLSerializer(fw, of);
            x.serialize(doc);
            fw.close();
            return true;
        } catch (Exception e) {
            return false;
        }
    }

}
```

Example C-49. Codeshare/Owner.pm

```perl
package CodeShare::Owner;

use strict;

my $index;                              # parsed index file
my $DC_NS = "http://purl.org/dc/elements/1.1/"; # Dublin Code namespace
my @ELEMENTS = qw(Title Creator Date Subject Description);

sub init {
  my($class, $root) = @_;
  open(F, $root) or die "$root: $!\n";
  $index = SOAP::Custom::XML::Deserializer->deserialize(join '', <F>)->root;
  close(F) or die "$root: $!\n";
}

sub traverse {
  my($self, %params) = @_;
```

Example C-49. Codeshare/Owner.pm (continued)

```perl
  my $start = $params{start};

  my $type = $start->SOAP::Data::name; # file|project|directory
  my $location = ref $start->location ? $start->location->value : '';

  # path to current structure. Empty for projects
  my $path = $type eq 'directory' ||
             $type eq 'file' ? join('/', $params{path} || (), $location) : '';
  my $prefix = $type eq 'project' ? $location : $params{prefix} || '';
  my $fullpath = join '/', $prefix, $path; # full path. Used to GET files

  my $where = $params{where};
  my $matched =
    $params{get} && $params{matched} ||
    $params{what} &&
    # check only subelements in Dublin Core namespace
    $start->$where() =~ /$params{what}/ && $start->$where()->uri eq $DC_NS;

  return
    # current element
    ($matched
       ? +{ type => $type,
            path => $path,
            ($params{get} ? (fullpath => $fullpath) : ()),
            map { ref $start->$_() ? ($_ => $start->$_()->value) : ()
                } @ELEMENTS
          }
       : ()
    ),

    # and everything below
    map { $self->traverse(start => $_, where => $where, what => $params{what},
                          path => $path, prefix => $prefix,
                          get => ($params{get} || 0), matched => $matched) }
      $start->project, $start->directory, ($type eq 'file' ? () : $start->file)
  ;
}

sub list {

  print("\nHandling a list request...");

  my($self, $what) = @_;

  [ map { my $e = $_; +{ map {$_ => $e->{$_}} qw(type path Title file fullpath) } }
      $self->traverse(start => $index, where => 'Title', what => $what, get => 1)
  ];
}

sub get {

  print("\nHandling a get request...");
```

Example C-49. Codeshare/Owner.pm (continued)

```perl
  my $results = shift->list(@_);

  [ map { $_->{type} eq 'file' && open(F, delete $_->{fullpath})
          ? ($_->{file} = join('', <F>), close F) : (); $_ }
      @$results
  ];
}

sub search { # same as info(), but returns only 'type', 'path' and 'Title'

  print("\nHandling a search request...");

  my $results = shift->info(@_);

  [ map { my $e = $_; +{ map {$_ => $e->{$_}} qw(type path Title) } }
      @$results
  ];
}

sub info {

  print("\nHandling an info request...");

  my($self, $what, $where) = @_;

  [ $self->traverse(start => $index,
                    where => $where || 'Title', what => $what || '.')
  ];
}

1;
```

Example C-50. Codeshare.pl (standalone HTTP Daemon)

```perl
#!perl -w
#Id:\perl\bin\perl.exe

use SOAP::Transport::HTTP;
use CodeShare::Owner;


print "\n\nWelcome to CodeShare! The Open source code sharing network!";
print "\nCopyright(c) 2001, James Snell, Paul Kulchenko, Doug Tidwell\n\n";


CodeShare::Owner->init(shift or die "Usage: $0 <path/to/index.xml>\n");

my $daemon = SOAP::Transport::HTTP::Daemon
  -> new (LocalPort => 8080)
  -> dispatch_to('CodeShare::Owner::(?:get|search|info|list)')
;
print "CodeShare Owner Server started at ", $daemon->url, "\n";
print "Waiting for a request...\n";
$daemon->handle;
```

Example C-51. Codeshare.cgi (alternative to standalone HTTP daemon)

```perl
#!/usr/bin/env perl
# -- Copyright (C) 2001 Paul Kulchenko --

use strict;
use SOAP::Transport::HTTP;
use CodeShare::Owner;

CodeShare::Owner->init('../Projects/index.xml');

my $daemon = SOAP::Transport::HTTP::CGI
  -> dispatch_to('CodeShare::Owner::(?:get|search|info|list)')
  -> handle;
;
```

Example C-52. Startserver.bat

```
@echo off

start "CodeShare Owner Server" perl cs_server.pl ..\Projects\index.xml
```

Example C-53. Startserver.sh

```
perl cs_server.pl ../Projects/index.xml
```

Example C-54. Codeshare_client.pl

```perl
#!/bin/env perl
#!d:\perl\bin\perl.exe

use strict;
use SOAP::Lite;
use File::Path;

print "\n\nWelcome to CodeShare! The Open source code sharing network!";
print "\nCopyright(c) 2001, James Snell, Paul Kulchenko, Doug Tidwell\n\n";

@ARGV or die "Usage: $0 CodeShareServer [commands...] [-dump [filename]] \n";
my $proxy = shift;
my $uri = 'http://namespaces.soaplite.com/CodeShare/Owner';
my $soap = SOAP::Lite->proxy($proxy)->uri($uri)->on_fault(sub{});

my($dump, $file) = @ARGV > 0 && @ARGV[-1] eq '-dump' ? splice(@ARGV, -1, 1) :
                   @ARGV > 1 && @ARGV[-2] eq '-dump' ? splice(@ARGV, -2, 2) :
                   (undef, undef);
if ($dump) {
  print STDERR "Wiredumps are logged in '$file'\n" if $file;
  $file ||= '&STDOUT';                   # STDOUT by default
  open(F, ">>$file") or die "$file: $!\n"; # open in append mode
  select((select(F), $|=1)[0]);          # select non-buffered output
  $soap->on_debug(sub{print F @_});      # debug goes there
  eval "END { close F }";                # close handle when we are done
}

print STDERR "Usage: { search | info | get | list | quit | help } [parameters...]\n> ";
```

Example C-54. Codeshare_client.pl (continued)

```perl
while (defined($_ = shift || <>)) {
  next unless /\w/;
  my($method, $modifier, $parameters) = m!^\s*(\w+)(?:\s*/(\w*)\s)?\s*(.*)!;

  last if $method =~ /^q(?:uit)?$/i;
  help(), next if $method =~ /^h(?:elp)?$/i;

  my $res = eval "\$soap->$method('$parameters', '$modifier')";

  # check for errors
  $@                              and print(STDERR join "\n", $@, ''), next;
  defined($res) && $res->fault  and print(STDERR join "\n", $res->faultstring, ''), next;
  !$soap->transport->is_success and print(STDERR join "\n", $soap->transport->status, ''),
next;

  # check for result
  my @result = @{$res->result} or print(STDERR "No matches\n"), next;

  foreach (@result) {
    print(STDERR "$_->{type}: @{[join ', ', $_->{Title} || (), $_->{path} || ()]}\n");
    if ($method eq 'get') {
      if ($_->{type} eq 'directory') { File::Path::mkpath($_->{path}) }
      if ($_->{type} eq 'file') {
        open(F, '>'. $_->{path}) or warn "$_->{path}: $!\n";
        print F $_->{file};
        close(F) or warn "$_->{path}: $!\n";
      }
    } elsif ($method eq 'info') {
      foreach my $key (grep {$_ !~ /^(?:type|path)/} keys %$_) {
        print "  $key: $_->{$key}\n";
      }
    }
  }
} continue {
  print STDERR "\n> ";
}

sub help {
  print "Short help about search, info, get and list commands is here\n";
}
```

Index

We'd like to hear your suggestions for improving our indexes. Send email to *index@oreilly.com*.

About the Authors

James Snell is a software engineer on IBM's Emerging Technology team, where he has been focused full time on the architecture, strategy, and development of web services technologies. Prior to joining IBM, James worked for a variety of custom enterprise system development companies, designing and building knowledge management, accounting, manufacturing, and system integration solutions. He has been actively involved with Internet-based development projects since 1994. He currently lives in Central California with his son and beautiful wife, Jennifer.

Doug Tidwell is a senior programmer at IBM. He has more than a sixth of a century of programming experience, and has been working with markup language for more than a decade. He was a speaker at the first XML conference in 1997, and has taught XML classes around the world. His job as a Cyber Evangelist is to look busy and to help people use new technologies to solve problems. Using a pair of zircon-encrusted tweezers, he holds a Master's degree in computer science from Vanderbilt University and a Bachelor's degree in English from the University of Georgia. He lives in Raleigh, North Carolina, with his wife, cooking teacher Sheri Castle (see her web site at *http://www.sheri-inc.com*), and their daughter, Lily.

Pavel Kulchenko is an open source developer, best known for his SOAP::Lite, XMLRPC::Lite, and UDDI::Lite modules for Perl. Since obtaining his physics degree and discovering Perl in 1993, he has consulted for a variety of companies in both the U.S. and abroad. With years of software architecture and development experience, including about two years of working with SOAP, he is a frequent writer and speaker on web services and SOAP::Lite.

Colophon

Our look is the result of reader comments, our own experimentation, and feedback from distribution channels. Distinctive covers complement our distinctive approach to technical topics, breathing personality and life into potentially dry subjects.

The animal on the cover of *Programming Web Services with SOAP* is a sea sponge. There are thousands of species of sponge (Phylum *Porifera*). Sponges are simple, multicellular animals that feed and breathe by filtering water. They are covered with tiny pores called ostia, which lead to an internal system of canals coated with sticky cells called choanocytes, or collar cells. These cells facilitate water through the canals with constantly moving flagella, picking up oxygen and pieces of food, and carrying out carbon dioxide and waste. The water passes out of the sponge through larger pores called oscula.

Free-standing and encrusting sea sponges live at the bottom of the ocean, in deep and shallow waters. Free-standing sponges can grow to gigantic sizes, and crab, shrimp, sea slugs, and starfish are often found living inside. Encrusting sponges attach themselves to rocks, shells, wood, and kelp. Some sponges produce toxic chemicals, possibly to give them a bad taste to predators. Other sponges have sharp, prickly spines as their only defense.

Colleen Gorman was the production editor and copyeditor for *Programming Web Services with SOAP*. Linley Dolby and Matt Hutchinson provided quality control. Phil Dangler and Camilla Ammirati provided production support. John Bickelhaupt wrote the index.

Ellie Volckhausen designed the cover of this book, based on a series design by Edie Freedman. The cover image is an original illustration created by Susan Hart. Emma Colby produced the cover layout with QuarkXPress 4.1 using Adobe's ITC Garamond font.

Melanie Wang designed the interior layout, based on a series design by David Futato. Neil Walls converted the files from Microsoft Word to FrameMaker 5.5.6 using tools created by Mike Sierra. The text font is Linotype Birka; the heading font is Adobe Myriad Condensed; and the code font is LucasFont's TheSans Mono Condensed. The illustrations that appear in the book were produced by Robert Romano and Jessamyn Read using Macromedia FreeHand 9 and Adobe Photoshop 6. This colophon was written by Colleen Gorman.

Whenever possible, our books use a durable and flexible lay-flat binding.

XML

HTML & XHTML: The Definitive Guide, 4th Edition

By Chuck Musciano & Bill Kennedy
4th Edition August 2000
677 pages, ISBN 0-596-00026-X

This complete guide is full of examples, sample code, and practical hands-on advice for creating truly effective web pages and mastering advanced features. Web authors learn how to insert images, create useful links and searchable documents, use Netscape extensions, design great forms, and much more. The fourth edition covers XHTML 1.0, HTML 4.01, Netscape 6.0, and Internet Explorer 5.0, plus all the common extensions.

Building Oracle XML Applications

By Steve Muench
1st Edition September 2000
810 pages, Includes CD-ROM
ISBN 1-56592-691-9

Building Oracle XML Applications gives Java and PL/SQL developers a rich and detailed look at the many tools Oracle provides to support XML development. It shows how to combine the power of XML and XSLT with the speed, functionality, and reliability of the Oracle database. The author delivers nearly 800 pages of entertaining text, helpful and timesaving hints, and extensive examples that developers can put to use immediately to build custom XML applications. The accompanying CD-ROM contains JDeveloper 3.1, an integrated development environment for Java developers.

DocBook: The Definitive Guide

By Norman Walsh & Leonard Muellner
1st Edition October 1999
648 pages, Includes CD-ROM
ISBN 1-56592-580-7

DocBook is a Document Type Definition (DTD) for use with XML (the Extensible Markup Language) and SGML (the Standard Generalized Markup Language). DocBook lets authors in technical groups exchange and reuse technical information. This book contains an introduction to SGML, XML, and the DocBook DTD, plus the complete reference information for DocBook.

Programming Jabber

By DJ Adams
1st Edition December 2001 (est.)
300 pages (est.), ISBN 0-596-00202-5

This book will offer programmers a chance to learn and understand the Jabber technology and protocol from an implementer's point of view. Every detail of every part of the Jabber client protocol is introduced, explained, discussed, and covered in the form of recipes, mini-projects or simple and extended examples in Perl, Python, and Java. *Programming Jabber* provides a walk-through of the foundation elements that are common to any messaging solution, including a detailed overview of the Jabber server architecture.

Programming Web Services with XML-RPC

By Simon St.Laurent, Joe Johnston & Edd Dumbill
Foreword by Dave Winer
1st Edition June 2001
230 pages, ISBN 0-596-00119-3

XML-RPC, a simple yet powerful system built on XML and HTTP, lets developers connect programs running on different computers with a minimum of fuss. Java programs can talk to Perl scripts, which can talk to ASP applications, and so on. With XML-RPC, developers can provide access to functionality without having to worry about the system on the other end, so it's easy to create web services.

Programming Web Services with SOAP

By James Snell, Doug Tidwell & Pavel Kulchenko
1st Edition December 2001 (est.)
352 pages (est.), ISBN 0-596-00095-2

In typical O'Reilly fashion this book moves beyond the theoretical and explains how to build and implement SOAP web services. 0The book begins with a solid introduction to SOAP, detailing its history and structure, followed by an introduction to the three major types of SOAP applications: SOAP-RPC, SOAP-Messaging, and SOAP-Intermediaries. Each SOAP application is illustrated with an in-depth implementation.